A Reasonable Belief

A Reasonable Belief

Why God and Faith Make Sense

William Greenway

WESTMINSTER
JOHN KNOX PRESS
LOUISVILLE • KENTUCKY

First edition
Published by Westminster John Knox Press
Louisville, Kentucky

15 16 17 18 19 20 21 22 23 24—10 9 8 7 6 5 4 3 2 1

Scripture quotations from the New Revised Standard Version of the Bible are copyright © 1989 by the Division of Christian Education of the National Council of the Churches of Christ in the U.S.A. and are used by permission.

Book design by Sharon Adams
Cover design by Allison Taylor

Library of Congress Cataloging-in-Publication Data

Greenway, William.
 A reasonable belief : why God and faith make sense / William Greenway. -- First edition.
   pages cm
 ISBN 978-0-664-26027-9 (alk. paper)
1. Faith and reason--Christianity. I. Title.
 BT50.G64 2015
 231'.042--dc23

2015002757

♾ The paper used in this publication meets the minimum requirements
of the American National Standard for Information Sciences—Permanence
of Paper for Printed Library Materials, ANSI Z39.48-1992.

Most Westminster John Knox Press books are available at special quantity discounts when purchased in bulk by corporations, organizations, and special-interest groups. For more information, please e-mail SpecialSales@wjkbooks.com.

*For Sylvia Bailey Greenway
and in loving memory of William N. A. Greenway Sr.*

Contents

Preface

By the late twentieth century, confessing faith in God was thought by many to mean you were credulous, ignorant, or afraid to face hard truths. It was widely believed that anyone who was honest, intelligent, well educated, emotionally strong, and reasonable would dismiss faith in God. The reasonableness of rejecting faith seemed so certain that, for instance, the distinguished Cambridge University historian Quentin Skinner, writing in a prominent scholarly journal and with merely a gesture to some of the West's foremost intellectuals, felt free to assert flatly that faith in God is "obviously self-deceiving and erroneous."[1] In fact, Skinner said bluntly, we may now conclude, "not merely that theism must certainly be false . . . [but] that it must be grossly irrational to believe otherwise" and thus that "anyone who continues to affirm it must be suffering from some serious form of psychological blockage or self-deceit."[2]

In the early twenty-first century, the case against faith still appears so strong that people of faith, even many pastors, secretly worry over the reasonableness of faith. They do not want to be skeptics. They want wholeheartedly to believe. Indeed, even many Nones (those who answer "None" when asked for "religious affiliation" on surveys) would love to be able to believe, would love to be free of the worry that faith can be gained only at the expense of reason. Novelist and self-identified None Eric Weiner, for instance, notes in a New York Times article that in his "secularized, urban and urbane world, God is rarely spoken of, except in mocking, derisive

1. Quentin Skinner, "Who Are 'We'? Ambiguities of the Modern Self," *Inquiry: An Interdisciplinary Journal of Philosophy* 34 (June, 1991): 148.
2. Skinner, "Who Are 'We'?" 148.

tones." Yet, Weiner continues, "We Nones may not believe in God, but we hope to someday."[3]

For those who hope for a wholly reasonable faith, there is good news. The streams of modern rationality that make faith seem irrational are running dry. Indeed, in some elite philosophical circles disdain for faith is itself increasingly viewed, even by atheists, as confused and simplistic, even haughty. Though this development remains largely unknown outside the sphere of professional philosophers, elite philosophers have for two decades now been talking with surprise (and, for many, with alarm) about a "theological turn" in cutting-edge philosophy.[4] As noted philosopher Simon Critchley, an atheist, says in his poignantly titled book, *The Faith of the Faithless* (2012), "The return to religion has perhaps become the dominant cliché of contemporary philosophy."[5] From this perspective, the celebrated and notorious "new atheists" represent not the cutting edge of modern thought but the last gasp of powerful intellectual currents in modern Western rationality whose weaknesses are rapidly becoming obvious. The sun is already setting on our secular age.

But what comes next? If the old certainties about the irrationality of faith have proven to be not so certain after all, what does this mean for the future of faith? To start with, it *does not* signal an automatic return to the truth claims of any particular faith tradition or grant free reign to irrationality or superstition. We will not escape into a nonexistent past where everybody "just knew" that what they believed was true. It *does* challenge people of faith to articulate clearly, reasonably, and movingly the reality and significance of faith. That is the task this book takes up. To the question, "Is faith reasonable?" I answer with a sure and spiritually resonant yes. I defend the following affirmation: *given the current state of human understanding, and based solely upon what is reasonable and good according to common public standards, every person of faith can be utterly confident that it is wholly reasonable and good to affirm, give thanks for, live, and testify to faith in God.*[6]

I need to clarify precisely what I mean by key terms such as "faith" and "good." I need to clarify what I mean by closely associated terms such as "belief," "grace," "salvation," "spiritual," "moral," and "revelation." I need to

3. Eric Weiner, "Americans: Undecided about God?" *New York Times*, December 11, 2011, SR5.

4. Dominique Janicaud, *Phenomenology and the "Theological Turn": The French Debate*, trans. Bernard G. Prusak, (New York: Fordham University Press, 2001); French edition, *Le tournant theologique de la phenomenologie francaise*, (Paris: Editions de l'Eclat, 1991).

5. Simon Critchley, *The Faith of the Faithless: Experiments in Political Theology* (New York: Verso, 2012), book jacket and p. 8.

6. If this conclusion is true, then even those who stand apart from faith should affirm that faith is reasonable and good.

clarify what I mean by the most audacious term of all, "God" (or to use the more reverent Jewish spelling, "G-d"), the term that signifies an Other whose ways transcend our ways (Isa. 55:8–9), whom we now see only "in a mirror, dimly" (1 Cor. 13:12), whose peace "surpasses all understanding" (Phil. 4:7). In a word, my confession is classic: God is love. But unfolding with precision the profound, multi-layered meaning of this deceptively simple formula and its exact relation to faith requires careful reflection.

I am a modern Westerner and a Christian theologian formed by the Christian and Jewish traditions. In my concluding chapters I analyze and am inspired by the teachings of Jesus Christ. All spiritual reflection proceeds from some such historically conditioned position or another. No human thinks and speaks from a perspective above or outside his or her culture. Insofar as diverse cultures and faith traditions are truly dealing with the same transcending Other, however, it is reasonable to expect all faiths to have been inspired by the same G-d. I cannot speak definitively for other religions, but I suspect that the essence of Christian spirituality is continuous with the essence of Jewish, Islamic, Hindu, Buddhist, and many other spiritualities. If so, then this defense of faith is not only for Christians. It may also represent the essence of a spiritual passion at the heart of diverse faiths. Nonetheless, any given author can only speak from within the conceptual contours of one religious tradition or another (including secular humanist and atheist traditions), and I speak as a Christian.

Since battles over the relationship of faith and science are prominent, let me offer a preliminary sketch of my understanding of the relationship among faith, science, and reason. First, I will not reject any specific discoveries of modern physics, chemistry, biology, psychology, or of any other modern science. I accept deep space and time (we are made of stardust), the biological theory of evolution (monkeys, you, and I share a common ancestor), even the possibility that the cosmos is teeming with life.

Second, as will become clear, the boundaries of scientific reflection do not exhaust the boundaries of reasonable reflection. Accordingly, while I will think through faith within the boundaries of what is reasonable, I will not think through faith within the boundaries of science. Where ideas pertain to natural realities (in the modern sense of "nature" or "physical," including genes and memes) I defer to the authority of science. But where ideas pertain to spiritual realities, I will evaluate them in accord with what is reasonable with regard to spiritual realities (I will define and defend my invocation of "spiritual realities").

Third, since I am remaining within the boundaries of what is reasonable and good in accord with generally accepted standards, I will not countenance any "leaps of faith" or presume from the start the truth of any particular tradition, creed, scripture, or religious authority. I limit my explorations to what theologians call "general revelation" (awakening to the divine available to any and all who open their hearts and minds) in contrast to "special revelation" (knowledge directly conveyed by a deity). I neither affirm nor contest the reality of special revelation. I neither affirm nor contest the truth of beliefs insofar as they depend upon special revelation. Making no judgments about special revelation, I strictly delimit my exploration of faith to the bounds of what is reasonable and good according to common public standards.[7]

The argument unfolds in two major parts. The first part, "The Secular Condition," begins by unfolding how modern Western rationality argued itself into the condition of secularity, a condition wherein faith in God is thought to be unreasonable. My argument in these chapters focuses on the influence of René Descartes (1596–1650), the famed "father of modern philosophy," and upon the modern, naturalistic appropriation of his cosmology in the nineteenth and twentieth centuries. I paint with broad strokes, but by the end of these chapters I will have described basic intellectual developments that resulted in the widespread emergence of the secular condition. Notably, by the end of this discussion I will already have made clear why affirmation of spiritual realities is not necessarily irrational.

In the second part, "The Essence of Reasonable Christianity," I begin by explaining developments in twentieth-century philosophy that unexpectedly led to the "theological turn" in late twentieth-century Western philosophy. In particular, I consider the philosophy of preeminent Jewish philosopher Emmanuel Levinas, which proved instrumental in stimulating the theological turn. Levinas thought that modern rationality had cut us off from our humaneness, from our existence as moral beings. A survivor of the Nazi camps, he sought to awaken us to the most basic, undeniable, and significant aspect of lived experience, namely, to the way in which we are "taken hostage" by concern for others (i.e., by love for neighbor).

For Descartes, the most real and important thing in the world is theoretical certainty: "I think, therefore I am." For Levinas, it is the way in which we are seized by love for others, most especially those crying out to us in desperate need and terror. If this is true, then above all there is no reasonable basis for the secular age's denial of a transcending moral reality (i.e., a moral reality that is not ultimately a product of natural conditioning and/or human culture). For Levinas (and for me), this is a critical clue to understanding how the reality of God comes to the human mind.

I supplement Levinas with insights into *agape*, grace, and faith inspired by the work of Christian theologian Jean-Luc Marion. Modern rationality

7. For reasons that will become clear, I do not speak in terms of "natural theology."

typically rejects the reality of *agape*, but I will argue that *agape* is real. *Agape* names the reality of our having been seized in and by love for others. At its heart, I will argue, faith in God is living surrender to having been seized in and by love for others. Select passages from 1 John 4 proclaim the essence of the faith I will defend:

> Beloved, let us love one another, because love is from God; everyone who loves is born of God and knows God. Whoever does not love does not know God, for God is love. . . . In this is love, not that we loved God but that [God] loved us . . . God is love, and those who abide in love abide in God, and God abides in them. (1 John 4: 7–8, 10a, 16b)

As these verses suggest, faith is not belief in or commitment to some thing. Faith is infinitely more intimate and precedes any initiating decision or intentionality on our part. In language I will develop, love is not something we create or do, but awakening and surrendering to that love in and by which we have been seized. As mystics across faith traditions have testified for millennia, the ultimate givenness in and by which one finds oneself seized is love, *agape*, the "gift of God" that yields faith.

When art restorers apply sophisticated solvents to cleanse the layers of dross that have accumulated over the centuries, the full brilliance of the ancient masters once again shines forth. I am joining in the process of purging layers of dross from modern Western rationality, a process that in elite philosophical circles has led to the "theological turn." I argue that this process is giving birth to a restored, spiritually attuned rationality, an awakened rationality that facilitates the unfolding of a philosophical spirituality. In the culminating chapters I consider classic teachings of Jesus in the light of this restored rationality, expecting that dimensions of Jesus' spiritual genius will shine forth with renewed brilliance. In like manner, while remaining within the bounds of general revelation, I consider what spiritual enlightenment an awakened rationality, and our study of the teachings of Jesus in light of that rationality, may bring to understanding of such central Christian concepts as original sin, the fall, good, evil, grace, forgiveness, *koinonia*, salvation, faith, eternal life, and resurrection.

I limit my explorations throughout to the bounds of general revelation, so this remains a *philosophical* spirituality. Nonetheless, insofar as the essence of this philosophical spirituality is continuous with the essence of Christian spirituality, I am able to specify how—not only generally, but thinking in an explicitly (not exclusively) Christian voice, and in accord with common public standards of what is good and reasonable—we can be utterly confident that it is wholly reasonable and good to affirm, give thanks for, live with, and testify to faith in God. A bit more poetically, I would say that, taking advantage of cutting-edge developments in late modern philosophy, I strive to articulate clearly and movingly (though most certainly not exhaustively) the reality, reasonableness, and surpassing significance of faith; and so I join in the historic quest to proclaim clearly how faith in God can empower us, fill us with joy, and inspire loving action.

Acknowledgments

This book was conceived and written over the course of a sabbatical year. Without the generosity of the Trustees and my colleagues at Austin Presbyterian Theological Seminary, it is quite possible I would never have found space and time to write this book, so my profound thanks go to our Trustees and to my colleagues at Austin. I am especially indebted to my editor at Westminster John Knox Press, Robert Ratcliff, not only for his keen and patient guidance as I strove to make the work as clear and understandable as possible, and not only for his enthusiasm and moral support, but also for his having the vision and energy to help this work rise from the ashes of a rejected proposal. Also at Westminster John Knox Press, I owe special thanks to Ann DeVilbiss, Emily Kiefer, Allison Taylor, Shelby Oney, Gerben Oosterbaan, and Julie Tonini for wonderful work editing, designing, and publicizing this book.

In indirect but critical ways, this work reflects the influence of professors who two to three decades ago played a pivotal role in forming my thought. First, I would like to thank several professors from my many years of graduate study (Masters of Divinity and PhD) at Princeton Theological Seminary. Thanks go to the members of my dissertation committee: to the late Diogenes Allen (chair), Wentzel van Huyssteen, and Mark Taylor. I would also like to thank five other professors who were pivotal in shaping my understanding at Princeton Seminary: Nancy Duff, Karlfried Froehlich, Steven Kraftchick, Daniel Migliore, and Peter Paris. I also owe thanks to four professors who were particularly critical to my intellectual formation at Houghton College: Brian Sayers, Carlton Fisher, Richard Perkins, and Lionel Basney. In addition, I owe special thanks to two other professors who in recent years have emerged as bastions of personal encouragement and crucial advice: Patrick Miller (Princeton) and John (Jack) Leax (Houghton).

I also want to express thanks to the passionate and intellectually critical members of *Koinonia*, the adult education class I taught from 1994-2004 at University Presbyterian Church in Austin, Texas.

Last but not least, I owe special thanks to Cindy, Xander, Jessica, Sherlock, and Kalico, who, during the year in which this book was being written, filled our home with fun, love, and support and who continually awakened me to the gift.

I have dedicated this book to my parents, who were—and in the case of my mother continues to be—unwavering pillars of love, confidence, and support. I dearly wish my father could have lived to see this book, but he fully understood and lived out the faith described herein, so it would have added nothing essential to our joy made complete.

William Greenway
Winter 2015
Austin, Texas

PART I

The Secular Condition

1

Modern Western Rationality's Eliding of Spiritual Realities

"Secularity"—that social and cultural situation in which spiritual reality is deemed nonexistent and nonsensical—didn't just happen overnight. It is the result of long-term shifts in how we understand what is and is not reasonable. These tectonic shifts are barely perceptible to ordinary reason. Unlike planet earth's tectonic shifts, these shifts are never earthquake sudden, but over the centuries their impact can be just as earthshaking. For instance, in the West we can go from the sixteenth century, when the whole of society was passionately debating how one is saved, to the early twenty-first century, when even believers worry over the reasonableness of faith.

At the heart of the shift to a secular age is a shift in what is considered to be reasonable that not only undercuts the reasonableness of faith in God but also undercuts the reasonableness of affirming free will, creative originality, altruism, moral reality, and moral responsibility. Henceforth I will call these "spiritual realities."[1] Notably, no new and challenging argument suddenly made spiritual realities seem like nonsense. The secular worldview arose slowly and indirectly. Certain background ideas about what was reasonable came together in such a way that they gradually rendered all spiritual realities intellectually suspect.

By the secular condition, however, I mean something more than simply the secular rejection of spiritual realities. The secular condition describes a society in which vast numbers of people subscribe to a modern, naturalistic

---

1. In part 2 of the argument I will be calling these "sphere of spirit" realities, and within the sphere of spirit I will distinguish between poetic and spiritual realities (at that point "spiritual" will be used in its traditional, religious sense).

understanding of what is reasonable (which involves rejecting all spiritual realities) and simultaneously continue to affirm some or all spiritual realities. *In short, the secular condition describes the quandary of a host of people who affirm spiritual realities whose meaningfulness and reasonableness they cannot, if pressed, defend.*

This is all a bit abstract, so before detailing the history of the conceptual shifts that have resulted in the secular condition, let me try to make all this more concrete with two illustrations. My first illustration should make clear how a shift in conceptual frameworks elided the meaningfulness of faith in God. My second illustration should make clear how a shift in conceptual frameworks elided the meaningfulness and reasonableness of affirming spiritual realities such as free will, creative originality, altruism, moral reality, and moral responsibility.

Eliding Faith

First, consider the fate of "faith" in the modern West. What does "faith" mean? Even for many believers, "faith" means believing something beyond what is warranted by the evidence. Even many believers say they are taking something "on faith" or that they are making a "leap of faith," meaning that they are affirming a proposition despite a lack of evidence, that they are leaping beyond what is warranted by reason. This means that making an affirmation beyond the bounds of evidence and proper warrant—in short, being irrational—is what "faith" now means by definition. Meanwhile, that which is specifically affirmed by faith, the content that distinguishes various faiths, is typically described in terms of "beliefs."

So, for instance, what makes one's religion Christian or Hindu depends upon the differing *beliefs* of Christians and Hindus. To speak of "faith" with regard to Christianity, Hinduism, and other religions is to affirm that they all affirm truths without proper warrant, which is to say, what all religions share, what makes them "faiths" is, by definition, their irrationality. In accord with this mainstream modern Western understanding of faith, the phrase "a reasonable faith" is an oxymoron, for faith by definition is irrational, an affirmation that goes beyond what is warranted by evidence.

Even conservative Christians who are self-proclaimed enemies of secularism accept this devastating definition of faith. Consider the work of Phillip Johnson, Jefferson E. Peyser Professor of Law, *emeritus*, at the University of California, Berkeley. Johnson, a major proponent of intelligent design theory, is the author of books such as *Defeating Darwinism* and *Reason in the Balance: The Case Against Naturalism in Science, Law and Education*. This, however, is Johnson at the beginning of *Defeating Darwinism*:

> I therefore put the following simple proposition on the table for dis-
> cussion: *God is our true Creator.* I am not speaking of a God who is
> known only by faith and is invisible to reason, or who acted unde-
> tectably behind some naturalistic evolutionary process that was to all
> appearances mindless and purposeless. That kind of talk is about the
> human imagination, not the reality of God. I speak of a God who
> acted openly and who left his fingerprints all over the evidence. Does
> such a God really exist, or is he a fantasy like Santa Claus? That is the
> subject of this book.[2]

Johnson is an evangelical Christian whose books are published by conservative Christian presses. But Johnson rejects faith alone because it is irrational: "I am not speaking of a God who is *known only by faith* and is *invisible to
reason* . . . That kind of talk is about the human imagination, not the reality of
God. I speak of . . . evidence." For Johnson, if you only have faith in God you
are as rational as an adult who still believes in Santa Claus: "Does such a God
really exist, or is he a fantasy like Santa Claus?"

Johnson understands himself to be defending Christianity—"defending
the faith," as Christians often say—against naturalism.[3] But Johnson accepts
a modern definition where "faith" means "affirmation without evidence," he
accepts a modern ethics of belief whereby to believe in God only by faith is
irrational, and he calls for an argument for the existence of God. In short,
Johnson's argument against naturalism and defense of belief in God remains
within the boundaries of the rationality he means to reject. That is why Johnson ends up defending a version of Christian faith that considers faith alone
insufficient.

Let me hasten to stress that I am not questioning Johnson's lived faith or
personal spirituality. From my perspective, Johnson is a victim of modernity's
eliding of faith. His attempt to protect Christianity from accusations of irrationality by developing an argument for the existence of God (an argument
in which belief in God doesn't have to be based on "mere faith" but rather
is grounded in evidence and reason) is continuous with prominent efforts by
Christians ever since the scientific revolution of the seventeenth century to
develop arguments that prove God exists. For this reason, standard philosophy of religion textbooks treat a variety of so-called ontological, cosmological, and teleological arguments for the existence of God and also review a

2. Phillip Johnson, *Defeating Darwinism by Opening Minds* (Downers Grove, IL:
Intervarsity Press, 1997), 23.
3. Note that throughout my argument I will, like Johnson, use "naturalism" to
designate what is often called "naturalistic," "materialist," "physicalist," or "scientis-
tic" rationality. I do not use "naturalism" or "naturalist" in the common sense that
designates an expert in fauna and flora.

variety of theodicies, which are arguments that provide justification for belief in God in the face of the so-called problem of evil (i.e., where the existence of evil creates a logical problem for those who argue for the existence of God).

No proof of God's existence has succeeded, no theodicy has triumphed, but that is not the real problem for Christian (or any other) faith. The clarity of Johnson's statement of purpose helps to unveil the depth of the real problem, which only becomes visible when one realizes that if any proof of God's existence were to be successful it would immediately ruin faith. For then the belief that "God exists" would be a matter not of faith, but a matter of reason, a properly warranted conclusion of reason. I would then believe in God in the same way that I believe that it takes approximately eight minutes for light from the sun to reach earth. That is, if any proof for the existence of God were successful we would be dealing with a God who is the conclusion of a human argument, a God who is a valid inference of human reason, a God who is known reasonably only insofar as that God is within the grasp of human reason.

According to Judaism, Christianity and all the rest of the world's classic theistic faith traditions, any such god, any god drawn by human reason, would be a graven image, an idol. Notably when I say, "ruin faith," I am not concerned with ruining the anemic, modern version of faith, where "faith" means "affirmation beyond the evidence." This modern understanding already ruins faith, as does its demand for a God who is a valid inference of human reason (i.e., an idol). The conceptual power of the condition of secularity is so strong that it is no longer clear even to many people of faith what else faith could possibly mean, so they define faith in terms of affirmation of some set of beliefs they cannot justify. In sum, within the background conceptual framework of modern Western reason, any defense of the reasonableness of faith is quixotic, for we are left with a disastrous either/or: *either* faith in God by virtue of an affirmation that reaches beyond the evidence (and therefore irrationality) *or* reasonable belief in a God whose existence we have demonstrated (and thereby idolatry).

Let me reiterate that I am not questioning the lived faith or personal spirituality of the multitude of people who, like Phillip Johnson, have been ensnared by the modern Western rationality that drives us to this disastrous either/or. I am claiming that the ability to articulate the reality of faith accurately, and to defend how faith is reasonable, has been elided by tectonic shifts that have eventuated in the condition of secularity. Over the past four centuries, modern Western thought has surreptitiously evolved background concepts—in particular, concepts of "knowledge," "good," "nature," "reality," "cause," and "I"—that empty "faith" of spiritual content and make the phrase "reasonable faith" nonsensical by definition.

Skeptics may argue that I should not use the term "elided" because there are arguments against faith in God. No such arguments exist. True, university classes in religion regularly review convincing *arguments against arguments for* the existence of God. But those arguments for the existence of God themselves presume a modern Western framework of understanding and are almost wholly the inventions of modern Western reason. They were developed when people of faith were, for the first time, duped into thinking that the reasonableness of faith depended upon finding proof for the conclusion "God exists," and thereby into thinking that it was a good idea to try to prove the existence of God. To the contrary, since any successful argument for the existence of God would ruin faith and set up an idol, from the perspective I am defending all arguments that defeat arguments for the existence of God are beneficial, for they eliminate a threat to true faith.[4]

The demand for proof keeps most modern thinkers from noticing and taking seriously the fact that none of the world's major faith traditions—none of their scriptures, major theologians, or classic interpreters—ever attempted to prove the existence of God. It leads some people of faith to speak of a "leap of faith," "belief without proper warrant," a "leap beyond reason," and sometimes even to describe faith as "a decision [*my* decision] to believe [beyond the evidence]." It leads others to declare faith insufficient and therefore to try to prove the existence of God, to speak of "evidence that demands a verdict,"[5] to argue enthusiastically for creation science, and/or to attempt to infer the existence of an intelligent designer. All of this displays the influence of quintessentially modern Western understanding and is disastrous for faith.

In sum, a centuries-long, surreptitious shift in conceptual frameworks has created a predominant form of reason in the modern West that sets up a disastrous either/or: *either* faith in God by virtue of an affirmation that reaches beyond the evidence (and therefore irrationality) *or* reasonable belief in a God whose existence we have demonstrated (and thereby idolatry). This disastrous either/or is not the result of any particular argument. It is the result of a

4. St. Anselm and St. Thomas Aquinas purportedly offered proofs for the existence of God. I would argue that neither Anselm nor Aquinas offered anything like proofs in the modern Western sense (i.e., objective demonstrations based upon nature—where "objective" and "nature" are understood in the modern sense). Anselm's so-called "ontological argument" is situated in the middle of a prayer. This is not neutral argument, but faith seeking understanding. Aquinas' cosmological arguments, meanwhile, do not attempt to prove the existence of the triune God Aquinas has faith in but demonstrate the continuity between the findings of reason and faith in God. Neither of these medieval Christian theologians, nor any patristic or Reformation era theologians, attempt to develop objective, foundational proofs for the existence of God.

5. Josh McDowell, *Evidence That Demands a Verdict* (San Bernardino, CA: Here's Life Publishers, Inc., 1972).

long-term, largely hidden shift in Western conceptual frameworks that elides the possibility of speaking meaningfully about faith.

How, then, should we think about "faith in God"? The meaningful answer to that pivotal question is beyond the ken of modern Western reason, which frames the "either irrational or idolatrous" dichotomy. Answering that question is the task of the second part of this meditation. The first task is to make visible the deep, modern Western conceptual shifts that have elided the possibility of reasonable affirmation of faith in God, and by this point I hope I have lent some beginning clarity and plausibility to my claim that a major stream of modern reason has walled off precisely that possibility. Now I will use a second example to illustrate how tectonic shifts in conceptual frameworks in the modern West have elided conceptual space for affirmation of free will, creative originality, altruism, moral reality, and moral responsibility.

Eliding Spiritual Realities

Most Westerners will remember the familiar nature/nurture debate from high school biology class—or in more recent terminology, the genes/memes debate (where "memes" are the sociocultural equivalent of "genes"). The signal question is, "to what degree is our behavior determined by nature and to what degree is our behavior determined by nurture?" The debate is typically resolved amicably enough with the conclusion that it is almost always some combination of the two, and one is left to quibble over how precisely to apportion the influence of nature and nurture with regard to particular cases.

The standard framing of the nature/nurture debate, however, is not innocent. There is no problem with the two key questions, "to what degree nurture?" and "to what degree nature?" Certainly our actions are to a significant degree determined by nature and nurture. That legitimate conclusion is betrayed, however, when one frames the nature/nurture debate without qualification and so by default *poses as a question that exhausts the explanatory options*: "to what degree is our behavior determined by nature and to what degree is our behavior determined by nurture?" When the nature/nurture question is posed without qualification, then the question frames thought in such a way that answers can appeal *only* to the influence of nature and nurture, perhaps leaving some space for indeterminacy/randomness. That is, "to what degree nature and to what degree nurture?" is then framed such that one will answer "15/85 nature/nurture," or "40/60 nature/nurture," or "50/50," or perhaps "49/50 nature/nurture with 1 percent indexed to sheer randomness." In sum: the nature/nurture debate limits explanation of human behavior to *these two factors alone* (with perhaps a little wiggle room for randomness).

The implications of this are exclusive and/or straightforward and are anything but obviously true or spiritually innocent. The exclusive framing means, for instance, that when one asks about the sources of one's behaviors there is no possibility of asking, "to what degree free will?" "to what degree creative originality?" "to what degree a response to moral reality?" or "to what degree altruism or response to the call of the divine?" That is, built into the nature/nurture question as commonly taught without qualification is a background notion of a wholesale continuum of causal/random progression that elides any possible conceptual space for spiritual realities.

With the standard, unqualified nature/nurture framing, then, we have been shifted *from* the nondebatable claim that to a significant degree my behavior is determined by nature and to a significant degree my behavior is determined by nurture *to* the highly debatable claim that my behavior is *wholly* determined by some combination of nature and nurture, save perhaps leaving some minimal role for randomness.

In this way, without explicit mention, let alone any actual argument, but with a momentous if barely perceptible conceptual shift, we are moved into a framework wherein there is no space for affirmation of spiritual realities. We are moved to a position that leaves no space for saying, for instance, that my action was 48 percent nature, 46 percent nurture, 1 percent random and 5 percent (a critical, tilt-the-balance degree) free will and/or response to moral or divine reality.

We are so accustomed to thinking of the nature/nurture debate as exhausting the explanatory options that my suggestion that we accord something like 5 percent to free agency and/or response to moral/divine reality can look very odd, but in fact my proposal accurately reflects ordinary and historic understanding. For instance, when in a court of law we consider not guilt nor innocence but what sentence to impose upon the one convicted, we quite reasonably consider it proper to take into account nature (e.g., to what degree was the violence largely the result of the pressures of a brain tumor?), nurture (e.g., to what degree was the violence largely a result of sustained and horrific abuse endured as a child?), as well as free agency (e.g., to what degree is there no excuse for the behavior, to what degree is the defendant morally responsible?).

Moreover, with regard to many crimes (e.g., assault, murder, rape, incest), classic philosophical and religious theorists have understood the convicted to be guilty not merely of breaking socially mandated norms, but also of committing a moral offense. That is, with regard to such crimes (in contrast, for instance, to traffic violations) the offense is not primarily against community agreement (rules by which we agree to conduct our lives together) but against moral reality (things that are right or wrong in themselves). Such offenses are unlawful because they are immoral.

My delineation of precise percentages is fanciful, but the point is nonetheless clear. Posed without qualification, the framing of the nature/nurture question, far from being neutral, objective, obviously reasonable, and innocent, is spiritually devastating and philosophically dubious. For without overt argument or even explicit mention it elides conceptual space for free will, creative originality, altruism, moral reality, and moral responsibility.

The Secular Condition

The eliding of conceptual space for these spiritual realities runs contrary to common modern Western public understanding of what is reasonable, real, and good. With the exception of divine influence, this is true even among atheists, who are often very concerned with creative originality and with what is good and just. But is common public understanding wrong? If we are not abandoning the advances of modern science (and we are not), and if we are not embracing irrationality (and we are not), then is there something "faith" can mean other than "affirmation beyond what is warranted by the evidence," and is there a wholly reasonable way to think about some or all of these spiritual realities?

I hope my "meaning of faith" and "nature/nurture" illustrations have at least lent beginning plausibility to my claim that deep background shifts in modern Western rationality have elided our ability reasonably and meaningfully to affirm faith and spiritual realities. The task of the first part of my argument will be to identify and disarm aspects of modern rationality that support these tectonic conceptual shifts. As long as we are captive to these modern Western conceptual shifts, it will continue to seem that the only honest, reasonable, and courageous thing to do is to face up to hard truths and reject faith in God and the other spiritual realities.

In brief, I will strive to unfold the contours of modern Western rationality with enough precision to allow us to draw a clear distinction between *naturalistic* reasoning, which illegitimately elides spiritual realities, and *scientific* reasoning, which is wholly legitimate and vitally important. Once this distinction is drawn, I can explain why affirmation of scientific reasoning does not logically entail denial of spiritual realities.

I will attempt to do more, however, than merely establish that affirmation of spiritual realities is not necessarily unreasonable. I will attempt to delineate our understanding of spiritual realities, including our understanding of faith, in such a way that it is clear precisely what we are affirming and why it is wholly and most reasonable to affirm it. In the end, let me be careful to note, I will not demand anyone accede to the conclusion of an argument. Rather, having quite reasonably cleared away conceptual obstacles to faith, I will, in the final portions of this meditation, strive to awaken readers to the reality and character of wholly reasonable faith, a wholly reasonable faith that empowers us, fills us with joy, and inspires loving action. I turn first, however, to a far more detailed attempt to delineate predominant streams of modern Western rationality that elide spiritual realities, including faith, and attempt to unseat these streams of rationality insofar as they entail rejection of faith and other spiritual realities.

2

The Scientific Revolution and Early Modern Western Thought

René Descartes and the Birth of the Sphere of Nature

Descartes on Knowledge

The secular world has its beginnings in modern Western society in the seventeenth century. I use "modern" to name a philosophical age, the so-called "age of reason." René Descartes (1596–1650), author of the famous affirmation, "I think, therefore I am," is justly celebrated as the "father of modern thought" because he formulated key modern Western philosophical and scientific concepts. Descartes was obsessed with certainty, and he initiated what is often called a "quest for certainty" that endures to this day. Indeed, Descartes invented the modern meaning of certainty, distinguishing certainty from, for instance, being sure or being without any real or lived doubt about some matter.

We can only speculate over the reasons for Descartes's obsession with certainty. Descartes was a brilliant mathematician, and he was impressed by the certainty found in mathematical and geometric proofs. Descartes also traveled widely and was exposed to different beliefs and customs among diverse peoples. He noticed that while he could expect reasonable people from diverse cultures to grant the certainty of mathematical and geometric proofs, there was no basis for demanding like assent with regard to matters of faith, ethics, and politics.[1]

1. René Descartes, "Discourse on Method: or Rightly Conducting One's Reason and Seeking Truth in the Sciences," in *The Philosophical Writing of Descartes*, Vol. 1, J. Cottingham, S. Stoothoff, and D. Murdoch, trans. (Cambridge: Cambridge University Press, 1985), 114–16.

Perhaps most significant, Descartes was born into a world in which no one doubted that the earth was the unmoving center of the cosmos. This was accepted by all ancient authorities and seemed the most obvious of truths. In his teens, however, Descartes learned that the earth revolved around the sun. It is hard to overestimate the massive disorientation provoked by this new knowledge, which went rapidly from being marginal speculation on the part of Nicolaus Copernicus (Copernicus's heliocentric theory, *On the Revolutions*, was published in 1543) to being the leading astronomical theory in the early seventeenth century, most especially in the wake of the invention of the telescope and Galileo's observation of moons revolving around Jupiter in 1610. Unlike those so stunned by this possibility that they persecuted Galileo and lived in denial of the heliocentric hypothesis, Descartes recognized the earth-shaking, heavens-rending truth—with the likely result that he resolved never again to leave himself vulnerable to such error.[2]

In any case, there is no doubt that Descartes was obsessed with certainty and that on November 10, 1619, in Ulm, Germany, he had a series of waking visions that convinced him that it was his destiny to provide a foundation of certainty for all human knowledge. In the following decades Descartes published numerous works of note in mathematics and natural philosophy (what we would call science), but he is most celebrated for two philosophical works that focused upon knowledge and certainty: *Discourse on Method* (1637) and *Meditations on First Philosophy* (1641). With these two works, Descartes helped to define and create modern Western reason and science.

In order to set himself upon the firm path of knowledge, Descartes adopted a method of radical doubt. In *Meditations on First Philosophy* he imagined that an evil demon was deceiving him about everything. Nowadays in philosophy classes we talk about alien super-scientists and brains in a vat. For instance, I say I am sure my body exists, I have no real doubt my body exists, but I

---

2. With regard to the discussions of medieval cosmology and the scientific revolution in this and subsequent chapters, I am especially informed by the work of E. A. Burtt, *Metaphysical Foundations of Modern Science* (New York: Doubleday & Company, Inc., 1954); Herbert Butterfield, *The Origins of Modern Science*, revised edition (New York: The Free Press, 1997); John Hedley Brooke, *Science and Religion: Some Historical Perspectives* (Cambridge: Cambridge University Press, 1991); Louis Dupré, *Passage to Modernity: An Essay in the Hermeneutics of Nature and Culture* (New Haven, CT: Yale University Press, 1993); Edward Grant, *Planets, Stars and Orbs: The Medieval Cosmos, 1200–1687* (Cambridge: Cambridge University Press, 1994); David C. Lindberg, *Beginnings of Western Science*, 2nd edition (Chicago: University of Chicago Press, 2008); David Lindberg and Ronald Numbers, eds., *God and Nature: Historical Essays on the Encounter Between Christianity and Science* (Berkeley: University of California Press, 1986), and Charles Taylor, *Sources of the Self: The Making of the Modern Identity* (Cambridge: Harvard University Press, 1989).

cannot be certain that my body exists, for I may just be a brain in a vat in the laboratory of some alien super-scientist who is feeding me input that makes me think I have a body (movie fans can recall *The Matrix*). This is the kind of thought experiment on which Descartes embarked.

In such an experiment, we recognize that all our knowledge of the world, including even knowledge of our own bodies, is made up of *ideas*, ideas in our minds about other ideas and about realities that are outside of our minds, that is, ideas about an external world. If that is the case, how can we be sure of the truth of our ideas? How can we be sure that our ideas match up accurately with external reality? How can we be sure that we are not actually brains in a vat and that all the ideas we have, ideas about other people and an external world and even ideas about our own bodies and life history, are not the input of some alien super-scientist?[3]

In this context of radical doubt, where all that seems obvious and solid is brought into question, is there anything I can know with certainty? Is there anything I can count as knowledge? Yes, Descartes says, there is still something of which I can be certain: I can know with certainty that I exist, that I am some sort of thinking thing. Even if I am wholly deceived, even if I really am only a conscious energy pattern in the laboratory of some alien super-scientist, I am still something that can be deceived, some sort of thinking entity. I can be certain of this: *I think, therefore, I am.*

"I think, therefore, I am," Descartes concludes, is free of any possible doubt. It is certain no matter who, what or where I really am. This understanding of certainty as that which is not susceptible to even the most far-fetched, logical doubt, and the insistence that we should only claim to have knowledge where we have certainty, is what distinguishes knowledge as certain, objective, and universal in Descartes's modern sense. Namely, "I think, therefore, I am," is certain, because it is not susceptible even to logical doubt. It is an objective truth, for it is true no matter who or what I am. And it is a universal truth, for it is true no matter where or when I am. Thus it is knowledge, justified true belief, for it is objective, universal, and indubitable.

Even after other elements of Descartes's thought have been rejected, this standard for knowledge remains definitive in the modern West: knowledge is objective, universal, and certain. Our philosophical task is to reason objectively and to evaluate all of our truth claims in accord with this standard of

---

3. Though he evidently has the sense not to pursue the notion with regard to such analytic truths (i.e., that which is true by definition), Descartes even suggests our judgment that two plus three equals five, or that a square has four sides, could be the deceptive work of a super-powerful being ("Meditations on First Philosophy," in *The Philosophical Writings of Descartes*, Vol. II, J. Cottingham, R. Stoothoff, and D. Murdoch, trans. [Cambridge: Cambridge University Press, 1984], 14).

knowledge, and we should never affirm any proposition beyond the degree to which we can be certain of it.

But what of Descartes's own body? What of everyone and everything else? "I think, therefore, I am" does not get us very far. I still may really be a brain in a vat. Descartes saw this immediately. In response, working only from "clear and distinct ideas" about God and perfect goodness, Descartes proved that God exists and that God is good (or so he thought). Descartes, considering his proofs for the existence of a good God decisive, then argued that God would never allow an evil demon (or alien super-scientist) to deceive us, so while we can be confused in ordinary ways (e.g., we may think the earth is the unmoving center of the cosmos when actually it revolves around the sun and spins like a top), we can trust our senses, our basic logical and mathematical reasoning, our basic ideas of good and evil, and our knowledge claims, insofar as we keep track of the degree to which we have certainty about them.

Henceforth, we can know with certainty what we do and what we do not know. With regard to that about which we cannot be certain, we can be explicit about our lack of certainty and be precise about the degree of probability we can have regarding the possible truth of our opinions. This means we have no excuse for confusing knowledge (i.e., what we know) and opinion, and we should never claim confidence about the truth of our beliefs beyond what is warranted by the evidence. In sum, Descartes gave precise meaning to certainty, and in its light defined knowledge, opinion, and an ethics of belief. Now, let's get a bit more specific about all of this as it pertains to spiritual realities.

I, God and Knowledge

As is now apparent, "God" stands at the heart of Descartes's philosophy. Indeed, since proof for God has logical priority over confidence in our senses, Descartes maintains we can be more certain about the existence of God than about the existence of our own bodies. Descartes, who dedicates his *Meditations on First Philosophy* to "the most learned and distinguished men, the Dean and Doctors of the sacred Faculty of Theology at Paris," proclaims this a triumph for Christianity. He appeals to passages such as Romans 1:19–20:

> For what can be known about God is plain to them, because God has shown it to them. Ever since the creation of the world his eternal power and divine nature, invisible though they are, have been understood and seen through the things he has made.

Based on such passages, Descartes concludes that offering an argument for the existence of God is not only legitimate; it is superior to common appeals to Christian scripture or tradition, for non-Christians (and thoughtful Christians) will legitimately wonder why they should believe Christian scripture or tradition:

> It is of course quite true that we must believe in the existence of God because it is a doctrine of Holy Scripture, and conversely, that we must believe Holy Scripture because it comes from God; for since faith is the gift of God, he who gives us grace to believe other things can also give us grace to believe that he exists. But this argument cannot be put to unbelievers because they would judge it to be circular . . . in the passage, "that which is known of God is manifest in them," we seem to be told that everything that may be known of God can be demonstrated by reasoning which has no other source but our own mind. Hence I thought it was quite proper for me to inquire how this may be, and how God may be more easily and certainly known than the things of this world.[4]

In short, appeals to Scripture or to the gift of grace (which here means God placing into our minds propositional knowledge of God's existence), both of which presume the existence of God, cannot then be used as a basis for affirming the existence of God (which has already been presumed), for such would be fallacious, circular reasoning. A legitimate proof of God's existence must not presume God's existence. So it appears to be good that Descartes develops a proof for God's existence "by reasoning which has no other source but our own mind."

Descartes's proofs for the existence of God were immediately criticized and never took hold, but his standard of logical indubitability for knowledge, which inscribes into the definition of belief in God an either/or between irrationality (faith) and proof (knowledge), and also his definition of opinion and of an ethics of belief, namely, his resolution never to affirm anything as true beyond what is indubitably warranted by the evidence: all these quickly take hold and endure.

Descartes was the first person to offer, in the modern sense, an argument for the existence of God.[5] While it is unlikely Descartes's beliefs were orthodox, there is no reason to question Descartes's sincerity about God's existence. Despite all his talk about faith and grace being gifts of God, however, in the philosophy of Descartes, in contrast to mainstream Jewish and Christian theology, God is not the subject of faith, and faith is not the gift of grace. Insofar as our reasoning is not circular, God is an object of human knowledge,

4. *Meditations*, "Dedicatory Letter to Sorbonne," in *Philosophical Writings of Descartes*, Vol. 1, 3–4.
5. I owe this insight to Charles Taylor, *Sources of the Self: The Making of the Modern Identity* (Cambridge: Cambridge University Press, 1989), 156–57.

the conclusion of a human argument, a valid inference about which I can be certain using only my ideas and reasoning, for, again, "everything that may be known of God can be demonstrated by reasoning which has no other source but our own mind." Descartes closes his preface celebrating this fact:

> The point is that in considering these arguments we come to realize that . . . knowledge of our own minds and of God . . . are the most certain and evident of all possible objects of human knowledge for the human intellect.[6]

This sure sounds positive for theology. In contrast to Galileo, Rome never censured Descartes.[7] Indeed, multitudes of Christians over the next three centuries would work to develop their own versions of proofs for the existence of God. But once one realizes the subversive significance of Descartes's demand that faith be replaced by reason, that is, once one realizes that Descartes is rejecting the possible reasonableness of faith, once one notices how casually but definitively Descartes defines reliance upon faith and/or grace in terms of irrationality ("unbelievers . . . would judge it circular"), one realizes how Descartes sets us up to attempt to infer God and ruin faith, how he makes of human reason an idol, how he sets up the disastrous either/or identified above: either faith and irrationality or reason and idolatry.[8]

Descartes's "I think, therefore, I am," has other profound consequences for spirituality. For instance, there is his delineation and elevation of human I's. To Descartes, I is our one foundation.[9] God, I's inference, is constructed wholly out of I's ideas and allows I to escape the confines of its own immediate

---

6. *Meditations*, 16.

7. Perhaps, in this regard, it is notable that after Galileo was forced to recant (1633), Descartes suppressed his own recently completed defense of heliocentrism (which was only published posthumously) and within a few years had published *Discourse on Method* (1637) and the *Meditations on First Philosophy* (1641), which established the supremacy of human reason while marginalizing the appeals to scripture and tradition upon which Rome depended for their censure of Galileo, all in the course of demonstrating the existence of an infinitely good God. Of course, Descartes's work still met with considerable resistance from natural philosophers committed to Aristotelian cosmology, but it never generated the approbation that met Galileo.

8. What I am saying here is true to the main way in which Descartes has been read with regard to proving the existence of God. Two of the very philosophers I will use to explain how we may understand the reasonableness of faith, Emmanuel Levinas and Jean-Luc Marion, advance a revisionary interpretation of Descartes that stresses the inability of the human intellect to conceive of God. This highly technical debate is very suggestive, but it is beyond the purview of this study.

9. Please note that from now on I will use the word "I" not only in its traditional sense as the first-person personal pronoun, but also to denote the autonomous self that stands at the heart of Descartes's system.

ideas and confidently build up knowledge about the external world. In sum, I and its ideas are fundamental; "God" is a critical brick in I's tower of objective, certain, universal knowledge.

Because Descartes's atomistic I is foundational, in Descartes knowing itself means something distinctive. All knowing starts from I and flows outward. This basic, possessive, existential orientation is reflected in modernity's most common terms for knowing and knowledge. I say that I "get," "grasp," "understand," "comprehend," or "have it." Thereby, the "I think, therefore, I am" inscribes into modern thought both an individualistic and a possessive existential orientation, for it inscribes a grasping, seizing, intending I at the heart of every existence and at the root of every knowing and intention. This I is prominent in twentieth- and twenty-first-century Western thought.[10]

For the world's classic faith traditions, by contrast, "knowledge" of God and "knowledge" about one's true I is not grasped or seized but received. I find myself given a gift. The Cartesian understanding is devastating for traditional spirituality, for its existential orientation forgets the giftedness of our being and resists opening to wisdom. Descartes thinks instead that I is atomistic and self-sufficient and focuses I wholly upon what I can grasp, assert, or intend.

Moreover, as over the centuries it becomes increasingly clear that no argument proving the existence of God will be forthcoming, belief in God is increasingly understood to be dependent upon faith in the sense of deciding to accept something beyond reason. Belief in God, then, must ultimately be the product of I's decision (in this case, an irrational decision that violates modernity's ethics of belief). In other words, for modern Western reason, once one realizes that "God exists" (or "Scripture is true," "Church teachings are true," and so forth) is not dictated by reason, affirmation of any of these propositions can only come through I's decision to believe. Thus I's decision anchors I's belief in God, and the fact that this belief goes beyond the evidence is what makes it a matter of faith.

This aggressive, I-decision anchoring is clearly on display in a twentieth-century ditty popular among conservative Christians: "the Bible [or "God"]

10. I say "existential orientation" and not "spiritual orientation" because the orientation of modernity's atomistic, knowing I violates "spirituality" as understood by all the world's classic faith traditions. Buddhists, for instance, use *koans* (e.g., "What is the sound of one hand clapping?") in order to grow in wisdom through defeat of an analogous, knowing I; and traditional Jews and Christians have typically confessed with precision to "knowing themselves known" or "finding themselves found" by the G-d whose "love surpasses all understanding." With Descartes, however, "philosophy" stops meaning "love of wisdom" and becomes a quest for certainty (which names the so-called shift to "epistemology as first philosophy"); and his category of "knowledge" has no place for awakening to spiritual wisdom/love that first has us.

says it, I believe it, and that settles it." Since it is certainly not given that the Bible is true or that any particular proposition has been uttered by God, "*I* believe," I's decision, anchors this bare assertion. As we saw with Phillip Johnson, here even conservative Christians who mean to oppose modern reason remain ensnared by a modern rationality that elides spiritual realities. For, in accord with Descartes's understanding of I, of God, and of knowledge, the possibility of reasonable faith as given, of faith as the gift of grace, of faith that does not originate in "I deciding to believe" is conceptually elided.

The Sphere of Nature and the Sphere of Spirit

Descartes is also the father of modernity's infamous dualism between mind and body (also called the dualism between mental and physical, or between spirit and nature). This contrast is built into the "I think, therefore, I am," which begins with pure thought, not presuming the existence of any body. It renders each I as primarily a thinking existence discrete even from I's own body, and makes it the center of all knowledge. There is, then, independent mental/spiritual reality. We also have an idea of nonmental stuff, of physical reality. In the light of our certainty about the existence of a good God who would not deceive, Descartes also affirms ideas about physical reality, reality that is extended in time and space. Descartes concludes, then, that there are two ultimate types of reality: physical/natural and mental/spiritual.

Physical/natural reality makes up the sphere of nature, which is for the first time conceived by mainstream Western rationality in the modern (and now ordinary) sense. The sphere of nature includes everything that is extended in space, all planets, all energy patterns, and all bodies, including our own. All interactions within the sphere of nature are deterministic (or, in a later development, possibly random) and mechanistic (if in recent developments a highly complex and fluid mechanism). Accordingly, all explanation in this sphere is developed in mechanistic, causal terms. Causation is now understood in the billiard-ball sense of regular, mechanical, antecedent causation: the same causes in the same context always produce the same effect. Causal relations, then, are inviolable, so we can think in terms of "laws of nature" or of a "natural order" in the modern sense. A complete explanation for any phenomena is one that wholly explains the exact combination of causes that produces, always, a given effect. For the first time, mainstream Western rationality sees "nature" or "the universe" as a vast machine and conceives of "science" in the modern sense, namely, as the discipline that explores nature and thinks strictly in the categories of the sphere of nature.

In Descartes's sphere of nature there is, by definition, no conceptual space for living spirits and lived awareness of reality nor for freely willing agents, creative originality, altruism, moral reality, moral responsibility, or God. Descartes, however, affirms such spiritual realities.[11] Before all else, remember, "I think, therefore, I am" is pure thinking. What we know first, then, are spiritual realities. That is, we know ourselves first of all as thinking I's with free will, lived awareness of reality, and moral ideas and sensitivities (recall that an idea of perfect goodness lies at the heart of Descartes's arguments for God's existence). Indeed, realities of the sphere of spirit are more certainly known than are realities of the sphere of nature, which Descartes affirms only after proving (appealing to spiritual realities) that a good God exists.

One can think about Descartes's split between sphere of nature and sphere of spirit realities in terms of the distinction between physical sensations and lived awareness of those sensations. Sensations are, to some degree, physical phenomena common to people and machines. For instance, I program my smartphone to say "red" every time it sees red, and I ask you to say "red" every time you see red, and you both do so. The smartphone and you, however, do not "see" in the same sense. True, there is a natural dimension to the event for both you and the smartphone. In both cases, a wavelength hits an eye that communicates via electrical impulses (or the like) with a brain. Insofar as that is the case, you and the smartphone see red in precisely the same sense. Nonetheless, there is clearly something missing in this strictly natural description of your seeing of red. You have a lived awareness of red that the sphere of nature description of the process of sensing red, no matter how complex, does not capture. You have a lived awareness of red that your smartphone does not share (though if phones get smart enough, they may also gain a lived awareness of red, and then they too would need to be understood in terms of both nature and spirit).[12]

11. I speak of "spiritual" instead of "mental" realities because twenty-first century Westerners tend to think of "mental" in terms of brain events (which is a result of the eliding of the sphere of spirit and the re-inscription of the meaning of "mental" within the sphere of nature). "Spiritual," with both its religious overtones and the connotation that we are dealing with an extraphysical, extranatural reality that is not a function of brain states, better captures the Cartesian meaning. Of course, "spiritual" here is not used in the colloquial religious sense of, "he is a very spiritual person." (I will use "spiritual" in this religious sense in my closing chapters.)

12. This eventuality vis-à-vis so-called artificial intelligences is sometimes discussed in terms of "emergence" and/or "singularity." Often, however, the meaning of the "emergence" or "singularity" falls shy of the ontological distinction for which I will argue. For instance, for some, to assert "singularity" is to make a wholly epistemological comment indexed to a Turing test. As will become clear, I would argue that the full potential meaning of these terms is realized only insofar as they are part of an ontological comment that moves beyond the bounds of "nature" in the modern Western sense (which would mean, for instance, that "singularity" names the emergence of a being with ethical standing).

In Cartesian terms, the lived awareness of red is an aspect of the spiritual, in contrast to the natural dimension of reality. Today, philosophers call "red" as lived awareness and all other sensations, insofar as they are had in lived awareness, "qualia." In a sense similar to qualia, consciousness, thinking, free willing (you, but not the smartphone, *deciding* to accede to my request and say "red"), and moral sensitivity are all also spiritual realities.

Spiritual realities cannot be explained or even described using a wholly natural vocabulary and/or solely by reference to causation. In contrast to the sphere of nature, then, where *explanations* appeal only to causation, *understanding* in the sphere of spirit includes talk of free will and of reasons that influence without determining (i.e., of "reasons" in contrast to "causes" in the mechanistic, modern scientific sense). Understanding also includes talk of creative originality, good and evil, altruism, and lived awareness of color, sound, taste, scent, and touch (i.e., qualia).

Today, as I will presently explain in greater detail, almost every Westerner takes the categories of Descartes's physical reality to be obvious; and what seems to many to be radical and doubtful are spiritual realities. In Descartes's day, however, it was the idea of the sphere of nature that was radically new. People have always made rough distinctions between the physical and the spiritual and between bodies and spirits. But in the medieval age no one distinguished a discrete realm of the "physical" in the Cartesian sense. Before the seventeenth century there was no "nature," "physical," "universe," or "science" in what is today the ordinary modern Western sense. That is, "physical," "nature," and "natural order" in the modern sense were just as new in the seventeenth century as were more famous ideas like "inertia" and "gravity."[13]

In a vague way, almost everyone knows all this. For instance, almost everyone knows that inertia and gravity are celebrated modern discoveries, and almost everyone has heard the phrase "scientific revolution." But precisely what was so revolutionary? Apples have been falling from trees for millennia. People have always known this. What did the idea of gravity replace?

Our general inability to answer these questions is significant for our study because it helps us to recognize that there are elements of current

---

13. Democritus and the ancient atomists, and later the Stoics, among others, had seen reality as a machine in roughly this modern sense; but the schools of Plato and Aristotle, which despite their differences both saw reality as having inherent purpose and moral contour, prevailed in the Western world until the modern period. Thomas Hobbes, Descartes's contemporary, was a thoroughgoing materialist, but seventeenth- and eighteenth-century culture as a whole (unlike late twentieth-century Western culture) was not ready to accept Hobbes's materialism. It was ready to accept a mechanistic vision of the world that was one side of a two-part dichotomy, the other side of which was the sphere of spirit.

understanding that we presume without question. Such ideas are disproportionately potent insofar as we often do not even realize we can bring them
into question. Some of these ideas help to solidify aspects of modern rationality that elide spiritual realities, so understanding what was so distinctive and
significant about the scientific revolution of the seventeenth century will help
us to understand the rationality we are setting out both to affirm and properly
to delimit.

In the medieval period in Europe (twelfth to sixteenth centuries) the natural philosophy of the ancient Greek philosopher Aristotle, together with
Ptolemy's earth-centered picture of a spherical cosmos, appropriated to fit
Christian understanding, was predominant. It is this Aristotelian cosmology
that was revolutionized by Descartes and others in the seventeenth century.
So in the next section we will briefly review some key elements of the medieval, Christianized, Aristotelian cosmology.

Medieval Aristotelian Cosmology

In the Aristotelian, earth-centered cosmology, terrestrial reality (i.e., everything beneath the lunar sphere) is divided into four basic physical elements:
earth, water, air, and fire. The Greeks knew from repeated observation that
rocks fall through air and water. But not everything falls (remember we must
think all of this without any notion of gravity). Air bubbles rise through water.
Fire rises above air (in its purest form fire, like air, is transparent: put your
hand over a flame and you can feel fire rising through air).

Based upon such observations, the ancient Greeks concluded that the four
basic elements naturally arrange themselves in a specific order: earth, water,
air, fire. Fire moves upward because its natural place is above earth, water,
and air. Water stays above earth but falls through air because it is naturally
inclined to move to its proper place between earth and air. Ancient thinkers,
observing that water separates when falling from a height (e.g., observing tall
waterfalls) even realized that water accelerates as it gets closer to its proper
station. Elements stop moving once they reach their proper place in the cosmic order.

The question about apples falling from trees is complicated because one has
to explain how those apples (mostly made of earth) got to be hanging above
air in the first place. How did they get up in the air? The answer involves living, spiritual beings. The terrestrial sphere is full of spiritual beings. There
are three levels of terrestrial spirit: vegetative, animal, and human spirit.
There are many differences among the different spirits (e.g., only humans
possess language), but one quality common to all spirits is an ability to move
independently of the natural motion of the four elements.

Apples are mostly made of earth and water, which is why they fall (i.e., move toward their proper station beneath air in the natural order) when the stem breaks. But trees are living spirits. They have the power to move against the natural order. Trees grow up through air and sprout apples, moving "earth" upward and holding it in mid-air. Once the stem breaks, the apple falls through air to earth, for it naturally moves toward its proper place in the cosmic order (of course, unlike rocks, apples, which upon squeezing turn out to be largely made out of water, remain suspended if they fall in water).

Above the terrestrial sphere there is the sphere of the heavens. The moon, the closest celestial being, marks out the boundary between the terrestrial and heavenly spheres. Above the moon are the sun, the planets, and the stars. The heavenly spheres, like the terrestrial, are understood to be solid (affirmation of a "vacuum" in "space" is part of the scientific revolution). The heavenly spheres are made of a fifth element, ether, that is transparent and eternal in its perfection. The transparency of the ether is consistent with the increasingly refined character of the terrestrial elements. Earth, water, air, and fire are increasingly transparent (for "fire," again, think in terms of the transparent "fire" you feel and can sometimes see creating ripples in the air above a flame).

As simple observation reveals, and as peoples had recorded for centuries already by the time of the ancient Greeks, the moon, sun, and plenitude of stars have always moved in the same circular motion through the heavens. Mathematically, a circle describes movement without change or decay. It is perfect, eternal motion. In the shining transparency and eternity of the heavens we observe this perfection. There are a handful of exceptions amidst the plenitude of stars, but observers since the ancient Greeks had presumed the few apparent exceptions, the "wandering stars" (planets), share in the perfection and eternal motion of the whole, and so must also move in circles, if, for some reason, at an oblique angle in comparison to the rest of the heavenly host.

The ancient Greeks already saw the shining heavens, with their eternal motions, as superior to our terrestrial sphere, which is pervaded by violent confusion of the elements and continual change, decay, and death. In the medieval period, when this Greek understanding was combined with Christian understanding, heaven, the literal abode of God, was thought to be located just beyond the outermost sphere of the heavens, that is, just beyond the stars. Some thought that the stars were actually small holes in the fabric of the outermost sphere of the heavens, through which the glory of God's heaven shines. Remember, the stars are not that far away and, just as they look, they are tiny (much, much smaller than the moon or the sun). People thought that heaven and God were literally just above our heads, just beyond the sphere of the stars. Once one begins to understand how close heaven was literally thought to be, one begins to appreciate why Galileo's displacement of the heavens, and thus his total displacement of heaven, so upset ordinary folk. Where are God, heaven, poor little Annabel, and great-grandma now?

It can be difficult for us to imagine how intimately involved in earthly affairs God was thought to be in medieval understanding. Consider, for instance, this passage from an influential sixteenth-century text, *The Institutes of the Christian Religion*, published by the classically trained scholar and famous Reformed theologian John Calvin in 1559 (only six decades before Galileo observes moons orbiting Jupiter):[14]

> With what clear manifestations his might draws us to contemplate him! Unless perchance it be unknown to us in whose power it lies to sustain this infinite mass of heaven and earth by his Word: by his nod alone sometimes to shake heaven with thunderbolts, to burn everything with lightnings, to kindle the air with flashes; sometimes to disturb it with various sorts of storms, and then at his pleasure to clear them away in a moment; to compel the sea, which by its height seems to threaten the earth with continual destruction, to hang as if in mid-air; sometimes to arouse it in a dreadful way with the tumultuous force of winds; sometimes, with waves quieted, to make it calm again![15]

Calvin's sense that every lightning bolt is a result of a direct act of God is remarkable but clear enough. Note also the reference, unintelligible within a modern framework, to "the sea, which by its height seems to threaten the earth with continual destruction," being compelled by God, "to hang as if in mid-air." As Calvin reminds readers in his commentary on Genesis, since, in accord with medieval Aristotelian cosmology, water, "being an element, must be circular, and being the element heavier than air but lighter than earth, it ought to cover the latter in its entire circumference."[16] In other words, all earth should be covered by all water.

For Calvin, God and heaven are literally just beyond the outermost sphere of tiny stars, not so distant above our heads (for Calvin in Geneva, heaven is literally closer than London). Moreover, the only thing that keeps the oceans

14. Together with Luther, Zwingli, Melancthon, Anabaptists, and the Catholic Theologians of the Council of Trent, among numerous others, Calvin was part of the great theological renewal in fifteenth century Europe known as the Reformation and Counter-Reformation. Within one hundred years of the Reformation, the medieval cosmology and philosophy through which all Reformation and Counter-Reformation theologians understood God and the world lay in tatters.

15. John Calvin, *Institutes of the Christian Religions*, edited by John McNeill, translated by Ford Lewis Battles (Philadelphia: The Westminster Press, 1960), 59.

16. John Calvin, *Commentary on Genesis*, 1:6–9; *Commentary on Jeremiah*, 5:22; and *Commentary on the Psalms*, 33:7, as cited in Calvin, *Institutes*, 59.

from rushing back over the land and drowning us is continual direct action by God. Calvin reads the Genesis account of God "separating the waters" so that dry land might appear quite literally. If God were not still acting to hold the waters back, they would immediately rush back to their proper place in the cosmic order, covering all land (as God allowed to happen with the Genesis flood). For Calvin, it is as if, from a modern perspective, the Matterhorn were literally hanging in mid-air directly over our heads, suspended only by the continuing action of God.

The ancient Greeks and medieval Europeans quite reasonably presumed that we humans, being ourselves a part of nature, accurately reflected the character of natural reality writ whole. In other words, they thought that we humans, freely willing spirits shot through with moral sensitivities, intentions, and goals, were microcosms of a larger cosmos. They quite reasonably presumed that our nature was continuous with and indicative of the character of all nature. We are morally ordered, goal-oriented, free spiritual beings, and so, they quite reasonably presumed, the cosmos is morally ordered, goal-oriented, and shot through with vegetative, animal, and human (and perhaps angelic) spirit. Accordingly, the same sort of moral, purposeful, spiritual explanation was used with regard to all parts of reality, even with regard to what we, in the wake of Descartes, call "natural" or "physical" reality.

I have been using familiar words: "higher," "lower," "fall," "rise," "mathematics," "nature," "natural order," "elements," "physical," "body," and "spirit." At a superficial level, we mean the same thing as ancient Greeks and medieval Europeans when we use such words and say, "the rock fell from the top of the cliff face" or "heat rises." But insofar as the meaning of all these terms is connected to a wholesale understanding of reality, even such simple terms have momentously different meanings for medieval Europeans and us.

In medieval understanding, you could indeed speak of "nature," "natural order," and "natural philosophy," you could distinguish the "physical" from the "spiritual" and "body" from "spirit," and you could speak of "science" and "scientific explanation," but you could not use such terms in the modern sense. In medieval understanding there is no "nature," "natural order" or "physical" in the modern sense, for the cosmos is inherently moral. Traces of medieval understanding still show through in our modern use of words such as "base," "fallen," "lower," "higher," "refined," and "ethereal," all of which still carry for us both physical (in the modern sense) and moral meanings. But we, in light of Descartes's modern split between physical and spiritual spheres, automatically sort the meanings into the physical and spiritual, or even into the literal and the metaphorical.

Before Descartes and the scientific revolution of the seventeenth century, such a physical/spiritual division was virtually inconceivable.[17] To describe the earth as base (just above hell, which is at the absolute center) and the stars as high (literally next to heaven) was to offer an explanation that was simultaneously moral *and* (in the modern sense) physical, for the geography of the cosmos was understood to be inherently moral and the energy behind all movement was understood to be ultimately spiritual (e.g., earth moves toward the center because it naturally moves, as it should, toward its proper, relatively base place in the cosmic order). Likewise, one could literally say, "sin weighs us down." In this sense the whole cosmos is permeated with spirit, and some thought that the cosmos itself was, if at a level more primal even than vegetative spirit, alive. In any case, to say the heavens are "higher than" the earth is to say that they are morally and spiritually of a higher perfection.

For instance, our medieval friend and we may both see the same thing and say, "that rock fell from the top of the cliff face." But beyond the superficial level we see different realities, for we live in different conceptual worlds. For our medieval friend, that "falling" is not a localized, wholly mechanical event related to the mass of some planet and gravitational attraction. In medieval eyes rocks fall off cliffs not because of gravity, but for the same reason air bubbles up through water and flames rise through air: because the elements they are composed of are relatively base or ethereal, heavier or lighter in a moral sense that is simultaneously a physical sense, and all things are naturally inclined to move toward or remain in their proper station in the cosmic order.

The energy behind all movement in the cosmos is ultimately spiritual, whether flowing from the natural tendency of all elements to move toward or remain at their proper station within the natural order or due to the action of vegetative, animal, or human spirits. Accordingly, all explanation of all realities involved a spiritual dimension, and though both our medieval friends and we would distinguish a rock from beings with spirit, such as trees, dogs, or humans, the being of the rock as well as the being of the tree, dog, and human would still, for our medieval friend, be clothed with irreducibly moral meaning connecting it to the whole thoroughly spiritual cosmological order.

Hopefully, it is now clearer why I say that Descartes, who is often ridiculed for affirming a dualism that provides a place for affirmation of spiritual realities, should mainly be credited with helping to carve out "nature" in the modern sense. Descartes helped to construct the idea of a sphere of brute

17. Again, some philosophical movements stretching to ancient Greece had indeed thought in essentially modern naturalistic terms, but those movements never became mainstream intellectual movements (varieties of Platonic and Aristotelian thought dominated the Western world until the seventeenth century).

existence, of the physical, of the natural order, and of cause in the regular, mechanistic modern Western sense, a sphere explicitly designed to exclude all value, morals, and free will, the sphere within which one could construct and define modern science and scientific rationality. Thereby, Descartes helped to carve out the revolutionary, seventeenth-century sphere of nature at the heart of the scientific revolution and the Enlightenment.

I have been trying to explain some key aspects of the immensely complicated shift from medieval to early modern Western conceptual frameworks in just a few pages. So, before beginning to trace developments within late modern thought in the nineteenth and twentieth centuries, let me briefly review the early modern conceptual framework of the seventeenth and eighteenth centuries. Note that we are reviewing key understandings of the age of reason and of the scientific revolution. As we notice how these ideas in key respects are obviously very different from common understanding today, we see evidence of the slow but sure and momentous tectonic conceptual shifts between early and late modern Western rationality that we will be tracing in more detail in the following chapters. That is, while far less sudden and far less famous than the scientific revolution, the quiet, slow but steady shift from early to late modern Western rationality, the shift I am speaking of in terms of the eliding of the sphere of spirit, a quiet revolution *within* modern thought, is no less momentous than the scientific revolution of the seventeenth century.

In Sum: Early Modern Western Cosmology

Let's review and sum up the basic contours of early modern Western thought (i.e., of the seventeenth and eighteenth centuries) schematically. *First, Descartes helps to establish a new distinction between knowledge and opinion.* Knowledge is certain, objective, public, universal and timeless. Opinion, by contrast, is subjective, private, not necessarily universal, not necessarily timeless, and not certain.

Knowledge	Opinion
Certain (indubitable)	Possibly mistaken
Objective	Subjective
Public (i.e., visible to all healthy adults)	Private (i.e., visible only to some)
Universal	Not necessarily universal
Timeless	Not necessarily timeless

Second, Descartes's standard for knowledge and opinion suggests a correlate ethics of belief. One's degree of certainty regarding any contention—for example, "the earth revolves around the sun" or "God exists"—should correspond to what is warranted by the evidence. It is unjustifiable (not ethical) to affirm anything with a degree of certainty that is greater than that which is warranted by the evidence.

Third, for Descartes and for most seventeenth- and eighteenth-century thought, there is general agreement over what qualifies as objects of knowledge in contrast to matters of opinion. Objects of knowledge include: scientific facts, ethical truths, and the existence of God. Matters of opinion include innumerable trivial items, but among the most significant are particular religious doctrines (e.g., regarding Trinity, Eucharist, baptism, Torah, Muhammad) and social customs (e.g., dress and manners).

Objects of Knowledge	Matters of Opinion
Scientific facts	Particular religious doctrines
Ethical truths	Social customs
Existence of God	

While no single argument for the existence of God ever prevailed in the seventeenth- or eighteenth-centuries (or beyond), virtually no one doubted the existence of God or doubted that a valid proof for the existence of a God was out there, awaiting discovery. No one expected proofs would establish the truth of tradition-specific particulars about God, for instance, whether or not God was triune (such particulars were considered to be matters of opinion). The fact of God's existence, however, was thought to be a matter of knowledge. Many intellectuals in the eighteenth and nineteenth centuries were Deists precisely because deism was thought to remain within the bounds of knowledge, though no successful proof of God's existence was yet in hand.

This distinction between knowledge and opinion anchored eighteenth-century political understanding of the distinction between public and private realms (i.e., the realms of knowledge and opinion, respectively). On this basis, for instance, John Locke recommended toleration of diverse religions within society. That is, the different doctrines that distinguished Jews, Christians, and Muslims should all be tolerated because they were matters of opinion. At the same time, Locke explicitly rejected toleration of atheists, for the question of the existence of God was not a matter of opinion. God was (in theory) an object of knowledge, thus atheists were irrational. More crassly, Locke feared atheists' fidelity to ethical truths also could not be trusted, for they lacked all fear of divine judgment for wrongdoing.[18] In any case, scientific facts, ethical truths, and the existence of God were all considered to be indubitable (or "self-evident") objects of knowledge.[19]

Finally, Descartes invents "nature" in the modern sense when he distinguishes between two fundamentally distinct spheres of reality: the sphere of nature and the sphere of spirit. What is revolutionary in Descartes's thought is the marking out of a discrete, amoral, a-directional, purposeless sphere of physical, mindless, brute reality. All interactions among entities in the sphere of nature are mechanistic and causally determined (or possibly, in a later development, random). Accordingly, explanation in the natural sphere (i.e., scientific explanation) will be mechanistic and causal (and, in later development, probabilistic) and will concern entities insofar as they are "natural" (in the modern sense), and this includes all bodies (including humans insofar as they are bodily).

Sphere of Nature	Sphere of Spirit
Interactions: deterministic/random	Interactions: free will, moral, and personal
Mechanistic causation	Free, self-originating choices, moral and interpersonal influence

18. Here is Locke in *A Letter concerning Toleration*, originally published in 1689: "Lastly, those are not at all to be tolerated who deny the being of God. Promises, covenants, and oaths, which are the bonds of human society, can have no hold upon an atheist. The take away of God, though but even in thought, dissolves all" (John Locke, *A Letter Concerning Toleration* [Amherst, NY: Prometheus Books, 1990], 64).

19. The "establishment clause" of the United States constitution, then, should be understood in light of the contemporary public/private distinction that was anchored in the eighteenth century contrast between objects of knowledge and matters of opinion. More precisely, the clause should be understood to instantiate a refusal to allow any particular *church* (with its private opinions about doctrine) to gain *public* standing (since only objects of knowledge have public standing). Though only implicit in the public documents of the time (e.g., references to "creation" and "creatures"), there would have been no serious (i.e., rational) question that the nation was literally under God and that many of the nation's laws were made in accordance with ethical facts (the "under God" was only added to the pledge of allegiance in the middle of the twentieth century when real questions over God's reality first became culturally significant). In any case, scientific facts, ethical truths, and the existence of God were all considered to be indubitable (or, "self-evident") objects of knowledge. Locke explicitly rejected Descartes's belief that thinking and ideas were the fundamental reality (i.e., he rejected Descartes's "rationalism" or "idealism") and argued instead that "ideas" were a product of the faculty of reason's exposure to sense impressions (i.e., Locke was an empiricist), but in Locke the shift to empiricism did not yet have the naturalistic consequences already visible in Descartes's contemporary, Thomas Hobbes, and that became definitive for the condition of secularity in the late twentieth century.

Sphere of Nature	Sphere of Spirit
Novelty	Creativity
Eros/desire	*Agape*/altruism
Explanation: via appeal to antecedent, billiard ball causation (scientific in modern sense)	Understanding: via appeal to reasons, decisions, goals; and to moral, interpersonal, and divine influence
Entities: natural (e.g., planetary systems, sunlight, plants, animals [including human bodies])	Entities: spiritual (e.g., mind, I's, "God")
Certainty and probability	*More* certainty

In distinction to the sphere of nature there is a wholly different sphere of existence, the sphere of spirit. This is the sphere of mind, ideas, free will, moral reality, altruism, purpose, and communion with the divine. Explanation in this sphere is not developed in terms of antecedent causal streams, and in this sphere there is no causality in the mechanistic, either-determined-or-random sense. Explanations in this sphere continue to be offered in terms of decisions freely willed (i.e., I may have decided otherwise) in accord with more and less influential reasons, including personal goals and with consideration of interpersonal, moral, and divine sensitivities.

In sum, by the eighteenth century, due in particular to René Descartes but thanks also to the influence of many other thinkers (including Galileo, Newton and Locke), the broad mainstream of modern Western culture conceived of reality in terms of the Cartesian categories we have been unfolding. Namely, in terms of a fundamental divide between the sphere of nature and the sphere of spirit, and in Cartesian terms of knowledge and opinion and of an ethics of belief. In obvious contrast to our own late modern rationality, the arena of knowledge included not only scientific facts but also ethical truths and the existence of God. That is, both the existence of God and basic ethical truths were considered to be objects of knowledge, facts that could be established as certain by public (i.e., universal and objective) reason.[20]

With this understanding of the basic contours of early modern Western rationality in hand, we are in a good position to understand a slow-to-unfold, quiet, but equally revolutionary conceptual development within modern Western rationality, namely, the rise of naturalistic rationality that by the

20. While not precisely germane to this argument, it is worth noting that the "ethic of belief" and public/private split critically inform the development of secular democracies, where "secular" signaled not "nonreligious" but—among the overwhelmingly religious peoples of the eighteenth-century West—"religiously plural."

late twentieth century results in the full-blown condition of secularity. At the heart of this quiet revolution lies the ascendance of a naturalistic rationality that wholly elides Descartes's sphere of spirit. As is often the case, this momentous development is initially most visible in the light of a reaction against it, namely, the Romantic movement of the late eighteenth and early nineteenth centuries.

3

The Quiet Revolution in Modern Western Thought

From Romantic Depths to Authentic Self-Creation

In 1633, Galileo is condemned for saying the earth moves, Westerners live at the center of a small cosmos, and folks are getting about on foot and by horse and carriage, just as they had since the time of Aristotle, some two thousand years before. Just four hundred years later, we know that our sun is one among hundreds of millions of suns in one of hundreds of billions of galaxies, and we're jetting about the globe, driving rovers on Mars, and taking soil samples on speeding comets. Equally stunning advances have been made in biology, physics, geology, anthropology, sociology, psychology, and numerous other scientific fields. The power of describing, studying, testing, and explaining reality wholly in terms of Descartes's sphere of nature is undeniable.

By the end of the seventeenth century, Descartes's "rationalist" notion of a realm of innate, pure ideas, that is, the realm of the purely spiritual I that is thinking, "I think, therefore, I am," has been largely replaced with the "empiricist" conviction that all of our ideas are ultimately derived from thinking in response to sense impressions. That is, we are born with cognitive capacities, but we are not born with any ideas. Our brains are a blank slate until we begin to form ideas in response to sense impressions.

Like Descartes, however, empiricists do not reject the spiritual realm. Even if all our ideas do originate with sense impressions, it does not follow that there are no spiritual realities. Throughout the eighteenth and early nineteenth centuries, I is still considered to be freely willing and creative, ethical truths are generally considered objectively demonstrable, and, despite

33

increasing skepticism, many still think arguments for the existence of God, if not yet in hand, only await discovery.

In the mid-eighteenth century, however, the idea of rejecting the Cartesian sphere of spirit and thinking wholly in terms of a mechanistic world, an idea already visible in Descartes's seventeenth-century contemporary, Thomas Hobbes, begins to gather momentum. In 1747 the French philosopher Julien Offray de La Mettrie publishes *The Human Machine* (*L'homme machine*) and a few generations later, in 1814, French physicist Pierre-Simon Laplace famously claims that:

> An intellect which at any given moment knew all the forces that animate Nature and the mutual positions of the beings that comprise it, if this intellect were vast enough to submit its data to analysis, could condense into a single formula the movement of the greatest bodies of the universe and that of the lightest atom: for such an intellect nothing could be uncertain; and the future just like the past would be present before its eyes.[1]

Laplace reverses the Aristotelian assumption about the prime model for understanding reality. Aristotelians presume the entire cosmos is essentially like us, inherently moral and full of purpose and purposeful free spirits. As we have discussed, Descartes helped to carve out from the inherently spiritual, Aristotelian, medieval cosmos the mechanistic sphere of nature. Laplace thinks we should complete the transition, rejecting the sphere of spirit wholesale and envisioning a deterministic world where even trees, dogs, and people operate wholly in accord with the laws of the sphere of nature. To be sure, people are conscious, full of desires and intentions, but they are mechanistic since their every thought, desire, intention, and movement is determined. Hobbes, La Mettrie, and Laplace are among the earliest modern thinkers to reject the sphere of spirit and conclude that the categories of Descartes's sphere of nature are fundamental to reality writ whole, that is, they are among the earliest to embrace naturalistic rationality.

Given the limitations of contemporary physics, let alone chemistry and biology, which had barely even emerged as sciences in 1814, it is remarkable Laplace's claim did not emerge as a textbook example of "hasty generalization" (i.e., leaping too quickly from limited knowledge to expansive knowledge claims). Because his eliding of the spiritual sphere anticipates late twentieth-century naturalistic rationality, however, Laplace's claim is often treated as prophetic. The only major difference is that today one includes the

1. Pierre-Simon Laplace, *A Philosophical Essay on Probabilities*, F. W. Truscott and F.L. Emory, trans. (New York: Dover, 1951), as cited in Daniel Dennett, *Freedom Evolves* (New York: Penguin Books, 2003), 28.

possibility of randomness in reality, so not even a super-intellect could say precisely what the future will look like. Randomness, however, still fits snugly within the Cartesian sphere of nature (for randomness funds only indeterminism, not free will or any other spiritual reality).

The wholesale mechanistic view of the world, naturalism, does not garner widespread support in the eighteenth and nineteenth centuries. Affirmations of moral realism and confidence in public (i.e., objective, universal, certain) ethical truths remain prominent. In the late eighteenth century, for instance, the United States of America's "Declaration of Independence" proclaims people's inalienable rights to life, liberty, and pursuit of happiness to be self-evident truths, realities established by "Laws of Nature" (a "Nature" still regarded as inherently moral) and by "Nature's God" (the theoretically demonstrable "God" of objective, public reason).

The idea that "Nature" reflects the work of a "Creator" and thus manifests an ethical dimension endures in the eighteenth and early nineteenth centuries not only because of the power of traditional ideas, but also due to an almost universal consensus that mechanistic explanations alone could not explain the complexity of life. This consensus is buttressed by two easily understood scientific principles: 1) Natural systems tend toward greater levels of disorder (entropy), and 2) An effect cannot be greater (i.e., bigger, more complex) than its cause. In accord with these two principles William Paley famously argued in *Natural Theology* (1802) that for the same reasons it is reasonable, if one finds a watch, to infer the existence of a watchmaker, it is also reasonable, given the complexity of eyes, humans, and all the rest of creation, to infer the existence of a Creator.

Even atheists in the eighteenth and early nineteenth century deemed mechanism inadequate to explain the incredible complexities of the biological world. Famed skeptic and atheist David Hume (1711–1776), writing in the mid-eighteenth century, admits that the complexity of the eye immediately suggests a designer. Hume is quick to note, however, that this inference does not entail God in any traditional sense. Reasoning consistently from creation to creator, Hume jokes that this rough-jointed, pain-filled creation looks to him to be, at best, a committee job, or perhaps the hackneyed work of an infant deity who has long since moved on to adult endeavors.[2]

Reflecting seventeenth-century rationality's eliding of faith and shift to empiricism, both Hume and Paley think about God in terms of Descartes's sphere of nature. The "natural" in Paley's "*Natural Theology*" is "nature" in the Cartesian sense, and Hume's "eye" only demands explanation in the

2. David Hume, *Dialogues concerning Natural Religion*, Martin Bell, ed. (New York: Penguin Books, 1990), 75–79 (Part V).

mechanistic, causal terms of Descartes's sphere of nature.[3] That is why Paley is not famous for developing an argument for the existence of a God who is "love," or a "redeemer" whose "peace surpasses all understanding," let alone for defending the reasonableness of faith that is the gift of grace. Paley is famous for arguing for the existence of a being drawn in the image of the scientist, a watchmaker, God the super-engineer.

In the eighteenth and early nineteenth centuries, resistance to wholesale mechanism and affirmation of spiritual realities is empowered not only by seemingly inexplicable physical complexity, but also by enduring belief in objective moral reality, free will, and creative originality. Spiritual concern over and resistance to the wholesale mechanistic interpretation of reality emerging in La Mettrie and Laplace coalesced in Romanticism. The Romantics do not deny modern science. They abandon the medieval idea that the location of elements and spirits is inherently moral and that all physical movement is inherently spiritual. They insist, however, that the sphere of nature designates and science discerns nature only at a surface level. Objective meaning, beauty, and goodness dwell in the depths of nature and, thanks to the creative genius of spiritually free I's, such spiritual realities can be represented in words and images that awaken and resonate with the spiritual depths of humans' spiritual being. At the deepest level of reality, we are still spiritual beings in a spiritual world.

Over the course of the nineteenth and early twentieth century, the Romantic's search for good, beauty, and meaning in the depths of nature is displaced by the combined energies of two very different conceptual developments. The first conceptual development is nested within Romanticism itself. Namely, the Romantic's celebration of the creative genius of atomistic I's. This creates an internal tension in Romantic thought, for this celebration of individual autonomy and creativity is compromised by obedience to supposed imperatives arising from the depths of nature.[4]

This internal tension becomes unbearable in the face of the second conceptual development: with ongoing advances in the sciences, nature is increasingly seen as machine all the way down. If the Romantic opening to the supposedly spiritual depths of nature is actually a bow to a machine, then it does not mark impressive openness to deep spiritual truth, but servile confusion. So there

---

3. By this point, the specifically modern meaning of "natural" is clear, and so it will be clearer why in my introduction I refrained from using the phrase "natural theology."

4. I owe this specific point, as well as considerable general inspiration for this entire chapter, to Charles Taylor's brilliant analysis in *Sources of the Self: The Making of the Modern Identity* (Cambridge: Cambridge University Press, 1989), see especially parts IV and V.

should be no compromise of the celebration of individual autonomy and of the creative originality of artistic genius.

As all sense for the sacred depths of nature fades, the sphere of spirit I emerges in its enduring twenty and twenty-first century form: the individual, generative, freely creating I of poetic self-creators. The spiritual threat to this poetic I is inauthenticity, servile obedience to nature or nurture, the possibility that I will never be more than a product of blind causal forces, never be more than a conscious puppet, never be a real I at all. By contrast, the potential of this poetic I is individual autonomy and authentic existence, the potential to be the freely choosing creator of myself. This names the crowning glory of I as poetic self-creator.

In stark contrast to Aristotelian and medieval Christian thought, where good and authentic existence is found by aligning oneself with an inherently moral cosmological order or, in the Christian vernacular of Paul, where true freedom is found by freely allowing one's will to be aligned with the will of God, in twenty and twenty-first century Western thought there is widespread idealizing of authentic individual existence, of the value of separating oneself from the herd, of not allowing others to dictate who or what you will be, of seizing your autonomy, freely creating yourself, creating your own identity, being your own person, choosing even the standards by which you will value yourself. As the celebrated American philosopher and quintessential secularist, Richard Rorty, affirmed and summed up this conceptual trajectory, I's crowning potential possibility, the greatest potential source of I's dignity as a human being, "is the one Coleridge recommended to the great and original poet: to create the taste by which he will be judged."[5]

One of the most profound conceptual tensions that defines the condition of secularity, however, becomes starkly apparent precisely in contrast to this celebrated, autonomous, freely self-creating, authentic, poetic I. For this poetic I in a newly attenuated sphere of spirit is incommensurable with another, equally prominent twenty and twenty-first century I, the I of Descartes's sphere of nature, the naturalistic I whose reality fits most consistently with the powerful, sphere of nature, scientific stream of modern Western rationality. Thus we find this same Richard Rorty, who considers each I's highest poetic potential to lie in the radical self-creation of the very standards by which I will judge I's self, also affirming a deterministic, Laplacean world in which every future movement of our writing hand and larynx is, in principle, predictable:

5. Richard Rorty, *Contingency, Irony, and Solidarity* (Cambridge: Cambridge University Press, 1989), 97.

Physicalism [i.e., naturalism; materialism] is probably right in saying that we shall someday be able, 'in principle,' to predict every movement of a person's body (including those of his larynx and his writing hand).[6]

The incommensurability between the poetic I and the naturalistic I designates the basic conceptual tension of the secular condition, for in modern Western thought both I's continue to be affirmed. Modern Westerners tend to think in terms of the naturalistic I when thinking scientifically or philosophically but to think in terms of the conceptually incompatible poetic I in day-to-day understanding and valuing of life. I turn now to describe some essential contours of naturalistic reasoning and the naturalistic I.

Naturalistic Reasoning and the Naturalistic I

"Naturalistic reasoning" and "the naturalistic I" name the reasoning and the I that presumes that the sphere of nature (in the Cartesian sense) and the sphere of reality are coterminous (i.e., there is no sphere of spirit). In this section, I will unfold the contours of naturalistic reasoning and the naturalistic I in relation to several loci: a. biology; b. psychology; c. freedom and free will; d. phenomena and epiphenomena; e. explanation and causality; f. truth; g. moral reality, altruism, and ethics; and h. moral responsibility.

A. Darwin and the Science of Biology

The conviction that the boundaries of the sphere of nature and the sphere of reality are coterminous was already visible in Hobbes, La Mettrie, and Laplace. This naturalistic conviction, and the associated vision of the naturalistic I, gains unprecedented plausibility and momentum in the wake of Darwin's *Origin of the Species* (1859). Darwin's theory of evolution explains how, given the existence of any replicator, and without violating the principle of entropy or the principle that an effect cannot be greater than its cause, randomness in combination with natural selection could explain increases

---

6. Rorty continues, "The fact that we can predict a noise without knowing what it means is just the fact that the necessary and sufficient microstructural conditions for the production of a noise will rarely be paralleled by a material equivalence between a statement in the language used for describing the microstructure and the statement expressed by the noise. This is not because anything is in principle unpredictable, much less because of an ontological divide between nature and spirit, but simply because of the difference between a language suitable for coping with neurons and one suitable for coping with people" (Richard Rorty, *Philosophy and the Mirror of Nature* [Princeton: Princeton University Press, 1981] 354-355).

in biological complexity using exclusively the mechanistic categories of the sphere of nature.

Darwin's work marks the coming of age of biology as a science in the modern sense, for it offers an explanation of biological complexity that remains wholly within the boundaries of the sphere of nature. Darwin's discovery immediately undercut what was up to that point the still powerfully felt need to posit a designer. It is the elimination of this felt need that led Oxford University biologist Richard Dawkins to say that Darwin finally and without remainder "made it possible to be an intellectually fulfilled atheist."[7] In this way, evolutionary theory could reinforce the conviction that the boundaries of the sphere of nature and the sphere of reality are coterminous, that is, that there is no sphere of spirit, for evolutionary theory could be seen as helping to remove the need to see humans as anything other than a product of the sphere of nature and thus reinforce the naturalistic sense that humans are wholly sphere of nature I's.

B. The Science of Psychology

Shortly after the appearance of Darwin's work, psychology too comes of age as a science in the modern sense, namely, as the discipline that interprets human ideas and behaviors solely in terms of the sphere of nature. The mechanistic understanding of humans this involves is obvious in twentieth century psychologist Bernard Skinner's familiar and celebrated stimulus-response (S-R) behaviorism. For Skinner, pigeons are complicated toasters. Pigeons and we are clearly conscious in a way that toasters are not. But in terms of our behavior, and in terms of our existence as physical beings in a physical world, we are not different in kind. So for Skinner, pigeons are complicated toasters and we are very complicated toasters—conscious, but machine through and through.

Speaking technically for a moment, let me note that this mechanistic, sphere of nature understanding of humans is less obvious but equally realized in the speculative psychology of Sigmund Freud. For Freud, a relatively discrete center of awareness, sensation, memory, reflective capacity, and desire emerges (he is thinking literally of fetuses and infants) as a pleasure principle that encounters a reality principle and through various pressures (e.g., introjection, suppression) generates an I that reacts to situations throughout life as an enduring interplay of id, ego, and superego. Freud's I is in its entirety the focal point of an enduring nexus of energies generated through an unrelentingly mechanistic interplay of forces and counterforces. (Freud's later work with the "death instinct" and "life instinct" is equally mechanistic.) What we

7. Richard Dawkins, *The Blind Watchmaker: Why the Evidence of Evolution Reveals a Universe without Design* (New York: W. W. Norton & Company, 1986), 6.

undeniably perceive as moral reality or freely willed decisions are actually and wholly the products of a brute interplay of physical, social, and mental forces.

Psychology becomes far more sophisticated over the course of the twentieth century, but into the twenty-first century, mainstream Western psychology continues not only to understand itself as a science (nothing wrong with that) but as, in principle, *wholly* able to explain human behavior. Our inability to predict human behavior beyond a certain level is not chalked up to the fact that psychology is dealing with freely willing, creative, partly spiritual beings but to situational uniqueness, causal complexity, and, possibly, randomness. In accord with naturalistic rationality, I is understood to be wholly natural in the Cartesian sense, to be, if you are emotionally able and willing to face the hard truth, wholly machine.

C. Freedom and Free Will

To be sure, we humans are very special machines, for we are conscious, full of desires and intentions, and possess linguistic capacities far advanced over every other known species. But insofar as we understand ourselves wholly within natural parameters, what we are conscious of, what we intend and desire, and everything we think and do is the product of brute antecedent causal streams (i.e., the product of some combination of nature and nurture) plus perhaps some random quantum-jerkiness.

It is still possible for a naturalistic I to think of being unique, of being true to itself, of having novel ideas, even of having freedom insofar as I is not prevented from doing what it wants to do. But when using these terms I must remember that I and my wants, my every idea, my every decision, and my every movement are all wholly products of antecedent causal streams (along, perhaps, with some randomness).

We are distinct from other natural phenomena like toasters and weather systems because we are conscious, and we are distinct from other conscious phenomena (like pigeons) because we are far more conceptually capable, but that makes us only aware, self-aware, and complexly reasoning spectators, not generative agents. Granted, we are spectators who, despite knowing better, *feel like* we are freely willing. As we now know (according to naturalistic rationality), however, we are actually spectators who are not freely willing agents; we are spectators who automatically participate in the flux of reality in especially complex ways.

I can be isolated as an I insofar as I can be relatively distinguished from the rest of nature, an emergent and for some time continuing locus of consciousness, intentions, desires, and behaviors, and a proximate causal source of new events and ideas. As a relatively discrete focal nexus of diverse causal streams,

I am utterly unique and will be, like every weather system, novel. Strictly speaking, every successive moment in reality, like every successive moment in an avalanche, is novel. Because of our conceptual sophistication, however, the ideas and behaviors of an I are potentially novel in the more dramatic sense of "unanticipated" and "significant" that "novel" is usually used to denote, and in this stronger sense various I's remain the proximate, but not the ultimate or to any degree originating, source of novel ideas and events.

Insofar as the naturalistic I displaces the sphere of spirit I, the distinctions between "events" and "actions" and also between "novel" and "creative" are erased. For instance, we typically think of ourselves as distinct in kind from natural phenomena like weather systems because we engage in actions and can be creative. That is, we typically think there is a sense in which a hurricane too is a relatively discrete entity, is an event and is, every successive second, novel but never acting or creating. This common distinction trades upon the differences between natural and spiritual entities. Speaking precisely, "action," "acting," "creative," and "creating" are endemic to the sphere of spirit. "Novel," "event" and "behavior" (in the modern scientific sense) are endemic to the sphere of nature.

In other words, both weather systems and we can be relatively distinguished from the rest of reality. Ordinarily, however, we distinguish ourselves from wholly natural entities like weather systems because we consider ourselves to be best explained and understood using the categories of both the sphere of nature ("novel," "behavior") and the sphere of spirit ("creative," "acting"), whereas we consider weather systems and the like to be best explained using only categories of the sphere of nature. Insofar as the sphere of spirit is elided, however, distinctions between "events" and "actions" and between "novel" and "creative" are literally unthinkable. Thus, insofar as I's are understood wholly in the categories of the sphere of nature, I's, in the same fashion as weather systems, are unique, novel, and the proximate cause of events. We, no more than hurricanes, however, act or create in the spiritual sense, for we are wholly naturalistic I's.

All this means that while we have freedom within the sphere of nature, no I any more than any hurricane has free will in the spiritual sense. Though it is far from clear that the categories of the natural sphere are sufficient to account for the reality of consciousness, no one tries to deny that we are conscious beings with advanced reasoning capacities, desires, and intentions. This does distinguish us from hurricanes, but the fact that we are conscious does not mean that we are creative, acting, or freely willing. "Freedom" names our ability to behave in accord with our desires and intentions. We can lose our freedom if, for instance, accident or coercion keep us from being able to do what we desire or intend to do. "Free will," by contrast, names not our ability to do what we will to do but our ability freely to decide what we will will to do.

"Freely to decide what we will will to do" indicates something other than a reality that is causally determined and/or random. It involves reasoning and reasons (i.e., as factors that influence without determining) in combination with an originating capacity to choose at a given moment among various alternatives in order to yield degrees ("degrees" because nature and nurture always have massive influence) of creativity (self-originating creativity, not merely novelty) and action (self-determining action, not merely behavior). In short, "freedom" names the ability to do what we will to do, "free will" names the ability (within limits) freely to decide what we will will to do.

Because free will names a reality outside the bounds of determinate/random physical/psychological sequences, it is literally inconceivable within the bounds of the sphere of nature. We can see freedom, the ability to do what we desire or intend to do, or the loss of freedom, the frustration of our ability to realize our desires or intentions, using solely the categories of the sphere of nature, for our desires, intentions, behavior, and the violation of our freedom to do what we desire or intend to do are all visible within the sphere of nature.

Thinking solely within the sphere of nature, however, we can never see or even make sense of the idea of free will. For insofar as reasons exist in the natural sphere, they are equivalent to causes, and insofar as decisions exist in the natural sphere, they are equivalent to effects. Once "reasons" equal "causes" and "decisions" equal "effects," the naturalistic, deterministic/random, cause/effect relationship applies wholesale to the relation between "reasons" and "decisions." Thus, again, free will is literally inconceivable for naturalistic rationality.

Naturalistic I's, again, may have freedom, the ability *to do* what they will to do, but they never have free will, the ability to any degree *to decide* what they will will to do. For free will (in contrast to freedom), like creativity (in contrast to novelty), and action or agency (in contrast to behavior), and personal responsibility (in contrast to proximate causality), are all endemic to the sphere of spirit. Freedom, novelty, behavior and proximate causality, on the other hand, are endemic to the sphere of nature. The naturalistic I, then, is unique and has freedom, desires, intentions, and novel ideas, but it does not have free will, it does not create itself or anything else, and it is not personally responsible in the sense that you could ever have decided to have desired, intended, or done anything other than what you have desired, intended, or done.

D. All That Is: Phenomena (Things) and Epiphenomena (Ideas)

As is by this point clear, all the intentions, desires, ideas, decisions, and thinking of the naturalistic I are without qualification mechanistic/probabilistic realities. For naturalistic rationality, I am wholly a product of nature and nurture (and perhaps some randomness). To be clear, all ideas *as ideas* are real parts of the natural world. People really do believe in free will, action, creativity, self-creation, personal responsibility, and other spiritual realities, and all these beliefs are undeniably real as beliefs (ideas, memes) and so play a real causal role in the world, making a difference to what humans think and do. Insofar as the sphere of nature is coterminous with the sphere of reality, however, none of these beliefs can be about anything that in any sense exists independently of our ideas about it. The "realities" these beliefs are about are inventions of thought and exist only insofar as we think them. They are not *phenomena* but *epiphenomena*.

In other words, insofar as the sphere of nature is taken to be coterminous with the sphere of reality, all that is is divided into phenomena (basically, things, like the tissues and electrical signals that are our brains) and epiphenomena (basically, ideas, the products of brains). For instance, a child's stuffed animal unicorn, which exists physically in the world as cloth and stuffing in a particular shape, is not a unicorn, which is wholly an idea, unless some brain is seeing it as such. "Unicorn" is epiphenomenal. Similarly, "Canada," "Canada's GDP," and "free will" (as an idea) all name epiphenomena.

"Tree," "ocean," and "sun," by contrast, all name phenomena, for the realities signified exist independent of the thinking of any brains. To be sure, the "sun" would not exist *as such*, that is, as "sun," without some brain seeing it as such, that is, without some brain dividing up sheer reality into sun, sun's rays, space, earth, and so forth. But the realities that we call "sun," "sun's rays" and "earth" would all still exist, whether anyone ever sees them as such or not. So these all exist independently of our ideas about them. They are not epiphenomena, are not wholly derivative, are not wholly dependent upon being thought, but phenomena that exist, if not as such, whether or not anyone ever thinks them.

Now there is nothing terribly exciting about specifying that "unicorn" and "Canada's GDP" are epiphenomenal. That fact can be freely and harmlessly acknowledged, but not so with spiritual realities. To acknowledge that "free will" is epiphenomenal, for instance, ruins "free will." For "free will" purports to name a real capacity of entities in the world, a way certain sorts of entities within the world proceed from past to future that falls beyond the causally determinate/random/probabilitistic flow of reality in the sphere of nature. From the naturalistic perspective, that means that the idea of free will depends upon confusion, for in (natural) reality there is no free will, all reality is part of the determinate/random flow. So to acknowledge that spiritual realities such as free will, which purport to be more than epiphenomenal, actually are epiphenomenal ruins the idea of such spiritual realities.

The point here is that the commonplace division of reality into either phenomena (things) or epiphenomena (ideas) elides spiritual realities like free will. The eliding of the spiritual sphere I am tracing is visible in the difficulty of saying what free will *is* in relation to phenomena (things) and epiphenomena (ideas). If reality is in part accurately described in accord with the sphere of spirit, then "free will" is every bit as real a phenomena within the sphere of spirit as "sun" is a real phenomena within the sphere of nature. Predominant streams of modern Western rationality, however, consider the sphere of nature and the sphere of reality to be coterminous, and so they elide any space for thinking of free will as a spiritual phenomena. All phenomena are understood to be entities within the sphere of nature and, as we have seen, free will is inconceivable within the parameters of the sphere of nature. So free will is not a phenomena. On the other hand, to contend free will is epiphenomenal ruins free will.

To be clear, I agree that free will is evidently dependent upon the evolution of complex, sentient, natural entities, and in that evolutionary sense free will is dependent upon the evolution of brains. But, as we have seen, free will cannot be a property of brains in the naturalistic sense common to neuroscience, psychiatry, and modern psychology. This is true by definition for these and every other modern science, for modern science by definition operates wholly within the sphere of nature. Nor can free will be epiphenomenal, wholly and only an idea of brains, without ruining free will.

The awkwardness involved in trying to say what spiritual realities like free will are results from the fact that spiritual realities such as free will are, in the mainstream naturalistic sense, neither phenomenal nor epiphenomenal, neither thing nor idea. Affirmation of free will and other spiritual realities can sound ridiculous to modern Western ears, for insofar as the spheres of nature and reality are thought to be coterminous, there is simply no conceptual space for any reality that is neither phenomenal nor epiphenomenal in the naturalistic sense.

E. Explanation and Causality

The goal of any investigation within the sphere of nature, which is to say, the goal of any scientific investigation, is to provide a complete explanation for a given effect. In order to understand what this entails, it may be helpful to distinguish roughly between *necessary* and *sufficient* causes/conditions and also to distinguish between *correlations* and *causal connections*. A necessary condition is one that is necessary if there is to be a given effect. For instance, oxygen is necessary if one is going to have fire. But a necessary condition is not sufficient to produce an effect. Oxygen is a necessary but not a sufficient condition for fire, for one can have oxygen without fire. Sufficient conditions for an effect necessarily result in the effect. Wood, oxygen, and a temperature of eight hundred degrees constitute sufficient conditions for fire. That is, if you have wood, oxygen, and a temperature of eight hundred degrees, you will have fire. A basic goal of scientific explanation is to delineate *sufficient* conditions for a given effect.

One can, however, realize that wood, oxygen, and a temperature of 800 degrees always gives you fire without having scientific understanding of the event. That is, you could simply be aware—as most everyone has been for millennia—of the consistent correlation among these conditions and fire. To have scientific knowledge, you would also need to be able to delineate how the mechanisms work. You would have to be able to detail the causal relationships among wood, oxygen, and a temperature of 800 degrees that result in fire. A complete scientific explanation, in short, would involve both the ability to delineate the sufficient conditions for any effect and the ability to explain the causal mechanisms leading from the causes to the effect. Typically, once the sufficient conditions and all the causal connections have been delineated, an explanation of the relationship between causes and effects is considered complete or proven. Shy of such explanatory completeness, one can still use the ideal of such a complete explanation as a measure against which to judge various explanations (i.e., which fall closer to or further from the ideal of being proven).

My purpose here is not to give a detailed account of scientific method or standards for scientific proof but to consider the impact of this modern explanatory ideal, which is now clear enough for our purposes. The drive to provide complete explanations in the categories of the sphere of nature, the drive to delineate, without remainder, all the causal links that lead to all effects, is wonderful within the sphere of science. But it can also be problematic, for we can be bedazzled by the unqualified vision of such theoretical closure, by the dream of complete explanation, of what is often called a "final theory," a theory of everything that even atheistic scientists often refer to revealingly in terms of "knowing the mind of God."[8]

---

8. Consider, for instance, how in the closing lines of *A Brief History of Time*, Stephen Hawking subtly asserts that sphere of spirit questions fall within the brief sphere of nature explanation: "if we do discover a complete theory . . . Then we shall all, philosophers, scientists, and just ordinary people, be able to take part in the discussion of the question of why it is that we and the universe exist. If we find the answer to that, it would be the ultimate triumph of human reason—for then we would know the mind of God" ([New York: Bantam, 1998], 191). It is utterly unclear, however, how knowledge of something like a unified field theory would answer the "why" question, let alone any "ought" questions, and it is utterly unclear why determining a sphere of nature "complete theory" must come before we can even begin to explore sphere of spirit questions of meaning. Most naturalistic thinkers more consistently follow Sigmund

This drive toward theoretical closure, which carries with it a background notion of a closed causal continuum, though perhaps one shot through with points of indeterminacy, can lead us to believe that we can, in principle, explain everything in accord with the categories of the sphere of nature and can lead us to be repelled by the idea that there are gaps in or limits to scientific understanding of reality. Seized by a vision of bringing all existence within the grasp of scientific knowledge (at least in principle), it can be easy not to notice or to discount the fact that this naturalistic vision of explanatory closure entails rejection of all nonnatural realities, including spiritual realities such as free will.

F. Truth

The depths of the eliding of the sphere of spirit in modern Western rationality that we are tracing are also manifest in modern Western understandings of truth. Suppose I say, "light from the sun takes approximately eight minutes to reach the earth," and "eight minutes" is correct. Most everyone will agree that my statement is true. For we understand "true" to name a correspondence between a statement and either a phenomenal or an epiphenomenal reality (e.g., "sun" or "GDP of Canada," respectively). We generally understand how (in principle) to test the natural or social/historical truth of such statements, thereby falsifying or justifying our beliefs or at least determining the probability of their being true.

Now suppose I say, "strawberries are far tastier than blueberries," "Beethoven's music is far better than Pink Floyd's," or "Rembrandt simply does not match up to Picasso." These propositions, I say, are all true. You may, depending upon your personal tastes, agree that all of these statements are true. If you disagree, however, I have no basis for claiming that my contentions are true and yours are false, for these are all matters of personal taste. That is, "truth" in this context is indexed to each individual's preferences, so what is true for me may well not be true for you.

In a sense, even with regard to natural phenomena, all truth depends upon subjectivity. Unless beings like us distinguish not only epiphenomena like "Canada" and "Canada's GDP" but also phenomena like "sun" and "earth"

Freud's argument in *Future of an Illusion* (New York: W.W. Norton & Company, Inc., 1989) and see the urge to provide a humanly satisfying answer to the question, "why," as fundamentally confused, for nature just "is." I think Freud's naturalistic eliding of the sphere of spirit is unwarranted and severely warps his interpretation of religion (which is confined to religion insofar as it appears as a natural epiphenomena). Hawking's confused conflating of the two spheres at best signals an inchoate but dawning awareness of the insufficiency of understanding reality wholly within the conceptual bounds of the sphere of nature.

from the sheer flux of reality, there simply is no "sun" or "earth" as such. However, given our existence and our realized potential for discerning and naming reality, "Canada," "Canada's GDP," "sun," and "earth" all signify realities that are physically or historically "out there" independent of any individual's thought about them so that once we begin to talk about them as such, their independent reality is distinct enough to be used to test the truth of our statements.

This is all a bit rough—even, I will argue below, *revealingly* rough—but what I am trying to say here is familiar and generally uncontroversial. Namely, I am naming a common understanding of the sorts of "truth" one is dealing with in the hard/physical/natural sciences (which deal with phenomena/things), in the soft/historical/social sciences (which deal with epiphenomena/ideas), and finally where, strictly speaking, there is no truth or knowledge at all, only greater or lesser consensus of opinion (concerning cultivated, subtle, or informed tastes) over aesthetic judgment in the humanities (e.g., art, literature, music).

This understanding of the character of knowledge and truth relative to reality yields the familiar, modern hierarchy among modern Western intellectual disciplines. At the top of the hierarchy are the "hard," natural sciences, such as physics, chemistry, and biology, which deal scientifically with phenomena (intramural debates over which is the hardest of the hard or who begets whom need not concern us here). Below the natural sciences are the "soft," social sciences, such as history, economics, sociology, psychology, religious studies, cultural studies, and so forth, which deal scientifically with epiphenomena (e.g., the fall of Rome, GDP, adolescence, or with Christianity or French Impressionism as sociocultural phenomena). Finally, we leave the sciences and enter the humanities, which are concerned with the affective impact of phenomena and epiphenomena (e.g., rainbows as soothing, Mozart as invigorating, Monet as pleasing, Shakespeare as moving or entertaining).

I take these distinctions to be familiar and uncontroversial. The implications of this naturalistic understanding of truth for morality and ethics, however, is especially notable, for insofar as the spheres of nature and reality are coterminous, moral truths are epiphenomenal. If "moral" realities are epiphenomenal, then if I say that "pedophilia," "torturing for pleasure," and "racism" are immoral, I am not saying anything that is more or less true than when I say, "the GDP of Canada is *y*," for these truths would likewise be wholly relative to evolutionary and historical forces.

In short, in the light of naturalistic rationality's division of all reality into natural phenomena and epiphenomena, moral imperatives are revealed to be biological and sociocultural imperatives, wholly a product of nature and nurture. Moral imperatives, however, are understood to have normative authority because their truth is understood to involve appeal to a reality beyond the brute givens of evolution and tradition (genes and memes). Like "free will" and unlike "unicorn" and "GDP of Canada," then, overt acknowledgment that moral reality is epiphenomenal ruins moral realism. This brings us to the relationship of naturalism to morality and ethics.

G. Moral Reality, Altruism, and Ethics as Science

As we have seen in medieval Aristotelian/Christian cosmology, the cosmos is inherently moral. The elements are naturally inclined to move to their proper/right place in the cosmos, what is "higher" moves toward morally perfect being (heaven, the outermost sphere) and what is "lower" moves toward morally imperfect being (hell, the center of the disordered, terrestrial sphere). Spiritual beings (vegetative, animal, human) transcend elemental things because they can move against natural inclination, but they too should move toward their proper place in the cosmic order and in accord with the moral/natural/spiritual goals and ways of being appropriate to their kind.

Until Descartes and others in the seventeenth century carved the sphere of nature out of the cosmos, thereby inventing "nature" (and "the universe") in the modern Western sense, there was no essential divide between natural and moral/spiritual reality. Descartes helped to invent the essential divide, but he did not reject spiritual realities. He considered sphere of spirit realities such as "good" to be just as real as sphere of nature realities such as "earth." "Good" is a reality in the sphere of spirit, and "earth" is a reality in the sphere of nature. They are utterly different kinds of reality, but they are all equally real. Indeed, as discussed, Descartes thought we could know spiritual realities, including the reality of moral perfection,that is, the reality of God, with even more certainty than we could know natural realities.

By definition the two spheres are utterly distinct. Within the sphere of nature one is dealing with a physical, causally determined/random continuum, absent of any purpose or *telos* and absent of any moral dimension. That is, by deliberate and stunningly productive design, the sphere of nature sees reality only insofar as it is physical (i.e., matter, atoms, energy, strings, or some such) in the modern sense. Thus, for instance, precisely as we should not attribute spiritual significance to the physics of planetary motion, we should not attribute spiritual significance to any other workings of nature. Moreover, if, contrary to Descartes, the boundaries of the spheres of nature and of reality are coterminous, that is, if there is no sphere of spirit, then there is no "good" or "evil" in the spiritual/moral realist sense.

Some of Descartes's seventeenth century contemporaries, most notably Thomas Hobbes, already considered the spheres of nature and of reality to be coterminous. For Hobbes, accordingly, until people invent good and evil (that is, as long as people remain in the "state of nature") there is no good or evil, only the struggle for survival, the war of all against all. Eventually, for reasons indexed wholly to each person's individual good (enlightened self-interest), social contracts and political systems are developed and good/legal and bad/illegal are invented. But again, while Hobbes anticipates twentieth century conceptual developments, his wholesale naturalism remained marginal in the seventeenth and eighteenth centuries, gaining real traction only in the wake of Darwin.

On the whole, as evidenced by the prominence of ethical appeals to "natural rights" and "natural law" even into the twentieth century, the medieval Aristotelian/Christian sense that nature was inherently moral survived the seventeenth century revolutions in astronomy and physics. Thus in the late eighteenth century we find Hume still arguing against lingering Aristotelian tendencies to draw moral conclusions based upon natural facts. Hume famously argued that it is invalid to draw moral conclusions from facts about nature.[9] For instance, the fact that the earth *does* revolve around the sun does not mean that the earth *should* revolve around the sun, and the biological fact that humans *want* to have sex with multiple partners beginning from around age fourteen does not mean that they *should* have sex with multiple partners beginning from around age fourteen. This is commonly known as the "is/ought" distinction (i.e., "is" does not entail "ought").

As we have seen, the sphere of nature was carved out of the sphere of reality precisely by excluding all spiritual realities, including moral reality, from the natural sphere. By definition, moral values are endemic to Descartes's sphere of spirit, and physical facts are endemic to Descartes's sphere of nature. The rejoinder not to infer "ought" from "is," then, simply reminds us that insofar as we affirm nature in the modern sense—an affirmation that lies at the heart of the stunning advances of modern science, that is, an affirmation it would currently be irrational to reject—we must not think about nature in any value-laden sense.

In the early twentieth century, a version of the is/ought distinction was taken up in dualistic, Cartesian fashion in order to defend the autonomy and reality of the sphere of morals/"ought." Acceptance of this view in the early twentieth century was so powerful that violation of the distinction, that is, the move to construct ethics on the basis of inferring "ought" from "is," earned its own moniker: the naturalistic fallacy.[10] By the end of the twentieth century,

---

9. David Hume, *A Treatise of Human Nature*, L. A. Selby-Bigge, ed. 2nd ed. Revised by P. H. Nidditch (Oxford: Clarendon Press, 1975), Book III, Part I, final paragraph of Section I.

10. The naturalistic fallacy is related to G. E. Moore's *Principia Ethica* (Cambridge: Cambridge University Press, 1903) and his so-called "open question argument." Moore and Hume's philosophies are very different and so the precise relationship

by which time naturalistic rationality had become increasingly predominant, talk of a naturalistic fallacy had faded away, for there had emerged widespread consensus that the sphere of nature is the only sphere; there is no independent sphere that contains "ought." On naturalistic understanding, if there are to be any ethics at all it must somehow be rooted in nature in the naturalistic sense.

While the challenge to develop a naturalistic ethics only became acute in the late twentieth century, some ethicists had already recognized the challenge in the middle of the nineteenth century. In response they cultivated a new school of ethical thought, utilitarianism, that represents ethics' best run at securing intellectual credibility within the bounds of naturalistic rationality by establishing ethics as a science within the sphere of nature.

Utilitarian theorists found empirical traction for "good" and "bad" in the apparently universal tendency for every (living) individual capable of sensation and movement, to the fullest degree to which it is capable (differing among daisies, paramecium, pigs and people), to disfavor and move to avoid pain and to favor and move to gain pleasure (or, in more conceptually advanced creatures, to move to gain personal preferences, which may be sadomasochistic or even suicidal). The drive toward good and away from bad, what we may call, in a word, *eros*, describes a basic inclination/impetus/driving force of living individuals (the dividing line is fuzzy but, roughly, an impetus/inclination/driving force characteristic of paramecium and people, but not of planets and genes).

In this way, "good," "bad," and "*eros*," are all defined in relation to causality and observable phenomena, have meaning within the sphere of nature, and provide basic explanatory terms for the movement of living individuals. That is, insofar as I have explained how a behavior is related to what an individual senses or believes will be good or bad for it (rightly or no), I have wholly explained the behavior insofar as it can be explained in terms of the *eros* of living individuals (other sorts of explanations, for example, chemical or genetic, may also apply).

Not surprisingly, explaining altruistic behavior—note well, explaining altruistic *behavior*, not altruism in the spiritual sense—in wholly natural terms, that is, wholly in terms of *eros*, became a significant challenge in the twentieth century, and led to now familiar accounts of kinship altruism (which depends upon genetic explanation), reciprocal altruism (which has been unfolded by social scientists with regard to human communities in terms of elaborate economies of gift exchange, sometimes stretching out over generations), and

---

between the is/ought distinction and the naturalistic fallacy is far more complicated than I am indicating. My account is not inaccurate as far as it goes and is sufficient for present purposes.

group altruism (based upon the utility of various memes—for example, belief in karma, God, heaven and/or hell—that cause altruistic behavior and on the whole increase the survival potentials of a sociocultural group).[11]

Kinship, reciprocal, and group altruism, all of which explain altruistic behavior in wholly natural terms, should not be confused with altruism in the spiritual sense. For instance, since "reciprocal altruism" depends upon all parties' expectations of tit-for-tat exchange, that is, upon a closed loop economy, there is no distinction to be made between reciprocal altruism and a sort of psychological, sociological, and/or anthropological conservation of energy manifest in a felt sense of obligation to reciprocate and restore equilibrium. The psychological, anthropological, and sociological dynamics are wholly mechanistic. Indeed, it is precisely the causally mechanistic character of the account that makes reciprocal altruism (and kinship and group altruism) legitimate categories within the sphere of nature.

In sum, the advantage of defining "good" and "bad" in natural terms is twofold. First, "good" and "bad" become empirically visible realities in the sphere of nature. Second, eros, the motivation/cause of movement/behavior (i.e., toward pleasure/preferences and away from pain/suffering) is intrinsic to this definition of good and bad, so there is no need, after explaining how an individual is moving to avoid bad (for them) and gain good (for them), to offer any further explanation for their movement/behavior.

For ethics, however, there are major problems with defining "good" and "bad" in natural terms. On this naturalistic account "good" and "bad" are wholly relativized and stripped of ethical meaning. For "good" means "good for me" and "bad" means "bad for me," and what may be good for me may simultaneously be bad for others. Moreover, just as there is nothing altruistic about kinship, reciprocal, or group altruism, so there is nothing ethical about a wholly self-centered dynamic in which each entity pursues what is good for it and avoids what is bad for it (and this is true whether or not the self-interest is enlightened). Consistent with Descartes's dualism, then, insofar as ethics is naturalized (interpreted wholly within the sphere of nature), it ceases to be ethics in any ordinary (i.e., any spiritual) sense.

Recognizing the difficulties, utilitarians added extra criteria to their naturalistic understanding of good and evil.[12] For instance, "always act so as to

11. For an excellent discussion of these various forms of natural "altruism" see Elliot Sober and David Sloan Wilson, *Unto Others: The Evolution and Psychology of Unselfish Behavior* (Cambridge, MA: Harvard University Press, 1999).

12. For an excellent discussion of this difficulty, often discussed in relation to Henry Sidgwick's "dualism of practical reason," see Katarzyna de Lazari-Radek and Peter Singer, *The Point of View of the Universe: Sidgwick and Contemporary Ethics* (Oxford: Oxford University Press, 2014).

cause the greatest good for the greatest number." Given what is lost in the transition from the sphere of spirit to the sphere of nature, all such principles suffer a twofold failure. First, unlike the natural meaning of "good" and "bad," which could be anchored empirically in terms of pleasure, pain, and *eros*, such general ethical principles (whether utilitarian or other) have no empirical standing (i.e., "always act so as to create the greatest good for the greatest number" is not an empirical conclusion). So "good" and "bad" remain wholly relativized and stripped of ethical meaning. As a result, as a review of ethics textbooks will quickly confirm, by the late twentieth century there is no generally accepted justification for first principles in ethics.[13]

Second, utilitarians, along with every other modern ethical school, struggle to answer this question: Why act morally? Why act, for instance, so as to create the greatest good for the greatest number? With regard to cognitively advanced creatures, mainstream modern Western thought typically presumes that insofar as any human decision is rational—remembering again that rational decision requires only freedom, not free will—the decision will be made in accord with self-interest, that is, in accord with *eros* (this is presumed, for instance, by modern decision, game, and political theory).[14] Deliberate sacrifice of our own good, of our own desires, even, in the extreme, the giving of one's own life for others—in a word, varieties of altruism in the spiritual sense (not kinship, reciprocal, or group altruism) is, from the natural perspective, irrational and unmotivated (for it runs counter to *eros*).

In sum, for naturalism there is nothing beyond "is" or "fact." There is no "ought," "value," "good," "evil," or "love/altruism/*agape*" in any realist,

13. Lacking any sure foundations, modern ethicists typically proceed by first acknowledging (correctly) that no attempt to establish ethical knowledge on empirical grounds (or based solely upon reason) has succeeded, and second declaring their own theoretical commitments, and third discussing the strengths and weaknesses of their theories vis-à-vis concrete examples. Since there are no objective realities over and against which "strengths" and "weaknesses" can be evaluated, theories are typically considered solid or dubious depending upon their relationship with ethical conclusions "everyone" agrees upon. Standard ethics texts typically delineate the major ethical theories and then run through a standard set of scenarios, one or another of which exposes the shortcomings of all the major modern ethical theories. Finally, modern ethicists compare their theory with competing ethical theories. By the time all this is done it is easy to forget that from a naturalistic perspective the whole ethical enterprise is floating in midair, for no one has any empirical or scientific basis for declaring the strengths or weaknesses of any ethical theory. See, for example, the widely admired text of Tom Beauchamp and James Childress, *Principles of Biomedical Ethics*, 6th ed. (Oxford: Oxford University Press, 2009).

14. In recent years there has been work on nonrational or irrational decisions, but unless there have been brand new developments (and I would expect them eventually, for a promising start see the work of Elinor Olstrom) "rational" continues to be associated with self-interest.

extranatural sense. With the ascendency of naturalism in the late twentieth century, the very idea of an is/ought distinction and of a naturalistic fallacy comes to be viewed as confused. For insofar as all biological and historical reality is ultimately the function of a massively complex, wholly natural algorithm, insofar as our every thought and movement is a product of antecedent causal streams (plus, possibly, some randomness), insofar as the driving force animating living beings (to the degree they are capable of having inclinations or interests) is *eros*, insofar as all reality is either phenomenal or epiphenomenal in the naturalistic sense, there only is "is," and there is no distinct sphere of "ought."

There is no denying our experiences of ethical conviction and no denying that we are decisively shaped by our family's, friends', and culture's ethical convictions. In that sense, we all experience the force of a sphere of "ought." However, in accord with the naturalistic stream of modern Western rationality, namely, that stream which not only affirms the rationality of the sphere of nature but considers the boundaries of the spheres of nature and of reality to be coterminous, all our experiences of ought are wholly epiphenomenal products of nature and nurture.

H. Moral Responsibility

I have now sketched the contours of naturalistic reasoning and the naturalistic I in relation to biology, psychology, freedom and free will, phenomena and epiphenomena (all that is), explanation and causality, truth, moral reality, altruism, and ethics. Finally, let me explain naturalistic understanding of moral responsibility. With regard to moral responsibility note that, despite our complexity and our consciousness, which distinguish us from hurricanes and genes, and despite our self-awareness, which distinguishes us from plants and many other animals, and despite our advanced reflective capacities, which distinguish us, to varying degrees, from all other known species, it remains the case that insofar as the boundaries of the spheres of nature and of reality are coterminous, I can only be thought of as morally responsible in the same sense in which every other relatively discrete natural phenomena/individual is morally responsible.

For instance, like a weather system that is good (providing needed rain for crops) or bad (destructive flooding), I am the proximate cause of events (including works and ideas) that may be good or bad (as indexed to pleasure/flourishing or pain/suffering) for others. I can quite reasonably be regarded and treated accordingly, that is, as the proximate cause of good or bad for others, and I can quite reasonably be held responsible for the consequences of my behaviors (at both the phenomenal and the epiphenomenal level), just as a hurricane (wholly phenomenal) might be held responsible for many deaths.

Moreover, based upon my past behavior and the circumstances I am likely to encounter, judgments can be made about my character and probable future behavior (again, just as with hurricanes).

"Good" and "bad" exist for us humans, of course, in a way they do not for hurricanes, for we have cognitive capacities lacking in inanimate objects like hurricanes. Nevertheless, insofar as we do not exercise free will or agency/action in the spiritual sense, but only manifest at best reasoned behavior/mechanistic reaction, that is, insofar as I have only freedom, not free will, insofar as I am only ever a relatively distinguishable proximate cause of *events*, never to any degree the ultimate or originating source of any *actions*, then with regard to moral agency or moral responsibility there is no difference between me and nonsentient or nonliving entities like genes or weather systems. We are, despite our cognitive superiority and self-consciousness, morally responsible in precisely the same fashion that a weather system is morally responsible, for both weather systems and we are responsible as proximate causes, not as freely willing agents.

Much more could be said about the naturalistic understanding of reality, but by this point its essential character is clear. Moreover, in the light of this sketch of the essentials of the Romantic movement and the neo-Romantic celebration of authentic, freely willed, individual, poetic self-creation, it may be evident why I speak not of secular rationality but of the secular condition. Namely, insofar as late modern secular thought affirms both naturalistic rationality—which understands the boundaries of the sphere of nature and the sphere of reality to be coterminous (i.e., there is no reality other than natural reality)—and also celebrates authenticity and poetic self-creation, it is afflicted by conceptual incoherence. In elite philosophical circles many have bitten the proverbial bullet and abandoned all affirmation of free will, authenticity, and poetic self-creation. Such unmitigated naturalism, however, is not even the rule among elite philosophers, let alone for modern Western secular thought generally. On the whole, modern Western thought celebrates both authentic, poetic self-creation and also the unmitigated reach of modern science, which is to say, naturalistic rationality. Affirmation of naturalism, however, entails rejection of the possibility of free will, authenticity, and poetic self-creation. Thus, to repeat, I speak not of secular rationality but of the secular condition, for late modern secular thought both affirms naturalistic rationality and celebrates poetic self-creation, and it is thereby afflicted by conceptual incoherence.

4

In Defense of Poetic I's

Scientific and Naturalistic Rationality

For a prominent stream of modern Western rationality, the naturalistic vision of the I delivers the hard but undeniable truth about the ultimate character of reality revealed by modern science. In fact, as I will now explain, science does not and cannot directly reveal the truth of naturalism, and it is utterly reasonable to reject the naturalistic vision of reality. Above all, the belief that naturalistic conclusions are compelling results from a failure to distinguish between naturalistic and scientific reasoning. The failure to distinguish between naturalistic and scientific reasoning results from the amazing success of modern science in combination with the eliding of the key metaphysical contention I repeatedly made explicit when unfolding the naturalistic vision—namely, the contention that the boundaries of the spheres of nature and of reality are coterminous.

"Metaphysical contention" sounds complicated, but now that we understand Descartes's distinction between the sphere of nature and the sphere of spirit, we are in a good position to understand the meaning, significance, and dubious status of naturalism's metaphysical contention. This understanding is crucial, for if we do not understand the metaphysical contention we will be unable to bring the naturalistic vision into question, and if the naturalistic vision cannot be brought into question, then there is no reasonable way to affirm free will, creative originality, altruism, moral reality, and moral responsibility (let alone divine influence and reasonable faith).

What makes the metaphysical contention metaphysical is the fact that it transcends the sphere of nature, for it concerns the relation of the sphere of nature and/or the sphere of spirit to reality taken whole. That is, given modern Western rationality's essentially Cartesian framework of understanding, there is scientific reflection and explanation within the sphere of nature; there is (perhaps) spiritual reflection within the sphere of spirit; and then there is metaphysical reflection about the degree to which the sphere of nature, the sphere of spirit, or both taken together reflect the ultimate character of reality. Naturalism contends that the boundaries of the sphere of nature and the sphere of reality are coterminous, that is, naturalism contends that the sphere of nature solely and wholly reflects the ultimate character of reality. Because it concerns the relationship between the sphere of nature and reality writ whole, this is a metaphysical claim.

The metaphysical contention of Descartes is different. Descartes contends that there are two wholly incommensurable types of reality, the realities of the sphere of nature and of the sphere of spirit. As we have seen, before Descartes a Christianized Aristotelian metaphysic had predominated in medieval Western thought. The ultimate character of reality was thought to be basically congruent with our ordinary understandings of free will, moral responsibility, and moral reality. Descartes's great originality was in helping to carve the sphere of nature out from the Aristotelian cosmos, for Aristotelian metaphysics, like naturalistic metaphysics, is monistic. In contrast to naturalism, Aristotelian metaphysics had integrated what Descartes divided into the physical and the spiritual in one cosmological order.

What was decisively new and gave birth to ideas such as "nature," "physical," "cause," and "science" in the modern sphere of nature sense was Descartes's (and a few other seventeenth century geniuses') conceptual splitting off of the sphere of nature, the sphere in which explanatory appeal to purposes, goals, moral reality, and/or freely willed human or divine agency was prohibited. This conceptual revolution was so successful that in our day many forget that basic concepts of the sphere of nature (e.g., "nature," "universe," "physical," "cause") are themselves revolutionary conceptual constructions. In light of our brief study of Aristotelian metaphysics, we have some idea of one alternative way of envisioning reality, but few modern Westerners have any idea of Aristotelian or any other metaphysic, and so one has to work hard to explain how else people could possibly have conceived of what we now think of as natural or physical reality.

The modern sciences are endemic to the sphere of nature. That is, modern science uses the categories of the sphere of nature and operates wholly within the sphere of nature. Since modern science works from start to finish within the sphere of nature, modern science is in no position to address directly the greater-than-sphere of nature, metaphysical question about the relation of the sphere of nature to reality on the whole. Is reality wholly natural (in the modern sense)? Are there also spiritual realities such as free will, creative originality, altruism, good, evil, moral responsibility, and the divine? Is there, as Descartes believed, both a sphere of nature and a sphere of spirit? Or, as naturalism contends, is there only a sphere of nature?

Since again such metaphysical questions transcend the sphere of nature, and since science by definition works wholly within the sphere of nature, such metaphysical questions transcend the direct reach of any and all sciences. So the naturalistic vision does not reveal "the hard but undeniable truth about reality now revealed by modern science," and I am justified in saying, "In fact . . . science does not and cannot directly reveal the truth of naturalism."

Moreover, since the metaphysical question is not scientific and since there is no question that modern science does accurately reveal truths about reality—to reiterate, I am not questioning the accuracy of modern science; the question is whether or not modern science *exhaustively* reveals *all* truth about reality—taking a stand on the metaphysical question is not prerequisite to affirming modern science or engaging in scientific research. Like Descartes, I affirm the discrete integrity and true-to-reality accuracy of the sphere of nature. I wholeheartedly affirm and celebrate the methodologies and discoveries of modern science. I will not reject the natural I of the sphere of nature, only the naturalistic I of naturalistic reasoning. Notably, as illustrated by a host of celebrated scientists, beginning with Descartes, Pascal, and Newton, and including a host of others from the seventeenth century to the present, not only naturalists but also those who affirm spiritual realities can be first-rate scientists.

Scientific discoveries most certainly can and should change spiritual understanding. For example, hell is not in the bowels of the earth and heaven is not just beyond the outermost sphere of stars. God is not holding back waters that would otherwise flood the earth. The movement of elements up or down has no intrinsic moral meaning. One cannot validly infer from "is" (sphere of nature reality) to "ought" (sphere of spirit reality). Even if we do freely will, we are nonetheless massively conditioned and circumscribed by nature and culture (including the dynamics of kinship, reciprocal, and group altruism). Evolutionary theory, not direct creation of discrete species by God, best explains biological complexity and the diversity of species (even if evolutionary theory still stands in need of significant, perhaps revolutionary, scientific refinement). There may well be freely willing, self-creating, poetic I's of various kinds scattered throughout the universe. In these and a host of other ways, modern scientific discoveries rightly change spiritual understanding. This is neither surprising nor a reason to conclude all spiritual realities should be rejected.

By this point I can make clear why it is crucial to distinguish between affirmation of naturalism and affirmation of science. Affirmation of modern science requires only affirmation and respect for the integrity of the sphere of nature, namely, affirmation that ultimate reality is *accurately* described in accord with the vocabularies/rationalities of the sphere of nature (e.g., the vocabularies of the natural and social sciences). Affirmation of naturalism, by contrast, involves the claim that the sphere of nature *accurately, solely, and exhaustively* describes the ultimate character of reality. Insofar as the distinction between affirmation of science and affirmation of naturalism is elided, powerful and valid reasons for affirming modern science can be confusedly considered to be powerful and valid reasons for affirming naturalism, and rejection of naturalism can be confusedly castigated as rejection of science.

On the other hand, once the distinction between naturalism and science is made, one begins to sense the fragility of naturalism's metaphysical contention, for the powerful influence of naturalism in modern Western thought depends primarily upon eliding the metaphysical question. Insofar as naturalism is defended explicitly, three arguments come to the fore. In the wake of clarity about the distinction between affirmation of naturalism and affirmation of science, however, it becomes clear that all three arguments fail.

On the Three Main Arguments for Naturalism

First, proponents of naturalism argue that we have no real need for explanations outside of the sphere of science, for scientific explanation is exhaustively satisfactory. Second, and closely related, they object that the categories and understandings of the realm of spirit are superfluous because they add nothing to scientific knowledge. Third, proponents of naturalism assert that the dualism between the sphere of nature and the sphere of spirit is incoherent because one cannot explain how two radically different types of stuff can interact (philosophy's so-called mind/body problem).[1]

Ultimately, none of these objections has bite. The first argument is significant because, while there is no direct way for the modern sciences to establish the truth of naturalism, it does name an indirect way in which one could validly infer from the findings of modern science to the conclusion that the spheres of nature and reality are coterminous. If all aspects of life and existence could be wholly explained using only the categories and rationality of the sphere of nature, then appeal to any other spheres of reality would be superfluous. This would justify the conclusion that the sphere of nature and the sphere of reality are coterminous (i.e., this would justify naturalism).

---

1. For a classic presentation of these standard objections, see Gilbert Ryle's 1949 classic, *The Concept of Mind* (Chicago: The University of Chicago Press, 2002).

Philosophers call this quest to establish the wholesale adequacy of sphere of nature accounts of reality "compatibilism." It describes a legitimate, indirect path from science to naturalism. The compatibilist position, however, is far from being established, as enduring controversy among credentialed scientists and philosophers about free will, creative originality, altruism, moral reality, qualia, mind, and consciousness makes abundantly clear.[2]

The second argument, which objects that an appeal to the categories and understandings of the realm of spirit adds nothing to scientific knowledge, fails along with the first, for one can only sustain this objection if compatibilism is true. One often hears, for instance, that appeals to free will or altruism (in the spiritual sense) add nothing to biological, psychological, sociological, and anthropological explanations of behavior (i.e., yield nothing scientists can use in their scientific explanations). This is true, but it is also unsurprising and metaphysically irrelevant. For once one understands how the sphere of nature was created and how one distinguishes the sphere of nature from the sphere of spirit, one realizes that the spheres of nature and of spirit are incommensurable by virtue of deliberate and terrifically productive design. So one is not surprised that the vocabularies of the sphere of spirit (e.g., of free will, creative originality, responsibility, altruism, morality) do not provide answers to scientific questions or contribute to scientific explanation, for addressing questions posed in terms of the categories and rationality of the realm of nature has never been the aim of the vocabularies of the sphere of spirit. (They are appropriate to spiritual realities, with regard to which naturalistic vocabularies fall short.)

If compatibilism were true, then this second objection would have bite, for there would be no conceptual space for a sphere of spirit, and no vocabulary would be significant unless it contributed to explanation in the sphere of nature. Presently, however, compatibilism is not established, and the vocabularies of the sphere of spirit (i.e., of free will, personal responsibility, creative originality, altruism, moral reality, moral responsibility, and, I will argue, of faith and the divine) are essential if we are to describe a host of realities vital to human understanding of the ultimate character of reality. While it is possible almost everyone has been massively confused about the basic character

2. Indeed, compatibilism is rejected not only by philosophers who contest naturalism; it is also rejected by philosophers who affirm naturalism. This position—accepting naturalism while granting that it does not give a satisfactory account of free will, moral agency, or creative originality—is so common that it has its is own name, "hard determinism" (or, "hard incompatibilism"). The position is a bit bizarre because, as noted, one can validly affirm the truth of naturalism only to the degree compatibilist accounts are found to be wholly satisfactory, and hard determinists do not consider compatibilist accounts to be wholly satisfactory.

of existence, with regard to categories of spiritual realities taken whole (e.g., free will, creative originality, good, evil) the burden of proof lies squarely upon those who would reject such vital realities.

The third argument is based upon the so-called mind/body problem. If nature and spirit name two fundamentally different basic types of reality, physical stuff and mental stuff, as Descartes thought, then how can thoughts interact with, make any contact with, or have any influence upon bodies? In other words, if "mind" names a mental, utterly nonphysical sort of stuff, and "body" names a physical sort of stuff, how do minds have any impact upon bodies, and vice-versa? In colloquial terms, is it not impossible for one to hit a thought with a bat or to swing a bat (e.g., that bat lying on the ground over there) with a thought? Descartes infamously and unconvincingly appealed to the pineal gland as the point of connection between the mind and body.

While the third argument also ultimately fails, it does have bite with regard to Descartes's understanding of the spheres of nature and spirit. So before the third objection can be dismissed, I must make clear one critical distinction between my own and Descartes's affirmation of the two spheres. Descartes did not draw the distinction, as I have, between the rationalities/vocabularies of the spheres of nature and spirit and the sphere of reality. He believed his two spheres exactly represented two metaphysical realities.

In other words, Descartes did not think he was developing two rationalities/ vocabularies that, despite their incommensurability, allowed us to reflect upon and understand reality better than was possible with Aristotelian rationality. He thought he was describing the essential and final character of two realities in and of themselves. He did not think he was dealing with two vocabularies that stood apart from the transcending reality that they each dependably but incompletely represented. Instead, he thought he was delineating the essential and absolute character of the two kinds of stuff into which reality was divided: natural/physical and spiritual/mental substance. Philosophers refer to this as Descartes's "substance dualism." It was and remains unjustified, and it is indeed susceptible to the mind/body interaction objection.

While substance dualism is dubious, it is reasonable to suppose that the ultimate character of reality is best reflected by the discrete vocabularies and rationalities of the sphere of nature (e.g., biology, geology, psychology, sociology, economics) as well as by the discrete vocabularies and rationalities of the sphere of spirit.[3] It is reasonable to think this because no one has come close to offering an argument that would compel us to reject free will, creative originality, altruism, moral realism, and moral responsibility and also because no one

---

3. Notably, the classic *Natur-/Geisteswissenschaften* split also subtly but definitively elides this sphere of spirit, for on either side of the divide one finds only science.

has come close to offering an argument for rejecting modern science. Notably, many Westerners who attack modern science are really attacking not science but naturalism. Indeed, public clarity about the distinction between affirmation of science and of naturalism may help to avert attacks upon science.

On the other hand, there is no reason to conclude that there are no other or better ways of understanding reality than with our neo-Cartesian appeal to the discrete vocabularies/rationalities of the sphere of nature and the sphere of spirit. Someday we may develop a radically new vocabulary (or new set of vocabularies) that will allow us to forge beyond the present incommensurability and better address all the realities currently named by the vocabularies of the spheres of nature and of spirit within a radically new, presently beyond-imagining conceptual framework.

If that happens, we will move beyond a neo-Cartesian framework of understanding as dramatically as the Cartesian framework of understanding moved us beyond the Aristotelian.[4] This gives no cause for general skepticism about human understanding. In the first place, the neo-Cartesian vocabularies of the spheres of nature and of spirit are incredibly rich, useful, and full of promise. In the second place, even if we were someday to develop a new vocabulary (or set of vocabularies) that was even richer and more useful, it is most reasonable to expect that by far central affirmations from the spheres of nature and spirit would all be largely taken up and preserved, if to some degree transformed, within the new conceptual framework(s).[5]

---

4. It is important to be clear, however, that the move beyond the present categories will be a move beyond the Cartesian nature/sphere dichotomy just as surely as the Cartesian cosmology was a move beyond the Aristotelian. That means that it will be a move beyond science in the modern sense. In this regard I would object that Thomas Nagel manifests an inconsistent devotion to naturalism/materialism when in *Mind and Cosmos: Why the Materialist Neo-Darwinian Conception of Nature is Almost Certainly False* (Oxford: Oxford University Press, 2012), after suggesting that we may simply be "at the point in the history of human thought" where "our successors will make discoveries and develop forms of understanding of which we have not dreamt" (an idea I would affirm) he then inexplicably goes on to specify that these will be "new forms *of scientific understanding*" (3; emphases mine). Along the same lines, Nagel later identifies as a "*naturalistic* alternative" to materialism the position that he advocates: a "*natural* teleology" (91–92, emphasis mine). Nagel, as he realizes—"The idea of teleology as part of the natural order flies in the teeth of the authoritative form of explanation that has defined science since the revolution of the seventeenth century" [92]—has definitively stepped beyond any modern meaning of "natural," "naturalistic," or "scientific," and so the use of new terminology is called for (i.e., Nagel's talk of "new forms of *scientific* understanding" is imprecise and misleading). Notably, consistent with his latent naturalism, and despite his charitable tone, Nagel quickly dismisses the theistic "alternative," which he only imagines in the modern mechanistic terms of creationists and intelligent design theorists (94–95).

5. Note the congruence of this approach with a "principle of charity" (Donald

In sum, the third objection, namely, that Descartes's substance dualism posits an unthinkable diptych in reality, does have bite. It is wholly reasonable, however, to affirm a diptych in *our picture of* reality. Given the youth of human understanding—we only figured out the earth is not the center of the cosmos four hundred years ago, DNA sixty years ago, and so on—it is hardly surprising that we have not yet developed a single vocabulary adequate to understand all reality, so admission that there is a diptych in our picture of reality is hardly scandalous.[6] In any case, however, I need not worry over any mind/body problem because I do not contend that the human I is made up of two different kinds of stuff, the physical and the mental, though I do contend that the human I is at present most accurately and completely understood using the incommensurable vocabularies/rationalities of the spheres of nature and of spirit.

Neo-Cartesian, Descriptive Dualism

From this perspective, Descartes's genius was to distinguish and affirm two incommensurable, indispensable, and essentially accurate families of vocabularies, namely, the vocabularies/rationalities of the sphere of nature and of the sphere of spirit. Taken together but not mixed, these two discrete families of vocabularies currently provide our most complete, useful, and productive description of reality. For instance, the part of reality that we designate "brain" or "mind" is best described using both the vocabularies of nature and

---

Davidson) that is not confined by metaphysical naturalism (as it is in the philosophy of this same Donald Davidson). That is, to speak very technically for a moment, when Davidson asserts his anomalous monism his fidelity to his own principle of charity is compromised by an unjustified commitment to naturalistic metaphysics (see further next note).

6. Here I deliberately echo and disagree with Donald Davidson, who, in the "Introduction" to his *Essays on Actions and Events* (Oxford: Clarendon Press, 1980), argues for understanding human actions wholly in terms of naturalistic causes because, "Cause is the cement of the universe; the concept of cause is what holds together our picture of the universe, a picture that would otherwise disintegrate into a diptych of the mental and the physical" (xi). I am pointing out that we do not know whether or not cause (and this is "cause" in the modern, sphere of nature sense) is the cement of the universe (an unsupported metaphysical contention), and I am arguing that at present it is more reasonable to use two incommensurable vocabularies, each of which is vital to current human understanding, than to shave off one for the sake of denying an unsurprising "diptych" in *our picture* of the cosmos. Notably, Rorty, who often speaks of avoiding metaphysics, surreptitiously presumes Davidson's metaphysical naturalism and thus ends up affirming a monistic, naturalistic metaphysic that does not line up with the plurality of self-created vocabularies he affirms as vital to having a real I. At this conceptual juncture, Davidson and Rorty remain caught up in a fourth dogma of empiricism (i.e., metaphysical naturalism).

the vocabularies of spirit. There are not two things, a mind and a brain. There is one transcending (not transcendent) reality that currently defies singular description, one transcending reality that is currently most completely and usefully described using two incommensurable but indispensable vocabularies, those endemic to the sphere of nature (e.g., talk of brains and causes) and those endemic to the sphere of spirit (e.g., talk of minds and reasons).

There is almost certainly no mind/mental state without there being a correlate brain/physiological state, but it does not follow, for instance, that the physical, determinate/random understanding of causality applies wholesale to the progression of the reality that is in part accurately represented by brain state description, for that understanding of causality is endemic to the sphere of nature vocabulary of "brain." It does not necessarily apply to the transcending reality that "brain" (physical) and "mind" (spirit) talk are both about.

Since physical vocabularies of brain are clearly useful and so significantly accurate, if not exhaustive, in explaining the transcending reality of mind/brain, I is in some way physical. So it is not surprising that our spiritual capacities (e.g., for free will or altruism) can be obstructed or artificially stimulated physiologically. It is even possible (evil demon style) that we can be deceived about the reality of our love or free willing (i.e., human scientists are at the point where they can directly stimulate specific brain activity that fools us concerning our own thought). All that logically follows from such possibilities is the realization that we are indeed physical beings (i.e., in part accurately described in terms of the sphere of nature) whose thinking can be artificially manipulated and who are not infallible in our introspection. It does not follow that we are typically, let alone always, artificially manipulated or deluded about spiritual realities such as free will and altruism.

To be clear, I do not claim that free will or other spiritual realities are realized apart from bodies. Consciousness, free will, moral awareness, and other spiritual realities are evidently spiritual potentials of ultimate reality realized to varying degrees only by entities that have evolved sufficiently complex bodies and brains (which may not necessarily be organic). I do not posit disembodied spirits attached to material brains/bodies (that would be the substance dualism view). I reject the idea that the physical vocabularies of "brain/body" are exhaustive or exclusively valid when attempting to describe and understand the reality that "brain/body" and also "mind/spirit" vocabularies are both about.

This is *descriptive* dualism, a dualism of the spheres of nature and spirit, a dualism that affirms *both* physical vocabularies of brain and determinate/random causality *and also* spiritual vocabularies of mind, reasons, and free will, a dualism that affirms both sets of vocabularies as accurate but not exhaustively true to ultimate reality. Descriptive dualism is actually commonplace in real-life early and late modern Western public discourse. But this commonplace linguistic habit must be seen as mistaken by the naturalistic rationality that presumes that the spheres of nature and of ultimate reality are coterminous (i.e., that presumes there are no sphere of spirit realities).

Notably, naturalists often scoff at Cartesian dualism and speak as if they have moved beyond Descartes altogether. Naturalists remain, however, definitively if often unwittingly neo-Cartesian. For naturalism retains Descartes's idea of substance, in particular the identification of the sphere of nature with a fundamental type of physical/material (in the modern sense) stuff, and it resolves the mind/body problem by simply shaving off spirit/mind while retaining the sphere of nature in precisely Descartes's substantive sphere of nature sense.

Naturalism and descriptive dualism, then, are both neo-Cartesian. But each differs from Descartes in different ways. Whereas naturalism steps beyond Descartes by rejecting the sphere of spirit while retaining Descartes's substantive way of thinking and his sphere of nature, descriptive dualism retains Descartes's two spheres but rejects his substantive way of thinking. Again, descriptive dualism contends that the vocabularies of Descartes's spheres of nature and of spirit are both about reality, that reality is bigger and other than either of these spheres taken alone, and that at present it is most reasonable to expect that the overall character of reality is best described by affirming as relatively useful and dependable, if far from perfect or exhaustive, both the family of vocabularies endemic to Descartes's sphere of nature (e.g., the vocabularies of the natural and social sciences) and also the family of vocabularies endemic to Descartes's sphere of spirit (e.g., of free will, creative originality, altruism, moral realism, and moral responsibility).

Surely the vast preponderance of what humans do is explainable in natural terms. We should affirm the reality of the sphere of nature, the truth and accuracy of modern scientific discoveries, and the fact that all animals, including humans, are natural objects. We should acknowledge that we are in very large part the product of nature and nurture, genes and memes. We should accept the findings of the modern sciences, of biology, neurobiology, psychology, sociology, economics, and the rest. We should affirm the natural, scientific I. We should reject only the naturalistic I. For while it is reasonable to suppose that the vocabularies of the sphere of nature are accurate to reality, there is currently little reason to conclude that they exhaust the character of reality. Presently, it is not unreasonable to affirm that we are beings whose existence is best understood using the vocabularies/rationalities of both the sphere of nature and the sphere of spirit. (I will be strengthening my argument for this conclusion considerably in the next chapter.)

Eliding of the Sphere of Spirit

The widespread sense that the naturalistic vision is compelling results not from the development of any well-defended, widely accepted argument but from surreptitious eliding of the sphere of spirit. As biology, psychology, sociology, anthropology, history, economics, and even ethics and religious studies emerged as natural or human *sciences* precisely by limiting themselves to the categories of the sphere of nature, they typically failed to make explicit or even to remember that they had bracketed the metaphysical question. As a result, many modern Westerners are taught to think that reality simply *is* nature in the Cartesian sense of the sphere of nature and that scientific rationality simply *is* rationality.

"Nature," "physical," "cause," "explanation," "freedom" (not free will), "behavior" (not action), "novelty" (not creative originality), "rationality" (i.e., scientific rationality), "reality" ("phenomena" and "epiphenomena" in the material sphere of nature sense), "reasons" (understood as causes), "decisions" (understood as effects), "eros," "altruistic behavior" (i.e., kinship, reciprocal, and group altruisms), "I" (the natural I of the sphere of nature), and so forth: in short, the whole of what Descartes (and a few others) carved out of the medieval cosmos as the sphere of nature, all of these increasingly function as the unquestioned and exclusive basis in and through which all rigorous, reasonable reflection is believed to live, move, and have its being.

As a result of such eliding of the sphere of spirit and identification of scientific reasoning with valid reasoning, those who affirm spiritual realities are easily dismissed as superstitious or magical thinkers. By the late twentieth century the modern Western eliding of the sphere of spirit even subverts the thinking of those who affirm spiritual realities. We have already seen how the evangelical Christian Philip Johnson was led to declare faith insufficient and to demand evidence for belief in God. Similarly, the thought of today's preeminent defender of free will, noted philosopher Robert Kane, is likewise subverted by his acceptance of naturalistic standards.

In his justly celebrated book, *The Significance of Free Will*, Kane develops a precise and rich definition of free will and delineates the significance of free will for our understanding of personal responsibility and creative originality. Kane's project, however, is unnecessarily short-circuited by Kane's own fidelity to naturalistic rationality. Let me speak a bit more technically for a moment and quickly relate neo-Cartesian, descriptive dualism to current debates over free will.

Kane defends free will in the spiritual sense, speaking in terms of "ultimate responsibility," "self-forming actions," and "underived origination."[7] He even

---

7. Kane, *The Significance of Free Will* (New York: Oxford University Press, 1998), 74, 106.

notes the conceptual limits of the sphere of nature. When "described from a physical perspective alone," Kane says, *free will looks like chance.* "But," Kane continues, "the physical process is not the only one to be considered."[8] Indeed, I would agree: from the perspective of the sphere of nature one can only see determinism or indeterminism/chance, so free will will look like chance. But that is not the only perspective through which to see reality; one must also consider the perspective of the sphere of spirit.

Kane, however, explicitly rejects the sphere of spirit. He rejects "mental events that exist outside of (but can also intervene within) the natural order."[9] He insists that if we are reasonably to affirm free will we must explain "where [free will] might exist, if it does at all, *in the natural order,*" and we must explain how, *thinking within the categories of the natural order,* "a kind of freedom that requires *indeterminism* can be made intelligible."[10] In short, Kane insists we remain within naturalistic parameters.

Since, as I have explained, the sphere of nature by stunningly productive design deliberately excludes spiritual realities such as free will, Kane's naturalistic demands cannot possibly be met. As a result, Kane ends his book confessing himself unable to defend the reasonableness of affirming free will, though he has with unprecedented precision delineated its character and significance.[11] From the perspective I am defending, Kane is more successful than he believes himself to be, for affirmation of free will does not depend upon understanding free will in terms of the sphere of nature (that would be impossible by definition), for no argument has established even the probable truth of naturalistic metaphysics. Thus Kane's brilliant delineation of the meaning and significance of free will, which makes clear why affirmation of free will is currently essential to our most reasonable understanding of the ultimate character of reality, does not confront any objection remotely strong enough to warrant the conclusion that affirming free will is unreasonable. The unfulfilled burden of arguing otherwise lies squarely on the shoulders of naturalists.

The eliding of the sphere of spirit not only subverts the thinking of highly trained scholars such as Johnson and Kane, making their positions seem weaker than they are, but it also masks the tenuous character of arguments of proponents of naturalism, making their conclusions seem more powerful than they are. Consider, for instance, the widely celebrated philosopher and preeminent compatibilist Daniel Dennett. Dennett consistently makes clear

8. Ibid., 147.
9. Ibid., 115.
10. Ibid., 105 (first and second italics mine).
11. Ibid., 195, see also 150–51.

that he *presumes* a naturalistic perspective. For instance, in a typical move at the beginning of a book arguing that consciousness can be wholly accounted for in natural categories, Dennett specifies that he presumes:

> *materialism*: there is only one sort of stuff, namely *matter*—the physical stuff of physics, chemistry, and physiology—and the mind is somehow nothing but a physical phenomenon. In short, the mind is the brain. According to the materialists, we can (in principle!) account for every mental phenomena using the same physical principles, laws, and raw materials that suffice to explain radioactivity, continental drift, photosynthesis, reproduction, nutrition, and growth. It is one of the main burdens of this book to explain consciousness without ever giving in to the siren song of dualism.[12]

Dennett dedicates other books to unfolding his naturalistic vision of reality, for instance, *Darwin's Dangerous Idea* (everything is part of one causally determinate continuum [perhaps with a dash of randomness]); *Freedom Evolves* (no free will), and *Breaking the Spell: Religion as a Natural Phenomena* (no divine reality). In all of these books Dennett simply *presumes* the truth of materialism/naturalism.[13]

Since wholesale affirmation of the Cartesian sphere of nature and rejection of the sphere of spirit is Dennett's *beginning* point, there is absolutely no chance that his books on consciousness, free will, evolution, God, and I will not remain within the boundaries of the sphere of nature. In other words, the naturalistic conclusions of his arguments are built into his naturalistic presupposition. Insofar as Dennett is a compatibilist, this could be a legitimate approach. But it means that Dennett should acknowledge that affirmation of a compatibilist project such as his own is warranted only to the degree that he can offer a wholly sufficient explanation of all life and existence.

Given the enduring and widespread debate among philosophers and scientists, including even many of his fellow naturalists, over consciousness, free will, qualia, altruism, moral realism, and moral responsibility, at the present time the most anyone can reasonably affirm is that it is perhaps possible, but very far from certain, that Dennett's position is true. Empowered by the eliding of the sphere of spirit, however, Dennett consistently speaks as if his conclusions are ironclad. For instance, with regard to those, like Kane, who defend free will, Dennett simply proclaims that there is no "God-like power to exempt oneself from the causal fabric of the physical world" and dismisses

12. Daniel Dennett, *Consciousness Explained* (New York: Back Bay Books, 1991), 33.
13. Daniel Dennett, *Breaking the Spell: Religion as a Natural Phenomenon* (New York: Viking Penguin, 2006); *Darwin's Dangerous Idea* (New York: Touchstone, 1995); *Freedom Evolves* (New York: Penguin Books, 2003).

those who do not share his naturalistic presuppositions as unrepentant dualists: "unrepentant dualists and others actually embrace the idea that it would take a miracle of sorts for there to be free will."[14]

Presuming the very naturalistic paradigm under question and equating freely willed decisions with caused effects, Dennett goes on to ask, "How do 'we' cause these [freely willed] events to happen? How does an *agent* cause an effect without there being an event (in the agent, presumably) that is the cause of that effect (and is itself the effect of an earlier cause, and so forth)?"[15] Dennett speaks as if these rhetorical questions make obvious a devastating argument against free will. Dennett's rhetorical questions, however, only seem devastating if one is already thinking solely within the boundaries of the sphere of nature (which was originally designed to exclude free will by definition). That is, his rhetorical questions depend upon the presumed truth of his naturalistic premise (in this case, on the deterministic/indeterministic understanding of causation/randomness endemic to the sphere of nature). Dennett's conclusions, then, are already present in his materialist/naturalistic premise. Such circular reasoning offers no argument at all.

Elsewhere, when Dennett gestures toward an actual argument for his naturalism, he succeeds only in exposing its vulnerability:

> Agent causation is a frankly mysterious doctrine, positing something unparalleled by anything we discover in the causal processes of chemical reactions, nuclear fission and fusion, magnetic attraction, hurricanes, volcanoes, or such biological processes as metabolism, growth, immune reactions, and photosynthesis.[16]

Such stupendous extrapolation (i.e., from the reality designated by "volcanoes" to the reality designated by "brains/minds") has stood in the stead of solid argument for naturalism ever since Laplace. "Perhaps Laplace's assertion of naturalism was premature," someone may retort, "but Dennett speaks after two more centuries of stunning scientific advance." Certainly, but the increase in knowledge has not resulted in an unqualified increase in confidence—especially vis-à-vis so fundamental a category as causation. To the contrary, duly impressed scientists now commonly voice their suspicion that the world may be not only stranger than we have imagined, but it may also be stranger than we *can* imagine. In that context, the audacity of Dennett's stupendously hasty generalization from photosynthesis to reasoning, from hurricanes to consciousness, from immune reactions to the potentials of human brains/minds for free will, is patent.

14. Dennett, *Freedom Evolves*, 100.
15. Ibid.
16. Ibid.

Pejorative talk of "miracle" and "mysterious," moreover, loses its pejorative force when one remembers that Dennett does not argue for his naturalism; he presumes it. I am invoking "supernatural" powers only in the sense of "beyond the categories and rationality of the sphere of nature" powers. That is, consistent with my neo-Cartesian descriptive dualism, I reject currently unwarranted naturalism and affirm the categories and rationality of the sphere of spirit. I am not surprised that, from the perspective of the sphere of nature, the effects and talk of sphere of spirit realities such as free will or altruism look mysterious and miraculous. Far from this being a point against spiritual realities, such truncated vision is all one should expect, by definition, insofar as one is wearing sphere of nature glasses.

In short, when Dennett rejects free will, creative originality, personal responsibility, moral reality, altruism, or divine reality in the spiritual sense, he does not offer any direct argument against these realities. He only points out that they are incompatible with naturalistic premises he presumes to be true. Dennett unfolds the implications of his own presuppositions accurately, but he does not actually offer compelling arguments against those who do not share those presuppositions. Dennett's books are widely celebrated as philosophically rigorous arguments for naturalism. But they consistently and overtly presume naturalism, which is nowhere close to being established.

The belief that Dennett's books offer compelling arguments depends upon a quiet revolution in late modern Western thought that illicitly elides the sphere of spirit. Once one elides the sphere of spirit, Dennett's arguments and conclusions do look decisive. As of yet, however, there is no good argument for rejecting sphere of spirit vocabularies. So Dennett's conclusions remain unwarranted. Widespread praise for his books primarily reveals the degree to which modern Western culture is in the grip of naturalistic rationality.

Affirmation of free will and of the associated capacities/attributes of creative originality, personal responsibility, and personal identity (the poetic I) is massively significant in modern Western personal, social, and legal understandings. It is common for philosophers who reject free will in theory to acknowledge that they cannot live their daily lives without affirming free will in practice. Some philosophers even argue that while free will is an illusion, it is so critical to personal and sociocultural understanding that it is an illusion no one should pierce.[17] Given its significance and the practical impossibility of denying its reality in our daily living, it would only be reasonable to reject

---

17. In *Free Will and Illusion* (Oxford: Oxford University Press, 2000), for instance, Saul Smilansky maintains that free will is an essential illusion. "Within our lives, insofar as they are affected by the issue of free will, illusion is descriptively central and normatively necessary" (1) and "Humanity is fortunately deceived on the free will issue, and this seems to be a condition of civilized morality and personal sense of value" (6).

free will (and associated ideas of creative originality, individual authenticity, and poetic self-creation) if we were compelled to do so by a very strong argument. Despite the hyperbolic, naturalistic overstatement facilitated by the eliding of the sphere of spirit, no such argument exists.[18]

Let me add two caveats to this criticism of Dennett and like-minded naturalistic philosophers and scientists. First, let me acknowledge that religious traditions, including Christianity, are full of superstitious and magical thinking. People of faith, for instance, make indefensible claims about a variety of differing, all supposedly inerrant texts; attempt to construct a science of God; attempt to prove the existence of God; reject modern science; and use appeals to theology in order to justify oppression of women and in order to vilify "heretics" and adherents of other religions, and even, at the extreme, to lend divine sanction to acts of heinous violence. I welcome and affirm criticism of such profoundly problematic parts of faith traditions as means to clearer spiritual understanding.

Second, and closely related, since the sphere of nature does accurately, if not exhaustively, represent reality, and since we are partly, if not wholly, natural I's (again, we affirm natural I's, reject naturalistic I's), then, for instance, Dennett's work on freedom, evolution, religion, and so forth is all potentially accurate and pertinent. For instance, if *Breaking the Spell: Religion as a Natural Phenomena* could be re-edited so it was not an attack upon faith but an attack upon magical thinking, and if it provided an analysis of how sphere of nature dynamics function within faith communities—in short, if it was re-titled and re-edited and became *Religion insofar as it is a Natural Phenomena*—then I would affirm and eagerly learn from it.

Naturalistic Rationality, the Secular Condition, and Faith

I am now in a position to give a far more precise description of the secular condition and its relationship to faith. The secular condition blossomed in the late twentieth century as the result of prominent developments in nineteenth and twentieth century modern Western rationality (traced in chapter 3), which led to two affirmations widely celebrated as hallmarks of modern

18. I agree with philosopher Charles Taylor, who says that the suggestion that there is no free will is "too preposterous to be believed" (169). It is simply "unthinkable," Taylor continues, that "we have been talking nonsense all these millennia," (170). Any acceptable theory, Taylor maintains, must "save the phenomena," must, "be rich enough to incorporate the basis of . . . distinctions which, at present, mark the intentional world of human agents and which are essential to understand their behaviour" (174,177) (Charles Taylor, 'How is Mechanism Conceivable?' *Human Agency and Language: Philosophical Papers 1* [Cambridge: Cambridge University Press, 1985]). Unfortunately, in this essay Taylor, relating "causes" and "reasons" along Davidsonian lines, fails to step definitively beyond the boundaries of the sphere of nature.

thought. On the one hand, there is post-Romantic celebration of individual authenticity, autonomy, and poetic self-creation. On the other hand, there is strong and increasingly confident (especially in the wake of Darwin) affirmation of naturalistic rationality.

These hallmark affirmations are perfectly familiar. Beyond the esoteric halls of modern Western universities, however, the conceptual incommensurability between celebration of authentic, poetic self-creation (which requires affirming free will and creative originality) and affirmation of naturalistic rationality (which means rejecting free will and creative originality) remains largely unnoticed. Within modern Western universities, wholesale naturalism and rejection of spiritual realities has been ascendant for the last century, though not without consternation and some resistance.[19] It is the simultaneous embrace of these conceptually incommensurable alternatives that creates the secular condition.

The promise of descriptive dualism as an antidote for the secular condition is now apparent. First, affirmation of naturalistic rationality is not the same as affirmation of modern science, for it involves a metaphysical contention that is neither warranted by modern science nor necessary for engaging in modern scientific research. We can reject naturalism, then, while affirming the sphere of nature, the natural and social sciences, and I insofar as I am described by the natural and social sciences (i.e., the natural I). At the same time, since there is no good argument for rejecting so vital a reality as free will, it is reasonable also to affirm free will and to celebrate authenticity and poetic self-creation (i.e., the poetic I).

In short, given current human understanding, it is reasonable to contend that in describing reality we should use the incommensurable vocabularies/categories of both the spheres of nature and of spirit. This affirmation alleviates the secular condition by allowing us to settle without anxiety into descriptive dualist, sphere of nature and sphere of spirit ways of understanding. Without the burden of affirming a conceptual contradiction, we can celebrate the modern sciences and sphere of nature rationality, and we can also celebrate free will, authenticity, and poetic self-creation. We can affirm each

19. Speaking technically, the consternation is blatant not only among philosophical libertarians, but perhaps even more revealingly in the existence of a school of thought called "hard determinism" (or, "hard incompatibilism") which essentially designates the "it is hard to accept but determinism is true" camp. Along another trajectory, note how classic deconstruction (early Derrida) and the disappearance of the subject/author ("we do not speak language; language speak us"), which was confusedly attacked by many for being anti-scientific, is actually the manifestation of unmitigated naturalistic rationality within the humanities.

sphere as most likely accurate but not exhaustive in its description of the ultimate character of reality.

While this alleviates the secular *condition*, however, we are still left with
secular *rationality*, a refined version of late modern rationality that affirms the
natural I, the sphere of nature, and the natural and social sciences and that also
affirms the poetic I and celebrates free will, authenticity, and self-creation. I
have made progress insofar as I have succeeded in unveiling and derailing naturalistic rationality. However, with regard to my prime concern, the reasonableness of faith, the analysis to this point allows me primarily to explain with
more depth why "secular" connotes "anti-religious" or "anti-faith." Indeed, it
is only in the wake of the defeat of naturalistic reason, which has no conceptual
space for any spiritual realities and which has for so long stoked the flames of
a confused war between religion and science, that the full scope of modern
Western secular reason's antipathy toward faith becomes manifest.

To this point, largely in happy accord with both of the hallmark affirmations of modern Western secular reason, I have argued that it is reasonable to
affirm two predominant modern Western I's: the natural, scientific I of the
sphere of nature and the freely willing, self-creating poetic I of the sphere of
spirit. The natural I is, again, described with the vocabularies of the natural
and social sciences. The poetic I is described using the conceptually inter-
linked vocabularies of free will, reasons (that influence without determining; not causes), decisions (not effects), self-creation, authenticity, creative
originality, and personal responsibility. With rejection of naturalism and the
naturalistic I, one major reason for rejecting faith as unreasonable is defeated.
In the wake of the collapse of the naturalistic objection, however, we are left
not with a clear and reasonable path to affirmation of faith but with newfound
clarity about the tension between affirmation of authenticity, along with celebration of poetic self-creation, and affirmation of faith.

As explained, the poetic I emerged in the wake of Romanticism. The poetic
I abandons the Romantic appeal to the sacred depths of nature and is distinguished by its capacity for self-creation and its crowning potential freely to
choose even the tastes by which it will judge itself. To the degree the poetic I
is conditioned or determined by any outside forces, it is not really an I at all,
for to that degree the I is a product, a puppet. The poetic I exists only insofar
as it is freely self-created.

The self-creating, poetic I lives in tension not only with the impositions of
nature and nurture but in tension with any other external imperative as well,
including imperatives flowing from other spiritual realities. For the poetic
I, then, moral, altruistic, and/or divine imperatives are as much a threat to
authentic self-creation as are nature and nurture. It is no accident that in my
discussion of the hallmark affirmation of authenticity and poetic-self creation

I only mentioned two of the aforementioned spiritual realities, namely, poetic potentials for free will and creative originality, for at the heart of affirmation of authenticity and poetic I's lie ideals that are incommensurable not only with naturalistic determinism/indeterminism, but also with altruism, moral realism, moral responsibility, and the divine.

The spiritual realities split into two groups that I will henceforward call the "existential" (free will, creative originality) and, in the traditional religious sense, the "spiritual" (altruism, moral reality, moral responsibility, and/or the divine). Affirmation of poetic I's not only does not presume affirmation of all the spiritual realities, but it also unveils a tension among them, for the spiritual realities would limit and constrain poetic I's existential potentials. Insofar as I truly become an I only to the degree that I transcend all external conditioning and self-create my own authentic I, spiritual realities in the religious sense (all of which bring external pressures and norms into play) are a threat to authenticity.

The scope of modern Western secular rationality's antipathy toward faith is now more fully manifest, because it is now clear how both of the hallmark, incommensurable affirmations of modern Western thought, namely, affirmation of naturalistic rationality and affirmation of authenticity and poetic self-creation, are each in their own independent ways hostile toward faith. If I am to explain the reasonableness of faith, then, I need not only to derail naturalistic rationality but also to mitigate poetic/existential resistance to faith and to explain the needfulness and reasonableness of affirming altruism, moral reality, moral responsibility, and the divine. I now turn to take up this task in part two of my argument, "The Essence of Reasonable Christianity." In brief, I will argue that it is currently most reasonable to affirm not only *a sphere of nature* (and the natural and social sciences, and natural I's) and *a sphere of poetic I's* (who freely self-create themselves), but also a third sphere, what I will call *the sphere of agape* (the sphere of altruism, moral reality, and the divine).

I will argue for the reasonableness of faith and the sphere of *agape* in the same way I have just argued for the reality of free will and the sphere of freely self-creating, poetic I's. To be clear, I have argued that since naturalism is unwarranted and since free will designates a vital aspect of human self-understanding and since free will cannot be described or comprehended using the vocabularies of the sphere of nature, it is reasonable to affirm a discrete sphere/rationality/set of vocabularies appropriate to the reality of free will and poetic self-creation. In the same way, noting the insufficiency of both sphere of nature and sphere of poetic I's vocabularies, I will argue for the reasonableness of affirming a sphere of *agape* and developing spiritual vocabularies appropriate to sphere of agape realities.

Just as my affirmation of the sphere of poetry did not entail rejecting the sphere of nature or devaluing the sciences, but only a rejection of naturalistic rationality, so my affirmation of the sphere of *agape* will not entail rejecting either the sphere of nature or the sphere of poetic I's, and I will continue to celebrate and affirm modern science and to celebrate and affirm poetic self-creation. In sum, I will work in Part II to awaken all to the reasonableness of affirming not only the natural/scientific I and the self-creating, poetic I but also to the manifest reasonableness of affirming I living awakened to *agape*, the I of faith.[20]

Up to this point, I have argued that affirmation of poetic I's is reasonable because rejecting naturalism is reasonable. In the next chapter, I strengthen this contention by explaining not only why rejecting naturalism is reasonable, but also, going beyond that, explaining why affirmation of naturalism is unreasonable. At the same time, I will begin to make manifest the screaming insufficiency of understanding reality only in terms of the spheres of nature and of poetic I's. In response to this screaming insufficiency, in the following chapters I unfold the contour and meaningfulness of the sphere of *agape*, striving thereby to make clear why, given the current state of human understanding and based solely upon what is reasonable and good according to common public standards, every person of faith can be utterly confident that it is wholly reasonable and good to affirm, give thanks for, live, and testify to faith in God. Indeed, I will strive to make clear why every good and reasonable person should affirm and be an I of faith.

20. Mindful of Occam's Razor, we should not multiply vocabularies needlessly. In light of Edmund Husserl's critique of "psychologism" in *Logical Investigations*, Volume 1, however, it may be that we should also posit a discrete sphere (Husserl would say "region") of logical principles (e.g., insofar as there is reasoning, then, for instance, "if A=B and B=C then A=C," "not both A and not A," and so forth) (Edmund Husserl, *Logical Investigations*, Volume 1, J. N. Findlay, trans. [New York: Routledge, 2001]).

PART II

The Essence of Reasonable Christianity

5

The Sphere of Poetic I's

Levinas, Evil, Faith

In the late twentieth century, even secular philosophers began referring to a "theological turn" in a small but influential stream of European philosophy. Emmanuel Levinas (1906–1995), the major inspiration for my defense of moral realism, *agape*, and faith, helped to inspire the theological turn. Levinas was born into a close-knit family in a flourishing Jewish community in Kaunas, Lithuania, where he grew up next door to a little girl named Raïssa, whom he would marry. Lithuania was then part of czarist Russia, and the Jews of Kaunas were briefly displaced during the Russian Revolution of 1917. In the late 1920s, Levinas traveled for advanced philosophical study to France and then to Germany, where he studied briefly with the renowned philosopher Martin Heidegger. He then settled in Paris.

At the onset of World War II, Levinas was a French citizen with past service as a chief master sergeant. He was assigned to the French Tenth Army and had to leave behind his wife, Raïssa, his five-year-old daughter, Simone, and his wife's mother, Frida Levy, who also lived with them. On June 18, 1940, General Rommel's forces overwhelmed the Tenth Army and Levinas was captured. Levinas was sent to a German forced labor camp, Stalag XIB, where he was segregated in captivity with other Jews.[1]

During five years of captivity, Levinas, like so many of his Jewish fellows, received the letter letting him know a friend or family member had been

---

1. Salomon Malka, *Emmanuel Levinas: His Life and Legacy*, Michael Kigel and Sonja Embree, trans. (Pittsburgh: Duquesne University Press, 2006), 6.

deported to a concentration camp.[2] For Levinas, it was his wife's mother, Frida Levy, who was never seen again. After his release in April 1945, Levinas learned his parents, Dvora Gurvitch and Yekhiel Levinas, and his younger brothers, Boris and Aminadav—his entire immediate family—had been murdered by the Nazis (quite possibly machine-gunned into open pits) back home in Lithuania. Thanks to the courageous actions of the nuns of the Monastery of Saint Vincent de Paul, his wife and daughter, Raïssa and Simone, survived.[3]

In a large corpus of writings, Levinas writes only one autobiographical note. It is two paragraphs long. The second paragraph, in its entirety, says in reference to the terse biographical itinerary of the first paragraph, "It is dominated by the presentiment and the memory of the Nazi horror."[4] For Levinas, the experience of the Nazi horror marked an absolute end of innocence. Two decades later, in 1966, he writes, "Soon death will no doubt cancel the unjustified privilege of having survived six million deaths . . . nothing has been able to fill, or even to cover over, the gaping pit. We still turn back to it from our daily occupations almost as frequently, and the vertigo that grips us at the edge is always the same."[5]

Levinas considered the Holocaust to be a "paradigm of gratuitous human suffering."[6] He dedicates his most significant book, *Otherwise Than Being or Beyond Essence*, "To the memory of those who were closest among the six million assassinated by the National Socialists, and of the millions on millions of all confessions and all nations, victims of the same hatred of the other man, the same anti-semitism."[7]

Levinas agrees with Elie Wiesel, who in *Night* famously declared that God had died in Auschwitz, that God had been hung on the gallows right along with an innocent young boy. The boy had been given relative power over other captives in the concentration camp. Whereas it was common, Wiesel relates, for prisoners with relative power to be especially brutal, this boy was kind and beloved by all. Moreover, it turned out he was secretly working

2. Ibid., 262.

3. For the biographical details about Levinas's World War II experiences and captivity, see Malka, 64–81.

4. "Signature," *Difficult Freedom: Essays on Judaism*, Sean Hand, trans. (Baltimore: The John Hopkins University Press, 1997).

5. *Proper Names*, Michael B. Smith, trans. (London: Athlone Press, 1996), 120, as cited in Michael Kigel, "Translators Notes," in Malka, *Emmanuel Levinas: His Life and Legacy*, xviii.

6. Emmanuel Levinas, "Useless Suffering," in *On Thinking of the Other: entre nous*, Michael B. Smith and Barbara Hershey, trans. (New York: Columbia University Press, 1998), 97.

7. Emmanuel Levinas, *Otherwise Than Being or Beyond Essence*, Alphonso Lingis, trans. (Pittsburgh: Duquesne University Press, 1981), v.

with the resistance, which was why he was being hung along with two adult coconspirators.

Wiesel says the boy had the face of a "sad-eyed angel." All the captives are forced to watch the execution. At the final moment the two men shout out, "Long live liberty!" The boy remains silent.[8] The men's necks break immediately, but the boy is too light. As the boy writhes in the noose, the man behind Wiesel whispers, "Where is merciful God, where is He?" Half an hour later, still watching the brutal death agony, the man says it more urgently, accusingly. Wiesel hears an answer from within, "Where He is? This is where—hanging here from this gallows."[9]

In "Useless Suffering" Levinas asks, "Did not Nietzsche's saying about the death of God take on, in the extermination camps, the meaning of a quasi-empirical fact?"[10] Gods die in extermination camps. Gods die in the face of gratuitous suffering. As Wiesel makes clear in *Night*, the God of adolescent piety dies there. The God of the prosperity gospel, the God of human wish fulfillment, the God exclusively aligned with this or that particular faith, nation, or tribe (e.g., the Christians and not the Jews), the God who could or would intervene to stop the slaughter of six million innocents, the God whose existence we can use to explain evil or cover over the gaping pits, all those Gods, along with all human arguments that would justify God—all those Gods and all such arguments die, and should die, in the face of gratuitous suffering.

However, Levinas continues, simply to renounce "after Auschwitz this God absent from Auschwitz . . . would amount to finishing the job of National Socialism."[11] We are called not to abandon faith but to "a faith more difficult than before," a screamingly real faith forged in the fires of "evil" manifest in every "diabolical horror."[12] Notably, this describes the faith born of slavery in Egypt, the faith of the Jewish exiles in Babylon, the faith of the prophets, the faith of Jesus and of Paul and, for that matter, the faith of a multitude of traditions born in concrete contexts of oppression, suffering, and death, traditions such as Islam, Hinduism, and Buddhism. Such "faith more difficult" does not bring the peace of conceptual closure. Unseeing eyes stare up still from gaping pits. The vertigo still returns.[13] Any would-be comfortable understanding

8. Elie Wiesel, *The Night Trilogy*, Marion Wiesel, trans. (New York: Hill and Want, 2008), 81–83.

9. Ibid.

10. Levinas, "Useless Suffering," 97.

11. Ibid., 99.

12. Ibid., 97.

13. All the useless suffering endures as a fissure across thought and sense that cannot be humanly breached. It is in this sense that Levinas's theological reflections,

that would rest content in an acceptable picture of the whole should be traumatized and rent by the violation of gratuitous suffering. If such "faith more difficult" is to hope after some final, perfect peace, it will have to hope after a peace that surpasses all current human understanding.

Such faith, forged within wholesale awakening to diabolical horror, has no ears for modern Western rationality's "problem of evil." The standard focal "problem" in modernity's "problem of evil" is not any concrete evil, not the gaping pits, not the living wound. The "problem" in modernity's "problem of evil" is the *logical* obstacle that gratuitous suffering poses to arguments for the existence of God. Worry over the problem of evil is not worry about any particular concrete evil, which is why attempts to solve the problem of evil, so-called "theodicies," have nothing to do with resisting concrete evils. Notably, "theodicy" literally means "justification of God." To realize the tension between would-be theodicies and classic confessions of faith, one needs only to ask, "who here is justifying Whom?"

At a more disturbing level, the problem theodicies seek to redress is the human inability to posit God within a human vision of the whole that can be at peace with itself. Precisely the fissure at the living heart of the dynamic of impassioned concern that engenders Levinas's difficult faith is what modern theodicies so often resist, what they tempt us to hide away behind a haze of logical pivots pro *and* con, what they keep outside the walls of dispassionate, objective, pseudo-scientific classroom discussion. To be clear, what is too often pushed out of the room is the mute witness to useless suffering ever still staring up at us in all those unseeing eyes.

The difficult faith Levinas speaks of is born of more profound response to gratuitous suffering. Surely it is no accident that when Wiesel crafts his pivotal narrative of the hanging of the innocent boy at Auschwitz, his narrative of the death of God, he draws a figure of Jesus on the cross—*Night* is not merely autobiography as history: it is spiritual testimony.[14] Wiesel credits François

---

and all theological reflection, are never closed. Hence Levinas's biographer, Salomon Malka, is right to say that for Levinas ,"there is no last word" (286). Malka takes up a mistaken and widespread philosophical tendency toward spiritual/moral relativism, however, when he continues by suggesting that Levinas offers us a philosophy "where nothing is definitive, where nothing is fixed" (286). Part of the passion and power of Levinas's work in an amoral or morally relativistic age is his insistence that in response to the concentration camps, in response to hatred toward others, we are taken hostage by something very fixed and definite. At the same time, this pious and, for Levinas, essentially biblical response to gratuitous suffering in a very specific way rejects closure, never forgets the gaping pits.

14. Despite the clarity of the comparison, I would hesitate to name it were it not named and used even more explicitly by the Christian Francois Mauriac at the close of his foreword to *Night*. Francios Mauriac, "Forword to *Night*," in Wiesel, *The Night*

Mauriac, a Christian, for getting *Night* published. He dedicates *Dawn*, the second book in his *Night Trilogy*, to Mauriac. In his foreword to *Night*, Mauriac proclaims the cross the "cornerstone" of his faith and says he considers "the connection between the cross and human suffering" to be "the key to the unfathomable mystery."[15]

In his preface to the new, 2006 translation of *Night*, which retains Mauriac's foreword, Wiesel says he does not know if Auschwitz "*has* a response." What he does know, he continues in classic Levinasian terms, "is that there is 'response' in responsibility."[16] Accordingly, I will be unfolding the relation of faith to responsibility in response to real evils. I will not make the mistake of worrying over the "problem of evil" in relationship to arguments for the existence of God. Faith in God is reasonable, but faith in God is not the conclusion of an argument.

Because of gratuitous suffering, the gaping pits remain uncovered and the vertigo returns even for people of faith. There is no adequate theodicy, no conceptual closure, no contented understanding. Gratuitous suffering should be lamented as *utterly useless suffering for every victim*. Even Christians who hope in literal resurrection should be clear that they are confessing hope that *transcends* human understanding. At the same time, as Wiesel says, while there is not "a response" to evil, there is response. Just so, Emmanuel Levinas discerns in the dynamics of responsibility in response a faith more difficult, a faith forged in the fires of earthly hells, a faith wherein cross or extermination camp gallows can become a cornerstone.

I will return to Levinas, faith, and the horror of those gallows in the next chapter, where I will sketch the essence of reasonable faith in God. First, however, I need to put naturalism to rest. Since naturalism has prevailed in twenty and twenty-first century Western thought, many mainstream scholars dismiss Levinas' work and the theological turn as fanciful and unrealistic. Admittedly, Levinas nowhere develops a detailed refutation of naturalism.

Trilogy, 19. Levinas explicitly parallels the passion of the Jews under Hitler to the passion of Christ: "So *la passion des juifs sous Adolf Hitler* still belongs for me to the Passion of Christ and to holy history . . ." ("Being-Toward-Death," in *Is It Righteous to Be? Interviews with Emmanuel Levinas*, Jill Robbins, ed. [Standford: Stanford University Press, 2001], 137).

15. Mauriac, "Foreword to *Night*," in Wiesel, *The Night Trilogy*, 19. In stark contrast to all this, it must be said that Mauriac comes perilously close to the obscene suggestion that the Holocaust was good because it led to the rebirth of the political nation of Israel. For Wiesel's grateful comments regarding Mauriac's role in finally getting *Night* published, see Elie Wiesel, "Preface to *Night*," in Wiesel, *The Night Trilogy*, 8; the dedication is at page 138.

16. Wiesel, "Preface to *Night*," in Wiesel, *The Night Trilogy*, 13.

That is because he considered naturalism to have been definitively refuted in Martin Heidegger's celebrated work *Being and Time* (1927).[17]

Levinas considered *Being and Time* an epochal work even after Heidegger, a prominent German academic, enthusiastically embraced Hitler, worked to further Nazi objectives within German universities, abandoned Jewish students and friends, and failed even long after the fact plainly to name and denounce his National Socialist views and his complicity in the Nazi horror. Levinas was blunt in his judgment of Heidegger, but he still considered *Being and Time* an epochal work because in it Heidegger definitively discredited naturalism.

I concluded above that naturalism has not been proven true and that affirmation of the sphere of spirit was reasonable. In this chapter I will argue that Heidegger takes us a quantum step forward because in *Being and Time* he makes it clear that *affirmation of naturalism is unreasonable* and that *rejection of the sphere of spirit and of poetic I's is unreasonable. Being and Time* is vital to defense of faith because in it Heidegger brilliantly defends the extranaturalistic reality of the sphere of spirit.[18]

In brief, Heidegger argues that if there is time in the sphere of nature, then there must be sphere of spirit I's. Heidegger's analysis is especially potent because he justifies affirmation of the sphere of spirit and sphere of spirit I's not through appeal to esoteric spiritual phenomena, but through a philosophically rigorous analysis of time, a central reality for the sphere of *nature*. If time requires sphere of spirit I's then, since all sciences presume time, the practice of any science presumes affirmation of the reality of sphere of spirit I's (minds/souls/*res cogitans*). Heidegger was partly inspired by the analysis

---

17. There are two major English translations of *Being and Time*. First, John Macquarrie and Edward Robinson, trans., (San Francisco: HarperSanFrancisco, 1962) and second, Joan Stambough, trans., revised by Dennis Schmidt (Albany: State University of New York Press, 2010). All quotes here come from the Stambough and Schmidt version. Please note that all my page citations reference the pagination of the German original. These page numbers are included in the margins of both English translations.

18. Throughout I will be appropriating Heidegger's argument and language in order to maximize its usefulness for my argument. Since this book is intended for a general scholarly audience, I will not be using Heidegger's extensive technical vocabulary. For instance, what I call the "sphere of spirit" Heidegger would call the "ontological region of ontic being," and in terms of the argument I will be making from time, Heidegger would say that recognition of the temporal be-ing of some ontic beings amounts to the unveiling of Dasein and the ontological region of being, that is, the be-ing of being that is necessary if being is to be (for without Dasein nothing either is or is not). I am forsaking some precision and strength of argument for the sake of general intelligibility, but I would argue that nowhere do I misrepresent Heidegger in a way that allows me to cheat on behalf of my overall argument. To the contrary, a technical presentation would strengthen my position.

of time that comes down to us from the ancient Greek philosopher Aristotle. Aristotle provides a good point of entry into Heidegger's argument. The going gets a bit rough, but finishing off naturalism was never going to be easy.

If No Sphere of Spirit I's/Mind, Then No Time

I know how to answer if I am asked, "what time is it?" Matters are not so simple if the question is, "time, what is it?" The first question asks about clock time, the counting of time, the time that tells me whether or not I'm late, time "t" in scientific equations (e.g., $v=d/t$). Pretty much everyone is clear about time in this sphere of nature sense. For instance, we mutually agree to designate some interval of time to be a "second, "minute," or "year," and then we know what it means to say that I have three minutes to catch the bus. But what is it that I have? Having three minutes to catch the bus is very different from, say, having three cups of flour. I know how to answer the question, "what is flour?" I know what it is made of, how it is made, and so forth. What, however, is it that I have when I have time?

Aristotle notes that we typically speak of time being made up of past, present, and future. The past, however, *is* no longer, and the future *is* not yet: past time and future time do not exist. The present or "now," meanwhile, is not a part of time at all but a moving boundary when future instantly becomes past.[19] Time, then, is made up of two parts divided by a moving boundary. Neither the parts nor the boundary exist. In light of all this, Aristotle comments, one might "suspect that [time] either does not exist at all or barely, and in an obscure way. One part of it has been and is not, while the other is going to be and is not yet."[20] Just as clearly, he adds, time exists.

Aristotle notes the close tie between time and movement. Time is not identical to movement, for movement is either fast or slow, and time is used to define fast and slow.[21] On the other hand, time and movement are intimately related, for if there is no movement there is no time. If "the state of our own minds does not change at all, or we have not noticed its changing, we do not realize time has elapsed."[22] It is possible that since you read that last sentence

19. A bit more technically, the "now" cannot have any extension for, Aristotle argues, if the now were extended, then the now would have within itself a before, now, and after, and the now within the extension of *that* now would also have within itself a before, now, and after, and the now within the extension of *that* now . . . and so on without end (i.e., we are led to the nonsense of an infinite regress). Since the "now" has no extension, it too *is* not (Aristotle, "Physics," *The Basic Works of Arisotle*, Richard McKeon, ed. and trans. [New York: Random House, 1941], 289.
20. Ibid.
21. Ibid., 290.
22. Ibid., 290–91.

our brains and the entire perceivable universe froze for a millennium, as measured by an observer completely outside our perception. For us, however, there was no time. Time, then, is not movement, but neither is there time if there is no movement.

All of this, Aristotle concludes, helps us to clarify the essence of time: there is time when we discern motion and "the mind pronounces that the 'nows' are two," one before and one after.[23] The interval bounded by the before and after is time. Time, then, is the "number of motion in respect of before and after."[24] I may, for instance, number a certain duration of motion—perhaps the interval between the "nows" marked by the two extremes of the swing of a pendulum—as "one second." Then I use that number of motion in order to count minutes, hours, and days.

It is vital not to confuse numbering in Aristotle's temporal, numbering of motion sense with numbering in the counting sense. When we designate three points on a line we use numbers in the sense of counting. For instance: _____1_____2_____3_____. This is numbering and numbers in the sense of counting. Counting *presumes* numbering in the number of motion sense, but counting with numbers is not the same thing as numbering in the number of motion sense. "Number" in Aristotle's number of motion sense refers to *the primordial manifestation of an interval between now before and now after*. In contrast to the 1, 2, 3, number line, this figure represents primordial numbering in the sense of number of motion: *_____*. The asterisks denote the two "nows," before and after, and the interval manifest between marks the primordial emergence of number.

Note well that numbering motion, that is, time in the sphere of nature sense, *requires a mind that can discern/pronounce that there are two "nows," a "now" before and a "now" after*. Therefore, if there is time, then there is mind (i.e., I in the sphere of spirit sense).[25]

Heidegger recognizes the radical implications of this for modern Western naturalism, which thinks of mind as a sphere of nature epiphenomena.

---

23. In Aristotle's words, "we think of the extremes as different from the middle and the mind pronounces that the 'nows' are two," "Physics," 292.

24. Ibid.

25. Aristotle had a sense for this issue. It would be fair to ask, Aristotle says, whether or not there would be time at all if there were no one to number. For if there were no soul/mind (i.e., that which has the capacity to mark the "nows" before and after and discern the interval), there would be no time, "but only that of which time is an attribute." This, Aristotle immediately qualifies, would be an interesting question only "if *movement* can exist without soul, and the before and after are attributes of movement, and time is these *qua* numerable." Aristotle never pursues this question, for, as we have seen, in the Aristotelian cosmos there is never movement without soul (Aristotle, "Physics," 299).

Aristotle's answer to the question, "what is time?" burns a hole in the closed sphere of nature and thereby unveils the mysterious, bottomless vistas of the sphere of spirit, for it raises a pivotal question, "What is *mind* that *numbers motion*?" No watch or computer numbers in this sense. Indeed, for reasons I will now strive to clarify, nothing in the sphere of nature, no phenomena and no epiphenomena, *numbers* in this sense.

Let me try to unveil this vital but difficult point in more familiar terms. The contention that "time is relative to an observer" is fairly well known. This commonplace, however, is usually understood in terms of the relativity of times "t" among multiple observers (that is, it has to do with relative *counting* among observers with discrete frames of reference). The more radical realization, the realization of the radically distinct *kind of being* that numbers/ observes in the numbering motion sense, arises when one notices the *relativity of time* even if there is *only one* observer. Time is relative to that observer in the most radical sense: if there is no observer, there is *no time* (no observers anywhere, no time anywhere). The pivotal question about sphere of spirit I's once again rises up, "what *observes* in the sense of numbering motion in terms of before and after?"

If No Time, Then No Being as Such

Let me approach the same point from a different angle. First, I maintained earlier that ultimate reality includes from the beginnings of the universe dimensions of what we now describe in the vocabularies of both the sphere of nature and the sphere of spirit. Evidently, the spiritual dimension of ultimate reality only achieves its individualized, more sophisticated, numbering-capable mind potential insofar as it is associated with highly ordered physical complexity (e.g., human brains). There is no reason (leaving God aside for the sake of argument) to think any such sophisticated minds existed in the first three minutes of the universe (or for a very long time thereafter).[26]

26. My position here is very similar to the process philosophy of mathematician Alfred North Whitehead. Speaking roughly, Whitehead rejected the idea that when matter reached a threshold of complexity, mental properties that are utterly different in kind suddenly appeared. He argues that it is more reasonable to suppose that even the most basic particles possess a mental dimension and that it was the mental/spiritual potential of those building blocks of existence that was realized in the emergence of conscious minds when these particles/events reached a threshold level of organized complexity. That is essentially the position I am suggesting. While I think White-head's effort to develop a new single vocabulary is a good philosophical exercise that may someday bear fruit, I am arguing that presently it is most reasonable to embrace the incommensurable vocabularies of the sphere of spirit and the sphere of nature. Whitehead, through his student Charles Hartshorne, inspired a movement known as

Second, although we have advanced from numbering with sun and pendulums to numbering with atomic clocks, the Aristotelian understanding of time as the number of motion remains valid. Time as the number of motion is the time we are speaking of when we say we have three minutes to reach the bus. This is time "t" in scientific equations. This is the "time" that is relative to an observer (or "space" that is relative to an observer, for there is no "space" without someone to number an interval relative to "here" and "there," define it as "meter" and so forth; or all again a bit more complexly with "spacetime" relative to an observer).[27]

Finally, note that it remains true that there is no time (or space) without mind (i.e., that which is capable of numbering, an observer). Taken together, this yields a remarkable conclusion. If there is no observer/numberer/mind, then not only is there no numbering of motion and no time, there is no "now," no "then," no "here," no "there," no space, no thing, no things, no counting, no measuring, no "is," no "is not," no "extension," and no anything else in the sphere of nature sense.[28] Since there was no observer/mind in the first three minutes of the universe, there was no time—no numbering, no counting, no here, no there, no this, no that, and so forth—in the first three minutes of the universe.

This is not to deny the independent "reality" of what we *retrospectively number and count as* the first three minutes of the universe. What we call time, space, cause, here, there, this, that, and so forth all what we call "existed" in what we call "the first three minutes of the universe." We are not denying that what we would call "reality" would what we call "exist" whether or not there are minds, but it would not exist *as* reality. That is, while in a sense everything existed, nothing existed *as such*, that is, nothing existed *as* atoms, helium, gravitation, physical interactions, minute two, e= mc² or any other categories or objects of the sphere of nature.

Let me try a thought experiment in order to clarify the meaning of this "as such." Suppose that only earth has minds capable of numbering (e.g., of noticing the nows are two and discerning intervals). Imagine that precisely two

---

process theology. While I would affirm many insights of process theologians, many process theologians affirm an Aristotelian, ontic logos, a God within reality "luring" it forward toward an ultimate good. I find this conclusion unwarranted. For some process theologians, this God even has the capacity to "remember" all that has been (a radically other, "personal" God may have such a capacity, but I do not see how such a capacity can be attributed to an ontic logos). Let me stress that the preceding is very rough insofar as process theology (to which I am in many respects very close) is now so diverse a movement that some process theologians appear to affirm a literal afterlife and a personal God.

27. *Being and Time*, 110–13.
28. Ibid., 338.

years from now we detect, too late, a massive asteroid. Six months after that all numbering-capable minds are wiped out. There are no minds/observers/ numberers anywhere. *What we called* earth, sun, moon, oceans, mountains, the orbit of the planets and weather patterns, what we called the light of the moon on a mountain peak, the sound of a tree falling in the woods, the drift of the galaxies, causation, what from another level is wholly the play of sub-atomic particles, and on and on; all these would still what we called "exist," just as what we called "other things" "were" in what we called "the first three minutes."

None of these things, however, would any longer exist *as such discrete things and events.* Insofar as there is no mind to count, to mark a now and then another now, there would be no time. Insofar as there is no mind to mark a here in distinction from a there, there would be no space.[29] Nor would there be the earth, moon, and sun, or any of the things, laws, or principles of physics, chemistry, biology, mathematics, and all the other sciences of the sphere of nature, none would exist *as such.* In other words, since only I's "world" (Heidegger uses this word as a verb) without I's there would be no world (as such), only utterly, undifferentiated timeless, spaceless and is-less happening.[30]

Notably, it is literally impossible for intrinsically temporal/numbering beings like us to imagine the sheer (without time, space, place, things, or thought) utterly undifferentiated, timeless, placeless happening that was and would be cosmos without any mind.[31] Even in our wildest imaginings we think temporally and spatially out from some particular place and point.[32] Even the bare words "flux," "happening," and "exist" inappropriately suggest temporal and spatial dimensions to what evidently "was" in what we call the first three minutes and to what could "be" again after the end of time/minds/ observers (which could come on earth at any moment with a catastrophe).

---

29. Ibid., 350–52.

30. "'*There is*' ['*gibt es*'] *truth only insofar as Dasein is and as long as it is.* Beings are discovered only *when* Dasein *is,* and only *as long as* Dasein *is* are they disclosed. Newton's laws, the law of contradiction, and any truth whatsoever are true only as long as Dasein *is.* Before there was any Dasein, there was no truth; nor will there be any after Dasein is no more" (ibid., 226, emphasis in original, brackets in translation). Also, "because Dasein is 'spiritual,' *and only because it is spiritual,* can it be spatial in a way that essentially remains impossible for any extended corporeal thing" (ibid., 368, emphasis in original).

31. Because of the counter-factual recognition, which can only be stated inexactly (e.g., "all that we attribute to the first three minutes of the cosmos happened even though there was no observer"), this is neither idealism (everything is a product of mind in the strongest possible sense) nor realism (things exist independently of mind).

32. Kant observed this about the forms of intuition (i.e., space and time).

Nonetheless, before sphere of spirit I's emerged there "was" what we *retrospectively* call the universe. This is why I keep stressing the *as such*. It would be misleading to say simply, "without any mind there would be no universe," for what we now call the universe and describe in terms of the first three minutes "was" sheer, undifferentiated happening. It "was" only in the barest, most obscure possible sense, but it would be misleading to say there was nothing before minds. So I do not say, "without any mind there would be no universe." I say, "without any mind there would be no universe *as such*." Since there is a universe as such, that is, since there are the categories and forces that constitute the sphere of nature, there must be minds, sphere of spirit I's.

In sum, if there were only sphere of nature existence, then none of the objects and categories of the sphere of nature would exist as such. The being of the sphere of nature *as* the sphere of nature depends upon sphere of spirit I's. The sphere of nature *as such* exists only because there are sphere of spirit I's. All of this leads to *the momentous conclusion that decisively undercuts naturalism*: no "things" (*res extensa*) are extended in space and time and countable if there are no souls/minds (*res cogitans*) thinking/numbering them.[33] *Since we do think the things and categories of the sphere of nature, it is literally impossible that the sphere of spirit is not real.*[34] Let me spend just a bit more time trying to unfold this vital point.

On the "Forgetting" of Spiritual Being

Sphere of nature categories *as such* depend upon sphere of spirit seeing, numbering, distinguishing, and so forth. The sphere of nature *appearing as the sphere of nature* means that there are sphere of spirit I's, minds. All of this unveils a sphere of spirit dimension of ultimate reality that naturalism fails to notice.[35] This is not surprising.

The sphere of spirit can easily be missed, for no matter which way any I turns, whether I looks out at the world or turns its eyes inward and looks inside (introspects, psychoanalyzes, engages in neuroscience), all any I directly sees is sphere of nature reality. When I look in a mirror, for instance, the eyes I see are not different in kind from the eye of a camera. The body I see is a biological machine. Everything I see is sphere of nature being.

It is easy not to notice that I nowhere see the see-ing. When one points the eye of a camera at a mirror it does not *see* itself. I am indeed the physical eyes

33. *Being and Time*, 89-99.
34. When Descartes said, "I think, therefore I am," he did not sufficiently develop the "to be" verb, the vital be-ing, am-ing character of the "am" (*Being and Time*, 263-264).
35. The language of "forgetfulness" is Heidegger's.

and biological body I see in the mirror. I am also a psychological, sociological, cultural-linguistic self, and I reason with a physical, computing brain (these all name sphere of nature dimensions of I). Those eyes, that body, that sociocultural self, and that computer, however, are not what *sees*. When I look in the mirror nothing that I overtly see *sees*.

I, however, incontestably do *see*. My seeing, however, is never visible before me. That is, the seeing cannot be ahead of itself and directly visible to itself. Like the proverbial beam of light that cannot shine upon itself but knows it is a light source by inferring from the light it casts, I can only see my seeing *transcendentally*. "Transcendent*al*" is not the same as "transcendent." Transcendental realization names what must be the case given what is. I never directly see myself seeing, not even if I look at myself in a mirror, but since I am seeing when I look in the mirror, since I number, I realize after the fact, indirectly, but without any reasonable doubt, that I am not only a physical but also a seeing, numbering/temporal being.

In the same way, Heidegger explains, only sphere of spirit I's touch.[36] I may, speaking loosely, say that two chairs "touch" one another. Strictly speaking, the phrase is vague and potentially misleading. The chairs are *in contact*. Physically, they "touch." Perhaps at some elemental level there is even an exchange of particles and/or energy. But only sphere of spirit I's *touch* in the physical *and* sphere of spirit sense.

When I touch the chair the chair does not touch me. When I touch another human or even, I would argue (allowing for significant differences), when I touch my cat, that human or my cat are aware that they are being touched (not merely contacted) and so they are touching me too (unless they are unconscious or some such).[37] In short, other things (e.g., smart phones) may, like our physical bodies/brains, detect sound or light waves, record them, "share them," even "speak" things they "know" in the sphere of nature sense. Only I's, however, *also* touch, hear, see, number, remember, share, speak, and know in the sphere of spirit sense.[38]

36. *Being and Time*, 91–92.

37. What I am doing here is related to the philosophical distinction between primary qualities (number, motion, energy waves) and secondary qualities (the seeing of a certain wavelength as red or the hearing of a wavelength as middle C), and it is even more intimately related to the debate over qualia (i.e., the seeing of red as red). These debates, however, have primarily taken place among so-called analytic philosophers, who until very recently have not taken account of the Heideggerian insights I am discussing.

38. Since I am not positing some free-floating spiritual stuff, but a real, spiritual dimension of ultimate reality that is realized in sufficiently and appropriately complex physical things (e.g., brains), then if smart phones ever get smart enough we may need both natural and sphere of poetic I vocabularies (i.e., vocabularies of brain and of mind)

No *sphere of nature distinction* is discernible that differentiates between two chairs that are touching and me touching a chair. Like seeing in the sphere of spirit sense, touching in the sphere of spirit sense can only be known transcendentally, in the sphere of spirit dimension of some sphere of spirit I's physical touching. Sphere of spirit seeing and touching, then, indirectly but definitely reveal the irruption in sheer physical existence of sphere of spirit I's. The physical (e.g., smart phones) and physical categories (of physics, chemistry, and all the other sciences) only discern and name the physical, not sphere of spirit realities. Insofar as one thinks and sees only in terms of the sphere of nature, in the categories of empiricism and the natural and social sciences, one can only *see* empirical/physical things. At the same time, though it often remains unnoticed, the italicized "see" in the previous sentence names a sphere of spirit event.

In sum, sphere of spirit I's see, touch, taste, smell, hear, remember, speak, share, and know other I's and other things in both the sphere of nature and sphere of spirit sense. Wholly sphere of nature things do not see, touch, taste, smell, hear, remember, speak, share, or know anything in the sphere of spirit sense.[39] Furthermore, as I will try to clarify in the next section, wholly sphere of nature things only exists *as* discrete things (distinguished from sheer flux) insofar as there are sphere of spirit I's/minds.

The Forgetfulness of Naturalism

The "forgetting" of the sphere of spirit was visible in my discussion in chapter 3 of the naturalistic vision of "All that is: phenomena (things) and epiphenomena (ideas)." There, in concert with naturalistic understanding, I explained that *epiphenomena* (i.e., ideas, such as "unicorn," "GDP of Canada") are dependent upon the thinking of some brain for their existence. *Phenomena* (i.e., things, such as tree, ocean, and sun), I explained, exist independently of the thinking of any brains. Everything that is, I said, is either phenomenal or epiphenomenal. I then said, "To be sure, the 'sun' would not exist *as such*, that is, as 'sun,' without some brain seeing it as such, that is, without some brain dividing up sheer reality into sun, sun's rays, space, earth, and so forth."

Consistent with naturalism's forgetfulness of sphere of spirit I's, however, I did not there note the significance of this acknowledgment of the "as such," I

---

in order to describe them accurately. One could speak here in terms of "singularity" if it is specified that it is not an epistemological comment related to a Turing test but an ontological comment related to the emergence into be-ing of sphere of spirit I's.

39. I am describing Heidegger's distinction between the ontic (sphere of nature being only) and ontic which is also ontological (sphere of nature and sphere of spirit be-ings—i.e., *Dasein*).

did not stop to consider that neither phenomena nor epiphenomena, both of which are sphere of nature realities, have the capacity to see, touch, or number in the sphere of spirit sense (i.e., discern time, space, or any thing *as such*). I did not there consider that our entire discussion of "all that is" presumed the existence of I's other in kind from phenomena (things) and epiphenomena (ideas). I did not in that naturalistic context note that the "thinking" and "seeing" (in the sphere of spirit sense) of a sufficiently complex brain was not itself either a phenomenon (thing) or an epiphenomenon (idea). So I failed there to notice that phenomena and epiphenomena could not possibly exhaust the sphere of ultimate reality (all that is).

In sum, time in the ordinary, counting sense, time as the number of motion, as "t" in scientific equations, time in this sphere of nature sense turns out to be derivative, to be dependent upon what Heidegger calls an "opening" or "clearing" in the sheer, undifferentiated flux of being. The "opening" or "clearing" is whatever it is that numbers. This rupture/emergence of *there* and *then* within physical being is Aristotle's "mind," is the "observer," is the "clearing" in the sphere of nature that numbers, marks the nows before and after, that discerns "here," "now," "there," "then," and everything else amidst the otherwise raw, undifferentiated happening.[40] This "clearing" in the sheer physical being of the sphere of nature is the opening of the sphere of spirit onto raw happening that is thereby seen *as* the sphere of nature. It is the clearing in being that we have been calling "mind" or "observers," and such clearings are the *sphere of spirit I's which we ourselves are (i.e., in part minds, res cogitans)*.[41]

To be sure, I am a sphere of nature object, a product of nature and nurture. What makes me a sphere of spirit I, however, is the fact that I am *also* other than the sphere of nature that I see and number.[42] This spiritual dimension of the being of I's is what distinguishes the sort of being that exists spiritually from the sort of being that is solely a part of the sphere of nature. This is what distinguishes I's from rocks and chairs. This is what distinguishes what lives from what sheerly is. This is what distinguishes what dies from what passes

---

40. Finding ordinary talk of soul, mind, ego, I, self, and so forth too freighted with conceptual baggage to describe whatever it is that numbers motion, Heidegger refers to this manifestation of mind from beyond the sphere of nature as "Dasein" ("da" = "there," "sein" = "to be," "there-be-ing"). For the sake of readability I will continue to use I instead of Dasein, but readers should take care not to import conceptual baggage into this I.

41. *Being and Time*, 231.

42. This is how I am appropriating Levinas's "other than," which for me, in contrast to Levinas, means not, "other than any and all being" but "other than sphere of nature being," put positively, "sphere of spirit be-ing."

away. Only I's *die*. Mountains and stars *pass away*—and even they only ever exist as such and pass away *in the eyes/seeing of sphere of spirit I's*.[43]

Sphere of Nature Truth and Sphere of Spirit Truths

The openings in the sphere of nature that are I's like you and me reveal sphere of spirit truth—not "truth" as the correlation between some sentence and some natural state of affairs (e.g., "the moon is on average x miles from earth," "$e = mc^2$"). That is a valid and vital definition of truth in the sphere of nature.[44] I's number, see, touch, hear, and describe the natural world, and then I's compare those observations (and inferences and hypotheses drawn from those observations) to other observations of the world so that the world can either disprove or support those observations.[45] This describes empirical/scientific truth in the sense of correspondence between sentences and the sphere of nature.

Sphere of spirit truths, however, have to do with the reality of the very I's that do all of the observing, numbering, talking, and comparing. These are not truths about anything in the sphere of nature. These are truths of the sphere of spirit discernable transcendentally in light of the appearance of the world *as such*. These are not truths in the sense of correspondence but in the sense of an unveiling or disclosure (as in the Greek word translated "truth" in the New Testament, *alethia*, meaning "uncovered," "unveiled," or "revealed"). These are truths unveiled in the spiritual dimension of being, the

43. In contrast to my assertion here, Heidegger identifies Dasein only with humans. Mindful of evolutionary continuities amidst all life, and without denying the distinctive capacities of humans—evidently, among known life forms only humans and a few other species can count—I would nonetheless argue (together with Aristotle) that degrees of soul or be-ing characterize all flora and fauna. I cannot pursue this complicated and important question in detail here.

44. This is "truth" in the sense of what Levinas, following Husserl, calls the noetic/noematic relation; it is also truth in the sense of Tarski's "snow is white if and only if snow is white" as interpreted by Donald Davidson.

45. The notion of objective "empirical content" in empiricism's scheme/content dualism, which is here undercut by Heidegger, is undercut much later in the analytic world by Donald Davidson's assault upon empirical content, most famously in "On the Very Idea of a Conceptual Scheme," which ends with the question of whether there is anything left that might be called empiricism ("On the Very Idea of a Conceptual Scheme" in *Inquiries into Truth and Interpretation* [Oxford: Clarendon Press, 1990]). Davidson's implosion of empiricism is more unsettled than Heidegger's because Davidson remains naturalistic, so one never gets a clear idea for *who* is doing the radical interpreting. Snow is white if and only if snow is white? Says *who*? Or, along a distinct but parallel philosophical trajectory: there is nothing outside of textuality. *Who* textures?

clearings in being that are numbering, thinking, seeing I's.[46] These truths remain hidden to those who only think about and acknowledge truth in the sphere of nature, correspondence sense. Thinking with Heidegger in terms of both the sphere of nature *and* the sphere of spirit, what truths can we affirm about human I's?

The Sphere of Nature/Sphere of Spirit Character of I's

I's are accurately described using sphere of nature and sphere of spirit vocabularies. Since sphere of spirit vocabularies are applicable only to highly complex natural objects (including, above all, human beings), sphere of spirit I's evidently emerge/open only where there is significant physical complexity. What we call the first three minutes of the cosmos and everything that happened in them and for billions of years thereafter evidently had to happen to allow for the evolution of I's physically sophisticated enough to emerge as openings from and to the sphere of spirit. In this sense the sheer happening that we call the sphere of nature is necessary for the emergence of sphere of spirit I's that in turn discern the sphere of nature as such. It is no surprise, then, that an I's sphere of spirit potential depends upon the integrity of that I's complex physical being. I's, for instance, can be knocked unconscious, killed, or have their thoughts and actions manipulated by drugs or brain probes.

Heidegger, in accord with Descartes, Judaism, Christianity, and most every other modern Western understanding—in contrast, say, to Hinduism or Buddhism with their ideas of reincarnation or transmigration of souls (though the relationship here is complex)—understands sphere of spirit I's to be discrete realities identified with discrete physical bodies. I's are apparently physical in such a way that the extraphysical dimensions of ultimate reality are realized as I's/minds in the sphere of spirit sense. Still, each I emerges first as a wholesale product of nature and nurture. Moreover, all the truths of biology, psychology, sociology, and of all the rest of the natural and social sciences always apply to I's. There is no reason to contest these important truths. As Heidegger has made clear, however, we have very good reason to contest the naturalistic claim that I's are *wholly and ever* a product of nature and nurture.

Because I's emerge first as wholesale products of nature and nurture, I's first come to awareness already "thrown" into some particular existence. I first

46. Says Heidegger, "Thus unconcealment, α-ληθεια [*a-lethia*] belongs to the λογος [*logos*]. To translate this word as "truth," and especially to define this expression conceptually in theoretical ways, is to cover over the meaning of what the Greeks posited at the basis—as 'self-evident' and as pre-philosophical—of the terminological use of αληθεια" (*Being and Time*, 219). Notably, *alethia* is the word used for "truth" in the Greek New Testament. By contrast, Tarski defines truth in "theoretical ways."

come to awareness, for instance, as a Ming Dynasty female peasant, a nine-teenth century male English aristocrat, or as a twenty-first century female Palestinian. I emerge and gain understanding as one already thrown into biological, geographical, political, sociocultural, and religious being. I do not begin on my own two feet deciding who and what I will be. From the first, I's come to awareness already thrown into an identity, already formed and being formed in accord with nature and nurture.[47]

In this sense, Heidegger says, I's come to awareness already "entangled" and "inauthentic," for I am a product of nature and nurture; I understand myself in accord with the meanings of the "they." Heidegger sees no inherent problem with this. The threat is that I will never notice my potential as a poetic sphere of spirit I, that I will never be more than a product of the "they." The threat is that I will always think that the world of things, the world of nature and nurture, the world of the sphere of nature, is the whole and only real world (the error of naturalistic reason). The threat is that I will never recognize and seize and create my I amidst other I's and the world, that I will never "choose" to affirm that which I am and freely influence what I will become (Heidegger can presume delimited free will, naturalistic objections having gone by the by with naturalism).[48] In sum, the threat is that I will never be anything other than thrown, that I will wholly "fall prey" to the "they," that my inauthentic existence will never be supplanted by authentic existence for I will never seize and shape my own I.

Heidegger on Death and Care

Heidegger, a World War I veteran, thinks death has unique power to counter the threat that one will be forever lost to inauthenticity, for death has the potential to break one free to one's "ownmost" possible authenticity. The death Heidegger has in mind is not one's own literal death, for there literally is no you after that. Nor, says Heidegger, is it the death of others, for those deaths, however personally painful, remain too distant from surpassing concern over one's own ongoing living. Nor is the death Heidegger has in mind intellectual assent to one's own inevitable death, for the mere idea of death remains too abstract.[49]

The death that can wrest one free from the hegemony of the "they" is the real death that comes from the future and grabs you right in the living

47. *Being and Time*, 346–349 and 382–92.

48. "The they evades choice" (*Being and Time*, 391). I would argue that in *Being and Time* Heidegger is defending choice in what philosophers call the "libertarian" sense (which is basically the everyday, free willing sense).

49. *Being and Time*, 237–41.

now, the death that comes to you when the doctor takes a steadying breath and looks *you* straight in the eye and says about the troubling lump or the odd pain, "it is cancer and it is not treatable; six months." Such moments can bring gut-dropping realization that no one else can or will die your death for you, can bring sinking awareness in your living now that on one coming real day you will indeed die your own death.[50] Such awareness of death, says Heidegger, has the fullest potential to individualize an I, to rip it free of the hegemony of the they.[51]

Nothing, Heidegger argues, individualizes I's more radically than lived awareness right now of I's arriving death. Only you, of course, were born your birth, eat your meals, breathe your breaths, and a million other things. I's reaction to death is radical because of another quality of I's. I's do not dispassionately move through existence, doing first this and then that. Transcendentally, I's realize that they are not dispassionate. I's are living passions within being. I's, unlike rocks, chairs, and computers, are inherently care-full. I's are primordial loci of living care. When I do the most abstract science I am always doing so out of some care. Even utter listlessness is an orientation related to I's care-full temporality (rocks, chairs, and computers do not get listless). I's provisionally adopt even the dispassionate, objective stance of the scientist for care-full reasons.

This is not to deny that I's are also of the sphere of nature. Much of what I am—and I am even in part a community of other creatures—happens on autopilot. Even sophisticated activities happen on autopilot. I arrive for the ten-thousandth time at work and do not remember driving there. I realize that my body (including my brain) has been driving while my care/mind (also dependent upon my body/brain) has been elsewhere—unless a trumping care breaks in, perhaps a child's ball bouncing out into the street in front of me (then I am care wholly focused upon driving again).

We can imagine a physical body without the sphere of spirit I, a body that is, so to speak, *always and only* on autopilot, never concerned with anything, a-temporal, wholly part of sheer flux, now and forever without any awareness or moment of realization. Clearly, however, I's are not wholly on autopilot. I's can be rendered unconscious, suffer brain injury, or be manipulated with drugs or electrical probes to the brain. In spite of all these debilitating sphere of nature possibilities, however, ordinarily the living I is physical *and also* self-creating and care-full.[52]

50. Ibid., 240.
51. Ibid., 276–80.
52. Dasein is fundamentally structured as *Sorge* (ibid., 316–31).

In sum, the very real threat is that I may wholly and ever fall prey to the cares of the they. Living awareness that I am living-toward-death is potentially salvific because it can wrest me free from wholesale absorption into cares of the they and deliver me to myself as individual, finite, free, care-full living toward death. The they and inauthentic life play an important role in living, for they frame stable contexts of social meaningfulness that provide I's with their original thrown identity and provide contexts over and against which I's find concrete purchase for self-creating. Each I's ownmost potential, however, lies in its potential for authenticity, in its ability to choose to affirm and shape the character of its own utterly unique I living unto death.[53]

Heidegger: Quintessentially Secular . . . Plainly Dangerous

We have returned to familiar ground. Heidegger's acknowledgment of the inauthentic, thrown character of every I and the power of the they parallels modern recognition of the natural I and of the fact that we are almost overwhelmingly the product of nature and nurture. Heidegger's proclamation, furthermore, of I's concern for itself in its living unto death and of its delimited but real potential to choose to seize and shape its own authentic identity, parallels modern celebration of the poetic I. This is the familiar modern Western concern so clearly named by the celebrated American philosopher Richard Rorty (discussed in chapter 3), who agreed with Heidegger about the I's ownmost potential for self-creation and warned that insofar as an I does not seize its individual poetic potential it will never be a real I at all.

In Rorty's words, the true horror for poetic I's is to realize at the moment of death that instead of having "impressed one's mark," one has "spent one's life shoving about already coined pieces. *So one will not really have had an I at all.*"[54] Explicitly invoking Heidegger, Rorty equates failure to create oneself with "guilt" over remaining ever and only a product of the they.[55] For Rorty, this poetic guilt frames the fundamental "religious" question confronting every I: "What am I to do with my aloneness?"[56] One is lost insofar as one never becomes more than a product of nature and the they. Salvation, says Rorty, comes insofar as an I seizes its potential for poetic self-creation and

---

53. Ibid., 305-16.
54. Richard Rorty, *Contingency, Irony, and Solidarity* (Cambridge: Cambridge University Press, 1989), 24.
55. Ibid., 108.
56. Richard Rorty, "Introduction: Antirepresentationalism, ethnocentrism, and liberalism," in *Objectivity, Relativism, and Truth* (Cambridge: Cambridge University Press, 1991), 13.

creates the most interesting, _ownmost_ I possible.[57] Note the loneliness that characterizes Rorty's description of both our fundamental situation and our greatest potential.

Rorty detested Heidegger's embrace of Nazism. Rorty celebrated the American and French ideals of liberty, fraternity, equality, and justice for all. Rorty also remained faithful to mainstream modern secular affirmation of natural and poetic I's and the ideal of authenticity. Accordingly, if I's condemnation of Nazism and affirmation of American and French ideals is to be _authentic_, not merely the product of natural or social conditioning, then I must self-consciously decide to affirm those values as an essential part of the identity I is creating for itself. Then I may authentically choose even to risk or lose I's life in the fight against the Nazis. That fight and that death are authentic—true to one's own poetic I, true to self-creation—only to the degree they are _chosen_.

For Heidegger, for Rorty, and for modern secular reason, _the sphere of spirit wholly consists of poetic I's_. I's escape the dictates of nature and the they only insofar as I's seize their ownmost ability to answer the question of their primordial "aloneness" by self-creating themselves. Note that this leaves no space in ultimate reality for anything that is not either the blind product of sphere of nature forces (natural and social conditioning) or the results of autonomous choices of sphere of spirit, poetic self-creators. Therefore, _there is no role or conceptual space for agape and good or evil in a moral realist sense_.

I have detailed Rorty's paradigmatically modern Western secular understanding in detail because it is not Heidegger, the Nazi, but Rorty, who detests Nazism (i.e., Rorty, the "good" guy), who more clearly manifests the chilling implications of this devastating affirmation of the sphere of nature and poetic I's. For while Rorty contends I may authentically self-create an identity that detests Nazism and that is willing to risk death in a war against the Nazis, Rorty also realizes that his disagreement with Heidegger over Nazism _cannot be moral_ (for there is no moral).[58] The disagreement is at best poetic,

---

57. Rorty exhorts us to heed the poetic "wisdom of the novel," the wisdom of, "Blake's exclamation, 'I must Create a System, or be enslav'd by another Man's'" (Rorty, _Contingency, Irony, and Solidarity_, 109, citing Blake, _Jerusalem_, plate 10, line 20).

58. In a largely naturalistic vein, Rorty introduces the final chapter of _Contingency, Irony, and Solidarity_ by saying that, "[t]he fundamental premise of the book is that a belief can still regulate action, can still be thought worth dying for, among people who are quite aware that this belief is caused by nothing deeper than historical circumstances" (Rorty, _Contingency, Irony, and Solidarity_ [Cambridge University Press, 1989], 189). Not only is this premise unsubstantiated in the book, but I would also argue that Rorty fails to substantiate the transition from contingency and irony to solidarity in any significant sense. Note how even in this dramatic statement Rorty remains tragically self-enclosed, portraying I's dying not for others but in fidelity to I's own beliefs.

the result of different self-creating choices, for Rorty can only interpret his disagreement in terms of his and like-minded poetic I's *choosing* of anti-Nazi values.[59]

If one affirms, with naturalism, only the sphere of nature, or if one affirms, with mainstream secular thought, only the spheres of nature and of poetic I's, then, while one may not *like* Heidegger's Nazism, *there is no basis for raising a moral objection to Hitler or Heidegger.*[60] The inability to raise a moral objection to the Nazi horror is on its face absurd, disturbing, and dangerous to peace on earth. It is so absurd, disturbing, and dangerous that it should have provoked Rorty, as it provoked Levinas, to ask whether this moral incapacity was evidence of a momentous error afflicting modern Western secular reason.[61]

Forgetting Moral Reality, Agape, and Faith

Heidegger moves us a decisive step forward, for he affirms the modern natural and social sciences while simultaneously defending the sphere of spirit and unveiling I's as passionate, poetic loci of care living amidst sphere of nature reality and other I's. Thus Heidegger alleviates the secular tension between, on the one hand, the affirmation of modern science and the natural I and, on the other, affirmation of authenticity and self-creation and the poetic I.

59. I say "at best poetic" because in his quintessentially modern secular philosophy Rorty, by turns, affirms poetic self-creation and, inconsistently, wholesale determinism.

60. At one point Rorty allows his enthusiasm for the purported "wisdom of the novel," which he tends to idealize in terms of realization among poets of infinitely unconstrained and diverse poetry, to drive him to a revolting conclusion. Rorty asks whether "the wisdom of the novel encompasses a sense of how Hitler might be seen as in the right and the Jews in the wrong?" and answers, "yes, I am afraid that it does." Rorty hopes no such novel is written soon, for the pain for survivors would be "too much." However, Rorty continues with relentless devotion to unconstrained poetic self-creation, saying, "such novels will someday be written. If we are to be faithful to the wisdom of the novel, they *must* be written" (Richard Rorty, "Truth and Freedom: A Reply to Thomas McCarthy," *Critical Inquiry* 16 [Spring 1990]: 639).

61. I would argue that Rorty, rejecting Levinas, never gets to the solidarity he strives for, despite what appear to be his plainly moral and mostly Christian convictions (in this sense Rorty may have done well to reflect more deeply on the consistency of his stance as an openly "*free-loading* atheist"). I *suspect* (not sure) that Derrida, on the other hand, is largely persuaded by his encounter with Levinas in the sixties and early seventies, and in the wake of that turn affirms something like moral realism when he says things like, "Justice . . . is not deconstructible" (Jacques Derrida, *Deconstruction and the Possibility of Justice*, Drucilla Cornell, Michel RosenFeld, and David Gray Carlson, eds. [New York: Routledge, 1992], 14–15, as cited in John Caputo, *Deconstruction in a Nutshell: A Conversation with Jacques Derrida* (New York: Fordham University Press, 1997), 131.

In Heidegger, primordially atomistic I's, individualized most profoundly and authentically in the living face of their own deaths, are the source and centers of all care and hence of all meaningfulness. The Heideggerian care that is unveiled to its fullest extent in the living wake of encounter with one's future death is care for self. For Heidegger, for Rorty, and for mainstream modern secular rationality, there is no greater care than this.[62] In sum, for Heidegger, Rorty, and mainstream modern secular rationality, the sphere of spirit is wholly made up of poetic I's, and a sphere of spirit wholly made up of poetic I's has no more place than does naturalism for *agape* and moral reality.[63]

As mentioned, because of the predominance of naturalistic rationality in modern Western thought, many Western philosophers consider Levinas's philosophy fanciful. That is why I made the difficult detour through Heidegger, for Levinas depends upon Heidegger's refutation of naturalism and defense of the sphere of spirit. Levinas, however, moves beyond Heidegger. Scandalized by Heidegger's and secular reason's inability to object morally to the Nazi horror, Levinas initiates a more penetrating transcendental exploration of poetic I's and uncovers an enveloping *moral* region of the sphere of spirit.

By the end of the last chapter I had delineated the character of both naturalistic rationality (which contends that the spheres of nature and of ultimate reality are coterminous) and secular rationality (which affirms both the sphere of nature and the sphere of poetic I's). In defense of secular rationality, I had argued that it was *reasonable* to affirm a sphere of poetic, self-creating I's, for as of yet no argument has established the truth of naturalistic rationality. At this point I have taken a decisive step forward. For in the wake of Heidegger's work I can, in defense of secular rationality, conclude that affirmation of naturalistic rationality *is unreasonable*. At the same time, in light of the insights of Levinas, we gain a clear sense that secular rationality is insufficient, for it is unable to account for profoundly significant dimensions of reality that are as wholly and primordially given as are the realities of the spheres of nature and of poetic I's.

Levinas does not contest the accuracy of the vocabularies of the sphere of nature or the vocabularies of poetic self-creation in the sphere of spirit.

---

62. For many predominant streams of modern Western rationality, a "rational decision" is by definition a "self-interested decision."

63. Heidegger's brief discussion of *mitsein*, with-being, which distinguishes Dasein vis-à-vis things-at-hand (other ontic being) and other Dasein (other ontological beings) with emphasis upon the way in which meaning is partly sustained by the social structures into which we find ourselves thrown, provides insufficient basis for argument against this claim (see "Chapter Four: Being-in-the-World as Being-with and Being a Self: The 'They,'" *Being and Time*, 113–30).

He realizes, however, that affirmation and use of only these two families of vocabularies is devastatingly incomplete. His transcendental explorations into the sphere of spirit unveil enveloping forces beneath, behind, and beyond the physicality and autonomy of secular rationality's natural/poetic I's. As I will argue in the next chapter, we need to speak not in terms of two spheres, the sphere of nature and the sphere of spirit, but in terms of three spheres, one sphere of nature and *two* spheres of spirit: 1) the sphere of poetic, self-creating I's and 2) the sphere of *agape*, the sphere of the discrete spiritual vocabularies of grace, morality, and faith. It is more reasonable to affirm these three spheres (i.e., the sphere of nature, the sphere of poetic I's, *and* the sphere of *agape*) than the two spheres of secular rationality (i.e., the spheres of nature and of poetic I's) because, as I will strive to make evident in the next chapter, *agape* is as independent and real a part of daily, given reality as gravity and poetic self-creation.

6

The Sphere of Agape

Death, Care-Consumed I's, and Agape

For Levinas, as for Heidegger, it is confrontation with death that illuminates the most profound dimensions of ultimate reality. In stark contrast to Heidegger, for Levinas it is the tragic or unjust death *of others* that unveils the most significant truths about the ultimate character of reality. In the presence of the terminally ill child in the oncology ward or of helpless refugees caught amidst the terrors of ethnic cleansing, the meanings of the they, the meaningfulness of authentic, self-creative choices, and I's absorption in passionate concern for self are all rent asunder. The reality of *agape*—in such contexts forcefully felt in its violation—is disclosed.

If I am to be true to Levinas and to real life, I am at this juncture transported to the extermination camps, to the mass graves, and to that dead boy hanging from the gallows. As became clear in chapters four and five, sphere of nature and poetic vocabularies have no conceptual space for a *morally realist* naming of the death camps as evil. Therefore, Levinas concludes, sphere of nature and poetic vocabularies are screamingly inadequate when it comes to describing the concrete reality of my having been taken "hostage" by the Face of that boy, and by the Faces of multitudes of other wounded people (I explain my capitalizing of "Face" below).

Levinas's "hostage" language reflects the fact that I do not want to look up at that gallows. I do not want to see that boy's Face. I do not want to be consumed with passion and pain. I want to look away, to deny, avoid, forget and never again open my eyes to such horror. Insofar as I do not cover over the reality, however, the vertigo returns, blank eyes stare out of gaping pits, and I am *awakened*, haunted, taken hostage by the Faces of all those suffering, persecuted, and murdered. In being taken hostage by the Face of that boy, the self-absorption of Heidegger's I, an I consumed with care for self, is rent asunder. A more primordial reality, the enveloping reality of *agape*, passion for the boy, here manifest in violation, is unveiled. Care for the boy consumes and displaces care for self. I am now living care for that boy, hostage to his Face.

Not only do I not want to be taken hostage by that boy's Face, I do not *choose* to be taken hostage. The passion by which I am seized is neither self-concerned nor self-originating. I do not first encounter the boy in a dispassionate fashion and then decide whether or not to be taken hostage by his Face. I do not begin from a neutral stance, assess the situation in light of some set of ethical or religious beliefs, and then decide that what I am seeing is horrific violation. I do not *decide* to be passionately care-full. Before evaluation, decision, or intention I am already taken hostage by that boy's Face, rent by the horrendous violation.[1]

Insofar as I is taken hostage by care for another, the atomistic walls of the poetic I are broken open. I does not choose the passion, originate the passion, desire the passion, or have the passion. I, then, is not only an opening to the extranatural sphere of poetic I's; I is also an opening to an enveloping dimension of the sphere of spirit extending out beneath, behind, and beyond I. This dimension of ultimate reality is unveiled as something more and other than a collection of poetic I's. I's subsist amidst an expansive spiritual reality that has definite contour, for this reality is manifest insofar as I's are taken hostage to concern for others.[2] In sum, I's are hostage to a care that *does not originate in I's*, that *does not stem from self-concern*, and that *is passionately for others*. This describes the reality of *agape*, a reality that is manifest in and that is as real as

---

1. Speaking technically, this priority of the moral names Levinas's assertion that ethics is first philosophy.

2. Notably, I am broken free from the determinations of the they when I am taken hostage by care for others in a far more direct and forceful fashion than when I am broken free from the they, as Heidegger would have it, through the abstract reflections that follow living confrontation with my own death. (This sphere of spirit care for self should not be confused with sphere of nature pursuit of bodily pleasure and flourishing and avoidance of bodily pain, threat, and decline, which is common to all creatures.) One should distinguish between I's sphere of nature tendency to avoid pain and mortal threat and to pursue pleasure and mortal security, which is basic to the physical constitution of every I, from Heidegger's sphere of spirit, poetic guilt over wholly falling prey to the they, and the realization in the living awareness of death of a call to create one's own poetic I. It is this latter, spiritual recognition that takes considerable imaginative work (i.e., that is far from obvious), whereas I am forcefully, directly, and regularly taken hostage by Faces.

the nonmaterial, nonintentional force that takes me hostage to care for that boy's Face.

Agape is not *I's* love. *Agape* is not *I's* response to the Face of the boy, as if some reflection and decision preceded *agape*. I does not have *agape*. *Agape* has I. Insofar as I do not harden my heart (more on this presently), nothing surpasses the passion for that boy's Face that has taken me hostage, not even concern for my own survival. Taken hostage by *agape*, the I is led, in Levinas's words, "to fear injustice more than death, to prefer to suffer than to commit injustice, and to prefer that which justifies being over that which assures it."[3] For Levinas, a Jew, the whole of Torah is about passion for neighbor that transcends even concern for personal pleasure and survival. In blazing contrast to Heidegger and mainstream secular thought, Levinas maintains that there is no greater love than this.

On this point Levinas is in full accord with a first century Jew who also summarized Torah in terms of love of God and neighbor and who likewise maintained that there is no greater love than the love that would lead one to give one's life for a friend. "Friend" here should be understood not in a personal but in a moral sense. Jesus is not speaking of personal preference or favoritism. The "friend" for whom one rightly sacrifices one's life is the friend of *agape*. Jesus calls upon us to love enemies (here again, not in a personal sense but in a moral sense, that is, "enemies of love") but delimits the sacrifice of one's life to friends (that is, friends of *agape*).

Levinas, working in the wake of Heidegger's opening of a realm of spirit, unveils the reality of *agape* in his description of being taken hostage by the Faces of others. In other words, in the event of having been taken hostage by a Face, a third sphere of ultimate reality that requires its own family of vocabularies becomes manifest: the sphere of *agape*. While all vocabularies are in and of themselves sphere of nature realities dependent upon sphere of spirit I's, it is now clear that three distinct vocabularies describing three discrete spheres of reality are necessary if we are to provide the most reasonable and satisfactory characterization of ultimate reality.

First, we need natural and social *scientific* vocabularies that pertain to ultimate reality insofar as we best understand it in terms of *the sphere of nature*, where what is basically given to human understanding is existence insofar as it is material (i.e., phenomenal and epiphenomenal). Second, we need *existential* vocabularies that pertain to ultimate reality insofar as we best understand it in

---

3. Levinas, "Ethics as First Philosophy," in *The Levinas Reader*, Sean Hand, ed. (Cambridge, MA: Basil Blackwell, 1989), 85. See also Levinas, "Non-Intentional Consciousness," in *On Thinking of the Other: Entre-Nous* (New York: Columbia University Press, 1998), 132.

terms of *the sphere of poetic I's* delineated by Heidegger, where what is basically given is temporal, thinking, freely self-creating I's. Third, we need *spiritual* vocabularies that pertain to ultimate reality insofar as we best understand it in terms of *the sphere of agape*, where what is basically given to human understanding is having been taken hostage by concern for others, that is, *agape*.

The two predominant versions of modern Western rationality discussed in "Part 1: The Condition of Secularity," can be defined in terms of the first two spheres. *Naturalistic rationality* affirms reality only insofar as it is described in accord with the sphere of nature (i.e., it affirms only scientific vocabularies). *Secular rationality*, vindicated by Heidegger, affirms reality insofar as it is described in accord with both the sphere of nature and also the sphere of poetic I's (i.e., it affirms scientific *and also* existential vocabularies). Because these two forms of rationality have long been predominant in modern Western thought, the ability of modern Westerners to discern and publicly affirm the sphere of *agape* and its spiritual vocabulary of faith and morals has been compromised. I am arguing that it is most reasonable to affirm a neo-Levinasian, re-enchanted, *awakened rationality* that affirms reality insofar as it is described in accord with the sphere of nature, the sphere of poetic I's, and the sphere of *agape* (i.e., I affirm scientific, existential, and also spiritual vocabularies).

As noted, because naturalistic and secular rationalities have been predominant in modern Western thought, many Western intellectuals still consider Levinas's philosophy to be fanciful and unrealistic. That, again, is why I made the difficult detour through *Being and Time*, for Levinas depends upon Heidegger's argument that naturalism cannot adequately account for itself (e.g., it cannot account for the numbering of motion presumed by any affirmation of the reality of time) in order to unveil the reality of an extranatural sphere of spirit. Levinas, realizing that neither scientific nor poetic vocabularies adequately account for having been taken hostage by the Faces of others, pushes beyond Heidegger, unveils the reality of the sphere of *agape*, and develops a *spiritual* vocabulary. The eliding of the conceptual space for a spiritual vocabulary, which forced people of faith to think and explain themselves in the alien vocabularies of the spheres of nature and of poetic I's, has been a major reason mainstream modern Western rationality has been so devastating for faith.

In the balance of this chapter, I will unfold the character of the sphere of *agape* using key concepts from Levinas's spiritual vocabulary, such as "awakening," "Face," "Saying," "said," and "Proximity." For the sake of clarity, when familiar terms are used to designate sphere of *agape* realities, I will capitalize the term. For example, "face" refers to sphere of nature realities (e.g., appearance, gender, nationality) and "Face" refers to sphere of *agape* reality (so where "face" designates a sphere of nature reality, "Face" designates a sphere of *agape* reality). Using Levinas as a springboard and working primarily in conversation with Jewish and Christian understanding (I would expect analogous concepts in other faith traditions), I will also unfold the character of faith, *koinonia*, church, revelation, idols, icons, good, evil, morality, ethics, and election. Despite my increasing use of overtly spiritual, largely Christian language, I will remain within the bounds of what can publicly be considered to be good and reasonable, that is, within the bounds of a *philosophical* spirituality.

Awakening to Faces: Faith, the Gift of Agape

For Levinas, modern Western rationality has had the devastating effect of deadening our sensitivities to agapic reality. Those who think only in terms of the spheres of nature and poetic I's need to be awakened to the sphere of *agape*. The power of Wiesel's horrifying narrative lies in its ability to *awaken* readers to the *Faces* of others.[4]

The Face is not a biological or sociocultural reality. Gender, nationality, family, height, age, and so forth are all features of one's face (small "f"). The Face of any face is that by which I am taken "hostage" in concern. The Face is discerned in and through awakening to *agape*.

As the SS officers who hung the boy and also as Heidegger (first in theory, then in practice, then in silence) illustrate, I's can harden their hearts. I's can focus their attention upon other desires and priorities. They can reject having been taken hostage. In this respect Levinas's "hostage" metaphor is less than helpful, for hostages are not free to reject being hostages. So instead of saying "hostage" I will say "*having been seized*." Moreover, I want to make explicit two points that remain implicit in Levinas. First, I am seized by *passionate concern for* others, that is, I am seized by *agape*. Second, the enveloping reality of the sphere of *agape* is the spiritual dimension of the ultimate reality *in which* poetic I's live and move and have their being. In order to make all three of these emphases explicit—potential to harden heart, *by agape, in agape*—where Levinas would say, "taken hostage by Faces," I will say, "*having been seized in and*

---

4. It would be fair for Levinas scholars to suggest that Levinas's "Other" is even more radically other than the ontological region of being. That reading does not allow us to make good sense of Levinas, for that Other is too Other to have any relation to us. On the other hand, a common stream of interpretation, in line with naturalism, reduces the "Other" to the sociopolitical other (i.e., other than me and my sociopolitical identity). That reading flies in the face of Levinas's explicit and repeated caution not to identify the other in terms of eye or hair color, dress, and so forth. In other words, that reading forgets the otherness of others and the Other.

by love for Faces." In this sense, when reading Wiesel's narrative I am seized in and by love for the Face of the boy.

Not only can I's harden their hearts to having been seized in and by love, this poetic potential is vital. I's freedom to resist is vital because it preserves I's authenticity. I am not enslaved to having been seized in and by love for the Faces of others precisely because my poetic potential means that I, in my free self-creating, could harden my heart.[5] There is a vital asymmetry here, for while I can choose to harden I's heart, I cannot choose to be seized by others' Faces, for I's having been seized in and by love precedes any thought, intention, or decision on I's part. Because I's can harden their hearts, however, when I's do not harden their hearts to having been seized in and by love, I's love for others is authentically I's even though it does not originate in I. I will call not hardening one's heart "surrender," but it is vital to remember that "surrender" in this context is not an action, but *not taking* an action, *not* hardening one's heart to having been seized in and by love.[6]

As is illustrated by Wiesel's narrative, I may find myself most dramatically seized in moments of crisis. I am the first on scene at an accident and I find myself seized by the Face of a child injured or weeping. I watch the news and I find myself seized by the Faces of the stunned survivors of the tsunami. In opposition to the hegemony of the self-creating, autonomous I of modern Western secular understanding, the passive tense is essential.[7] I do not *decide* to be seized by passion for others. I do not react to *an idea* of what is right or good. I do not initially react neutrally and then decide whether I should be concerned. The demand that we assume a dispassionate, neutral, objective attitude and decide whether or not to be concerned is the confused demand of much modern ethics (just imagine what we would think of someone whose initial response to an injured or weeping child was dispassionate neutrality). I do not initially react neutrally and then decide whether I should be concerned. I find myself immediately seized in and by love for the Faces of suffering, pleading, dying faces.

The context may also be wonderful. Perhaps I am walking by a church and I see joyous, smiling, laughing newlyweds running out to the limo beneath a

5. In Levinas's words, "if no one is good voluntarily [i.e., good does not originate in I's free will], no one is enslaved to the Good" (Emmanuel Levinas, *Otherwise Than Being or Beyond Essence*, Alphonso Lingis, trans. [Pittsburgh: Duquesne University Press, 1981], 11).

6. This is the sense in which, in Christian theology, grace is neither a work nor a negation of poetic I's autonomy and authentic loving.

7. The priority of the activity of some sort of I is central to virtually all modern Western philosophical trajectories and includes Descartes, Nietzsche, Brentano, Heidegger, Rorty, and Critchley.

light rain of birdseed, and I find myself happy and smiling too. I have been seized by the Faces of those newlyweds. Levinas claims Faces beckon even when I pass strangers on the street. Even then, awakened I's are called to say hello. Levinas is not suggesting we ride the subways of Manhattan saying hello to everyone. The awakened, however, feel the call of every Face even in Manhattan, where, sensitive to context, they are hopefully wise enough to know when to suppress the urge even to make eye contact.

The relationship among Faces may not be reciprocal. For instance, I may find myself seized by the Face of an infant who is as of yet incapable of seeing and being seized by concern for my Face. The Face may also be manifest in creatures we do not ordinarily think of as having Faces. Imagine you have come to my lecture and I have walked in and given everyone a brittle stick gathered from the parking lot. I ask folks to break the sticks into pieces. I get odd looks, but folks typically break the sticks in order to humor me.

Now, imagine I walk you outside to a very young tree, perhaps a foot-high maple or oak sapling. The sapling is in a splendid location, not in the way of anything, and I hand you a hoe and say (at some cost, even in the imagining), "Tear it out of the ground by the roots so that it cannot possibly recover." Usually, folks visibly recoil when they hear this request. Even with regard to a sapling, many look up with expressions of horror. They have been seized in and by love for the Face of the sapling. The Face of the sapling, like all Faces, *is manifest solely and precisely in awakening to having been seized in and by love.* Indeed, the manifestation of Faces is simultaneous with the manifestation of *agape*. Insofar as we are awake, from saplings to humans, our world shimmers with a sea of glorious Faces.[8]

8. I would argue that the *ethical* violation involved in the killing of a sapling (perhaps a human needs it for heat or shelter) would not be equivalent to like violation of the Face of a human. This raises the properly ethical question of how to adjudicate among the violation of the Faces of different faces. Such questions remain beyond the scope of this work, for I am focused upon awakening to moral violation wherever any life, even the life of a sapling, is destroyed. I should note that Levinas, still confined by modern Western anthropocentrism, did not extend his category of "Face" beyond the human species. The exclusion, while contextually unsurprising, is unjustifiable. Late in his life Levinas may have indicated openness on this issue (his tone of voice is not clear) when he said somewhere that he did not know whether or not a snake has a face. For those familiar with Levinas, let me note that the story of the welcoming dog, Bobby, who Levinas knew in captivity, speaks even more profoundly to this issue, for Levinas credits Bobby with seeing Levinas's Face, and in this sense the dog delivered to Levinas Levinas's own Face when its reality was being so violently denied by other humans—that is, Levinas to a degree receives his own Face when he sees Bobby seeing his (i.e., Levinas's) Face (Levinas, in "Interview with Myriam Anissimov," in *Is It Righteous to Be? Interviews with Emmanuel Levinas,* Jill Robbins, ed. [Stanford: Stanford University Press, 2001], 90 and Levinas, "The Name of a Dog, or Natural Rights,"

In short, *agape* beneath, behind, and around one is unveiled in having been seized in and by love for the Faces of others. The question for freely self-creating I's in the face of having been seized in and by love is whether or not they will harden their hearts. *The I who does not harden his or her heart, but who lives surrender to having been seized in and by love, is the I of faith. Faith is I living surrender to agape.*

Faith, then, is not something I create, assert, or intend. Faith is not knowledge I have or my assent to some set of beliefs. Beliefs are significant insofar as they are ideas we have about faith and allow for testimony and shared understanding. A systematic system of beliefs about faith constitutes a faith tradition. Assent to even the most wonderful and full system of beliefs, however, is not faith. Faith is living surrender to having been seized in and by love for all Faces, living surrender to the surpassing reality of *agape* in which I's live and move and have their spiritual being. In living surrender to *agape*, I am faithful. In living surrender to having been seized in and by love, I freely receive faith, the gift of *agape*.

The said and Saying

Levinas speaks of the distinction between natural (sphere of science) and existential (sphere of poetry) vocabularies on the one hand and spiritual (sphere of *agape*) vocabularies on the other, in terms of a contrast between the "said" (i.e., the natural or existential) and "Saying" (i.e., the spiritual). Within the sphere of nature, I's use the said to talk about phenomena and epiphenomena ("the GDP of Canada is x," "I need a cup of flour," "the earth is eight light-minutes from the sun," "$e=mc^2$"), and also to articulate their partly self-created, existential

Sphere of Nature	Sphere of Agape
face	Face
said	Saying
proximity	Proximity
beliefs	faith
icons	the divine
church/synagogue/mosque/temple	*koinonia*
ethics	the moral

Difficult Freedom: Essays on Judaism, Sean Hand, trans. [Baltimore: John Hopkins University Press, 1997], 151–53).

identities. All *vocabularies*—the scientific, the existential, and the spiritual—
are in and of themselves sphere of nature realities dependent upon poetic I's.
Spiritual vocabularies, however, are sphere of nature realities (e.g., *said* in word
or deed) that testify to the extranatural, extrapoetic, spiritual reality of *agape*.
In Levinas's terminology, spiritual vocabularies are said that strives to Say, said
that testifies to the love in and by which I has been seized.

The spiritual truth of *agape* to which the said testifies is not proven,
established through consensus, or seized by I's. It is not truth in the sense
of correspondence between a sentence and a sphere of nature reality (i.e.,
a phenomena or epiphenomena). The truth of *agape* is unveiled in having
been seized in and by love for a Face. Again, this accords with the Greek
word for spiritual "truth" in the New Testament, *alethia*, which means literally "unveiling."

The sphere of nature meaning of the said makes a difference for any Saying. Extraordinary circumstances aside, I cannot Say, "I love you" with the
said, "I hate you." Of course, it is possible for me *only* to said, "I love you"—
just words, we say. Or, using the said, I can *Say*, "I love you." People typically
have a strong sense for when someone is, or is not, *Saying* "I love you." Likewise, I can only said a prayer, or I can use the said to Say a prayer. I can only
said a hymn, or I can use the said to Say a hymn. "*Said*," names the natural or
poetic meaning of the words; "*Saying*" names the sphere of *agape* reality that
fires words and works of love with spiritual meaningfulness.

The spiritual meaningfulness of the Saying is not a product of human
intention. The Saying of prayers and hymns, for instance, is not ultimately
a communication of meanings, is not an intentional affirmation of a set of
beliefs, is not assent to a philosophy of life or a religion. The Saying of prayers
and hymns is not an event in which some I tries to communicate meanings
to other I's, or even to God, but I Saying in a said its surrender to having
been seized in and by love for all Faces (every person, every sapling). For
instance, insofar as my surrender is complete, I find the hymn or prayer *Saying* me. Strictly speaking, even when engaged in spiritual discourse or practice, I never Say, I only said the Saying in and by which I am seized. As I uses
the said to Say, in reality it is the truth of *agape* that is Saying (so, Christians
say, "not me, but Christ in me"). In this very strict sense, faithful faces *said* in
surrender, "Here I am, Say me without ceasing."[9]

Sometimes Saying is most obvious in its absence, when, as one sometimes
hears, there is singing without soul, liturgy without spirit, prayer without

---

9. I would argue that here we discern the essence of prayer (this "here I am," often
referenced by Levinas, is the "here I am" of Samuel 3).

heart, the words without the Word.[10] The all-too-frequent absence of Saying in churches has given rise in the modern West to some I's heartfelt protest that they are "spiritual, not religious," for many people who are skeptical of organized religion truly hear the Saying. Many people skeptical of religion treasure memories of self-transcending moments when the Saying of *agape* awakened their spirits and in surrender they found the prayer, the hymn, the confession, the response to horror, the acts of service, or the communion with creatures or creation *Saying* them.

Ideally, sphere of nature realities such as synagogues, temples, churches, mosques, and ashrams and their sermons, liturgies, and acts of public service are all diverse ways of trying to make the said *Say*, to give the spiritual reality of *agape* purchase and influence in the natural sphere (i.e., in what the apostle Paul calls "the world"). There is no spiritual escapism in this philosophical spirituality, for insofar as I surrenders to having been seized in and by love for all Faces—of children, cats, roaches, saplings—I lives and acts in the sphere of nature in the light of having been seized in and by love for every Face (i.e., in the light of the truth/unveiling/revelation of *agape*). In this sense I's are faithful insofar as they are *in* the world (i.e., in the spheres of nature and poetic self-creation) but not of the world, for they are *of* the sphere of *agape*.[11]

When one uses the said to Say, language can be secondary. Indeed, language is not even essential. For instance, an embrace can Say one's having been seized in and by love for another's Face far more powerfully than any words. Bedside in the hospice, or kissing one's child goodnight, words may only distract from the silent communion of the Saying. Profoundly meaningful liturgies often Say with speechless acts (embraces, kisses, kneeling—all Saying in silence). Indeed, the most intense moments of Saying often palpably demand silence, a radical minimizing of the distractions of the said.

As the problem stimulating the "spiritual, not religious" qualification suggests, the said can actively obstruct Saying, for the said (for instance, the belief, liturgy, commitment, affiliation, or philosophy) can itself become the focus of attention and the object of fidelity. In this case I's flounder, asleep to *agape*, self-contained within the spheres of nature and poetic I's, and so here

---

10. Along these lines one could also discuss the relationship between *apophatic* unveiling and *kataphatic* theology (by definition, there should be no such thing as *apophatic* theology), or the relationship between biblical exegesis (very important) and *lectio divina* (an attempt to open us to the *Saying* of a text).

11. This is how one could understand within philosophical parameters the "heroes of faith" in accord with the New Testament book of Hebrews, which celebrates those who remained faithful to that which remains unseen, that is, to that which is invisible to physical and existential understanding, namely, which celebrates those who remained faithful, sometimes unto death, to their election to the Faces that seized them.

one finds only said about said, religion about beliefs, atomistic I's trying to establish foundations for their own existence and meaningfulness: "I think, therefore I am," "I freely and creatively choose, therefore I am authentic." This describes the tragic self-enclosure (myopia) of modern Western naturalistic and secular rationality.[12] By contrast, those who are awakened and faithful are filled with the meaningfulness of having been seized in and by love for all Faces.

The distinction between said and Saying facilitates a distinction between idols and icons that can help us to guard against the problem "spiritual but not religious" reacts against.[13] *Idols* are said that does not Say, said that does not originate in or strive to testify to the sphere of *agape*, said that remains wholly within the natural and poetic spheres. *Icons*, by contrast, can be understood as said striving to Say, as said that originates in Saying as I's in surrender said in word and deed the Saying in and by which they have been seized.

The sophistication of the ancient Hebrews on this point is clear in their prohibition against graven images, for this is not merely a prohibition against golden calves and wooden statues. It is *a warning against confusing G-d with any word, thought, or concept.* This is how and why "G-d," which like every other word and idea remains a sphere of nature reality, with its strikingly visible caution against idolatry, strives to be an icon, always gesturing beyond itself to the transcending, spiritual reality of *agape*.[14]

When we remember that not only objects but also all human constructions, including all theologies, even the word/idea "G-d," are sphere of nature realities, we realize that even the most ideal beliefs can function as either idol or icon. If the meaningfulness of an idea or system of beliefs remains wholly

12. I would argue that such self-enclosure short-circuits Simon Critchley's poignant *Faith of the Faithless: Experiments in Political Theology* (New York: Verso, 2012). For instance, while on the one hand Critchley can say the faith of the faithless "is an openness to love, love as giving what one does not have and receiving that over which one has no power" (7), he also insists that the "faith of the faithless cannot have for its object anything external to the self or subject, any external, divine command, any transcendent reality . . . The faith of the faithless [perfected by suffering] must be a work of collective self-creation where I am the smithy of my own soul and where we must all become soul-smiths, as it were"(4).

13. With the distinction between idols and icons I am unfolding Levinas as inspired by Jean-Luc Marion's work on idol and icon in *God Without Being*, Thomas Carlson, trans. (Chicago: University of Chicago Press, 1991) 7–24.

14. The distinction between said and Saying also allows us to make sense of warnings not to confuse the letter with the Spirit, for these can be understood as warnings not to confuse the said with the Saying. In a similar fashion, within the Christian tradition the twentieth century Protestant theologian Karl Barth warns Christians not to confuse the words (i.e., of scripture) with the Word. For Barth, the words proclaim the Word, the Saying to which the words/said testify.

within the bounds of the spheres of nature and of poetic I's, which means that its meaningfulness is grounded in the intentions and desires of one or more I's, then it is an idol. If, however, the meaningfulness of an idea or system of beliefs flows from *agape*, if the idea and beliefs are said testifying to Saying, then they are icons.

Insofar as we are physical and poetic I's, all Saying will be thought and represented with some said or another. There is no possibility of being purely spiritual. I's of faith can only understand themselves in terms of some religious or theological said or another. However, for I's of faith, that is, for I's who are living surrender to having been seized in and by love for all Faces, every religious idea, every said of love in word and deed will be an icon, will be said testifying to the Saying of *agape*.

Koinonia: proximity and Proximity

Just as Levinas distinguishes the sphere of nature from the sphere of *agape*, distinguishes faces from Faces, and distinguishes said from Saying, he distinguishes proximity and Proximity. On the one hand, proximity, a sphere of nature category, has to do with physical closeness. On the other hand, Proximity, a sphere of *agape* category, names the relation to Faces in and by which one has been seized. You get a phone call from halfway across the world and suddenly, whether it is joy, grief, excitement, or fear, in your surrender to having been seized in and by love for that person's Face, you are right there with that person. Even if you are half a world apart, spiritually, nothing separates you. You are Proximate, though not proximate. In the same way, when you read *Night*, the Faces of the Jews caught in the Nazi horror are made Proximate. On the other hand, you can be, spiritually, a world apart from someone sitting right next to you, proximate but not Proximate.

When people are asked to share the most meaningful experiences of their lives, they tend to talk about intense experiences of having been seized in and by love for a Face. Intense moments of utter Proximity, when Saying screams through the said, can be fleeting in the rush of daily life. Nonetheless, whether joyous or horrific, they typically anchor testimony to the most significant and meaningful moments of people's lives.

Often Proximity is a reciprocal experience. You have surrendered to having been seized in and by love for a Face that has surrendered to having been seized in and by love for your Face. You are Face to Face. The spiritual Proximity of Face to Face relationships, where each I has surrendered to having been seized in and by love for the Face(s) of others who are simultaneously seized in and by love for I's own Face, describes the spiritual communion of what Christians call the *koinonia*. The *koinonia* is not an intentional community, not a community formed by affirmation of a common set of beliefs, by common nationality, by common blood, or the like, but a community sustained in and by shared surrender to *agape*, a community in Proximity, where all live awakened to the transcending spiritual union of the Face to Face.[15]

This is how we can understand Jesus when he says he will be present whenever two or three are gathered in his name. Jesus is not saying he will be physically present whenever two or three folks are in proximity. Jesus is saying the essence of his being, *agape* incarnate, is spiritually present whenever two or three are gathered in Proximity, Face to Face, all having surrendered to having been seized in and by love for all of the others' Faces, all taken up in the transcending communion of *agape*.

In modern Western society, even revelatory moments of spiritual Proximity can be subverted by naturalistic rationality: "What else could such experiences be, but phenomena and epiphenomena?" or "All such must be wholly the product of nature and nurture." After naturalistic rationality is displaced, such moments are quite reasonably affirmed as revelatory, as an unveiling of the truth of the sphere of *agape*, a sphere beyond the bounds of the vocabularies of the spheres of nature and of poetic I's. Such moments can pierce delusions of self-sufficiency, waken us from dogmatic slumbers induced by naturalistic rationality, rescue us from lost wanderings amidst appearances ("things of this world"), lead us beyond sphere of nature meanings and poetic self-creation, and anchor us to the reality and meaningfulness of *agape*, faith, Saying, Proximity, and *koinonia*.

Moral Realism: The Good, and Evil; the Moral, and Ethics

Moral realism and the meaning of the good can also be defined in relation to the sphere of *agape*: *agape* itself is the essence of the good, and good actions are actions that accord with *agape*. That is, good actions are actions in accord with surrender to having been seized in and by love for all Faces. "Evil," by contrast, names any violation of *agape*. Since evil exists only via violation of the good, evil is wholly derivative. Speaking precisely, there is not "good" and "evil" but "good" and "violation of good." There is a sphere of *agape*, but there is no sphere of evil. When we see the murder of the boy, the evil we see is the violation of the boy's Face, violation of the good we would have for the boy. Evil only exists in the violation of some Face. In and of themselves, natural realities and poetic I's are neither good nor evil. Insofar as natural forces or poetic I's violate Faces, however, they do evil.

15. Perhaps *kenosis* (i.e., the "self-emptying" Paul attributes to the essence of the Christ in Philippians 2:5–11) can best be understood as "surrender to agape."

It is helpful to make a distinction between "moral" and "ethics" that corresponds to the distinction between "Saying" and "said." "Moral" names the transcending reality of having been seized in and by love for a Face. "Ethics" addresses the need for faithful I's concretely to respond to Faces in a complicated and conflicted world. For example, Wiesel's surrender to having been seized in and by love for the Face of the boy is an unveiling of the moral. Wiesel's determining how best to respond to having been seized, giving due consideration to physical and sociopolitical realities and to all the other Faces involved, including his own, is ethics. Wiesel's eventual telling of the story is in part an ethical response to the awful violation of the boy's Face.

In other words, *ethical reflection* names the sometimes difficult and often uncertain reasoning needed when we must adjudicate among various faces of Faces (e.g., when is it ethical for me to kill that sapling or cat?), or when we must adjudicate among various human Faces (e.g., is it acceptable for us to kill that human in "the war on terror"?), or when it is not clear what does or does not violate a Face (e.g., vis-à-vis genetic engineering).

"Moral," then, names the reality of the having been seized in and by love that fires commitment to goodness and justice and fires the struggle against evil and injustice. "Ethics" names the reflection needed to determine how best to remain faithful to the moral in a complicated and conflicted world. Ethics without the moral would be empty, baseless, a wholly natural and/or poetic construction. The moral without ethics would lack historical concreteness, conceptual form, inter-subjective refinement and confirmation, and the capacity to address carefully the complexities of ethical quandary cases.[16]

To be sure, I's are sometimes forced to make intractably ambiguous and momentous decisions, wherein all options involve violation of one Face or another. Lack of perfect options or clarity vis-à-vis a range of ethical questions, however, neither undercuts moral realism nor entails ethical relativity. In our complicated, conflict-ridden world we will always face ethical ambiguity. Nonetheless, there are vast numbers of evils over which there should be no real doubt (the list is long and painful), and there are also vast numbers of goods over which there should be no real doubt. The hanging of that boy; the extermination camps; the greed, exploitation, oppression, and physical abuses that pervade history and surround us still: all of these are unquestionably evil. Feeding the hungry, clothing the naked, healing the sick, comforting the afflicted: all of these are unquestionably good.

In both science and ethics there are propositions about which we are very confident, propositions about which we are far less confident, and questions

16. In this sense, what Levinas calls "the ethics of ethics" I would call "the moral essence of ethics."

about which we are mystified. With regard to both science and ethics, there is nothing surprising about the existence of this spectrum from more to less sure understanding. We should track areas of relative surety or uncertainty in both science and ethics and make truth claims with appropriate confidence. In the light of the unveiling of the reality of the sphere of *agape*, however, uncertainty over some ethical questions provides no more reason for rejecting moral realism and asserting wholesale ethical relativity than uncertainty over some scientific questions provides reason for rejecting natural realism and asserting wholesale scientific relativity.

The spiritual realities signified by *agape*, good, and evil would no more be *as such* without I's than the physical realities signified by physics and chemistry would be *as such* without I's. In both cases, the I is essential. If there is no I, there is no *agape*, moral reality, or ethics *as such*; just as if there is no I, there is no time, space, or physics *as such*. At the same time, the realities described by natural and moral vocabularies are not wholly the product of I's. "Greed is evil" is just as real a truth vis-à-vis ultimate reality insofar as we can most accurately represent it using the vocabularies of the sphere of *agape*, as "e=mc²" is a real truth vis-à-vis ultimate reality insofar as we can most accurately represent it using the vocabularies of the sphere of nature. Sentences representing moral reality, then, are about a reality that is just as independently real, just as much related to an aspect of the ultimate, wholly autonomous character of reality, as sentences representing physical reality are related to an independently real aspect of the ultimate, wholly autonomous reality. "Greed is evil" is just as real a truth vis-à-vis ultimate reality as "e=mc²." *Agape* is as real as gravity.

Response-ability and Responsibility

In light of this analysis, it becomes clear that the common ethical vocabulary of "responsibility" is astoundingly precise, for ethics is not grounded in I's decisions, intentions, or initiative. Rather, ethics names decisions, intentions, and actions taken *in response* to having been seized in and by love for Faces. In I's having been seized the truth of the sphere of *agape* is unveiled and I's moral response-ability, which is to say, the inherently *moral* dimension of I's being, I's ability to be seized in and by love, is manifest.

My response-ability, my identity as in part a potentially moral, faithful I, names the self-creative, poetic character of I in its relation to the reality of *agape*. Response-ability names the capacity that allows I's to discern and freely surrender to the reality of *agape* and to recognize ethical choices. In other words, I's moral response-ability immediately raises the concrete question of I's ethical responsibility.

Because ethics springs from the reality of having been seized in and by love for others, those who have surrendered to having been seized are gripped by a passion to do good and to resist evil. For those who do not harden their hearts, response-ability immediately raises the question of responsibility, "*what* should I do?" Significantly, a question that never arises for those who have not hardened their hearts, a question that does arise for modern Western ethics, a question to which modern Western ethics has no adequate response is "why act morally?" This question never arises for our philosophical spirituality because the passion to act lovingly is an intrinsic aspect of having been seized in and by love for all Faces.

Finally, for Heidegger the uniqueness of each I—what Rorty calls "having an I at all"—is established only insofar as any I escapes the meanings of "the they" and creates its own authentic identity. Let me stress that awakening to the sphere of *agape* does not preclude affirmation of poetic self-creation and creativity—to the contrary, I celebrate poetic self-creation. Indeed, it is only poetic I's free choice that ensures the authenticity of I's surrender to having been seized. Given the reality of the sphere of *agape* and of I's having been seized in and by love, however, in addition to affirming the poetic potentials of authentic I's for creativity, one discerns the need to acknowledge the unique, moral *election* of each I in its response-ability and responsibility.

In addition to freely self-created poetic individuality, then, the uniqueness of each I is also established in the fact that when I am seized in and by love for the Face of another only I am seized at that precise point in time, space, and history, and only I have my particular understanding, talents, skills, and resources. Thus I am individualized insofar as I am uniquely elected by love. Others, all likewise uniquely elected, may be at my side. Insofar as I have been elected by the concrete call of specific Faces to unique responsibilities in the precise historical situations that make up the course of my life, however, I am utterly unique, irreplaceable, elected by love, and called to respond, "Here I am, *Say* in and through me."[17]

Agape, Evil, faces, and Faces

Finally, let me note one very significant corollary to my having been seized in and by love for Faces. Remember that the face (e.g., the eye color, nationality, species, all physical and sociocultural attributes) is irrelevant when I have been seized by a Face. Remember too that Levinas was a French officer (i.e., not a pacifist) and a Jewish captive. When he distinguishes the Face from the

17. While Levinas does not discuss individuation in terms of poetic self-creation, I am here glossing his understanding of individuation in terms of election.

face and calls upon us to surrender to having been seized in and by love for every Face, no matter their eye color, nationality, or uniform, Levinas knows he is speaking of having been seized in and by love for the Faces of his Nazi captors, of the murderers of his family, of those he believed he had no better option but literally to fight against. Levinas is saying that even as we may find ourselves forced in the name of what is good and just to fight for the sake of persecuted Faces we will, insofar as we remain awake, still be seized by the Faces of the faces we fight.[18]

While Jesus' teachings *may*, by contrast, entail pacifism, this gives we who are not pacifists a wholly reasonable way of understanding what Jesus is talking about when he speaks of loving those who are *and remain* enemies of what is good and just, even as our fidelity to the call of other Faces may force us literally to fight those who are enemies of the good. "Love your enemy" means surrender to having been seized in and by love for the Faces of even those faces who are enemies of the good, even if fidelity to other Faces forces us to fight them.

Spiritual Realism: Agape, Moral Realism, Faith

There is a screaming need to condemn violation of Faces. That is, there is a screaming need for *moral* condemnation of the violation of Faces. This is a condemnation essentially related to having been seized in and by love; a condemnation related to a reality not encompassed or broached by either the spheres of nature or of poetic I's. Moreover, this is a condemnation not excluded by any compelling, reductionistic, metaphysical argument (not even close). Since there is a screaming need for moral condemnation, and since there is absolutely no compelling argument against the reality of the sphere of agape, we are wholly warranted in concluding: 1) an awakened rationality's affirmation of three spheres of ultimate reality is more reasonable than *naturalistic rationality's* affirmation of only the sphere of nature and 2) an awakened rationality's affirmation of three spheres of ultimate reality is more reasonable than *secular rationality's* affirmation of only the spheres of nature and poetic I's.

In sum, we now have more warrant for and better understanding of the contention that it is *most reasonable* to conclude that three discrete families of vocabularies describing three discrete spheres of reality are required if we are

18. This may offer one way of explaining the "moral injury" soldiers and police officers experience after killing or wounding others even when their actions were unquestionably ethical and in proper fulfillment of their duties (e.g., in the sense we have described, it is possible for an action to be simultaneously ethical and not moral, the most relatively good choice when one has no wholly good option).

to provide the most reasonable, accurate, and adequate understanding of I's and of the character of ultimate reality. First, there are the *scientific vocabularies of the sphere of nature*, namely, the vocabularies of the natural and social sciences, of nature and nurture, and of I's as natural, bodily, historical realities. Second, there are the *existential vocabularies of the sphere of poetic I's*, namely, the vocabularies pertaining to temporal, numbering, logical,[19] seeing, touching, aesthetic, response-able, freely self-creating, and poetic I's. Third, there are the *spiritual vocabularies of the sphere of agape*, including the spiritual vocabulary of I's in relation to the sphere of *agape* that I have unfolded in this chapter in terms of Faces, faith, love/altruism/*agape*, said, Saying, revelation/unveiling/truth, icon, Proximity, *koinonia*, good, the moral, the ethical, election, response-ability, responsibility, and love of enemies of the good.

Is It Righteous to Be?

I believe we have made significant progress, for I think that, inspired above all by the wisdom of Emmanuel Levinas, we have unveiled the reasonableness of affirming the spiritual sphere of *agape*, and we have begun to unfold substantial vocabularies that unfold and manifest the significance and character of the sphere of *agape*. At this juncture, most especially in the wake of rehabilitation of moral realism, moral response-ability, and ethical responsibility, the challenge of the gaping pits can arise with a vengeance. For in a world suffused with pain, suffering, and injustice, awakening to moral realism and to the Faces of all creatures is awakening to vast magnitudes of evil, injustice, and suffering. Would not every I, perceiving the overwhelming suffering and injustice permeating reality, would not every I be overwhelmed with bitterness and despair, would not every I be broken? From the beginning, just by virtue of being born part and parcel of this vale of tears, every I is complicit with the evils of the world.[20] What moral person would not resonate with the apparent ethical sensitivity of Dostoevsky's Ivan Karamazov, who needs not multitudes, but for the tears of one child would give back his ticket to this world?[21] This is the sense in which Levinas says that, as an awakened,

---

19. As noted, reflection upon "logic" may warrant the positing of a fourth sphere.

20. This, says Levinas, is a "guiltless responsibility, whereby I am none the less open to an accusation of which no alibi, spatial or temporal, could clear me" (Emmanuel Levinas, "Ethics as First Philosophy," in *The Levinas Reader*, Sean Hand, ed. [Cambridge, MA: Basil Blackwell, 1989], 83).

21. Fyodor Dostoevsky, *The Brothers Karamazov*, translated and annotated by R. Pevear and L. Volokhonsky (New York: Vintage Classics, 1991), 244-45 (close of book V, section 4, "Rebellion").

response-able I in this world of suffering and injustice, "One comes not into the world but into question."[22]

The ethical question, then, is "the question of my right to be."[23] The ethical reply, in light of the fact that my own existence is inextricably tied up with all who exist and all who have ever existed, and in light of the fact that my personal existence is purchased at the price of the disproportionately massive suffering suffusing reality, the ethical reply is, "No, I have no right to be." My existence is unjust, and given the realities of existence, there is no way for me to render my existence justifiable. The issue is not accepting death but affirming life. Not "ask not for whom the bell tolls" but, as Levinas insists relentlessly, "*I* hurt them, *I* torture them, *I* kill them" (so, conservative Christians stress, *you* drove those nails into his wrists and feet). Indictment of existence and of our own selves screams out from and at us, a desperate, pained cry in an enveloping abyss. *How now joy, affirmation, yes?* Not amorality or moral relativism but supremely convicted moral sensitivity to all the suffering and injustice immediately delivers damnation. That is where every I awakened to all the suffering and injustice suffusing this vale of tears, beyond any possible protestation of personal innocence, lives.

While Levinas insists that each and every I is guilty, that the pits never close over, that the vertigo ever returns, he does not counsel despair and self-condemnation but joy and happiness. How is that possible?

Levinas's position parallels Christian understanding. The recognition that the world is not good but overwhelmingly suffused with evil: Christians call this the fallenness of the world. (The fall, in this philosophical sense, does not name an historical event but the way so many sphere of nature realities are manifest as evil in light of awakening to the sphere of *agape*.) Christians use the term "original sin" to refer to the fact that, since my existence is dependent upon the existence of this fallen world, I am complicit before I form any intention or take any action. (In contrast there is willful violation of Faces, that is, "personal" or "intentional" sin.) Traditional Christian confessions strive to be ethically honest in the face of the brutal realities of a fallen world and original sin, calling upon everyone to confess their complicity and to acknowledge that no one can claim a right to be, that no one can justify themselves.

As with Levinas, all this does not lead Christians to despair and self-condemnation but to joy and happiness. How, for both Levinas and Christianity, is that possible? Since the reply to the question, "is it righteous to be?" is, for each I, "no," why and how do wholly awakened I's, without hardening their

22. Levinas, "Ethics as First Philosophy," 81.
23. Ibid., 86.

hearts, find joy and happiness? Whence this salvation? We need to deepen our understanding of the reality of having been seized in and by love, for the answer to this question lies in what Christians call "grace." It will become clear that "grace" is an intrinsic dimension of the love in and by which we have been seized (it was already visible in Levinas's understanding of the way in which we are seized in and by love for the Faces of enemies).

In the next chapter, "The Truth of the Gift: Grace," I strive to unfold the way in which grace is incarnated in our daily living in the light of a remarkable essay on "the gift" (read "the gift" as "grace") by the Catholic theologian Jean-Luc Marion.[24] After sketching out the character of the gift, I try to add real-to-life substance to the analysis by reading Jesus' parable of the Prodigal Son in the light of this understanding of grace. In the following chapter, "Grace, Justice, and Forgiveness," I unfold the precise dynamics of forgiveness in relation to having been seized in and by love for all Faces. I then attempt to add real-life substance to the analysis and to illustrate that the essence of reasonable faith is wholly commensurate with the essence of Christian faith by reading Jesus' parable of the Unforgiving Steward in the light of this description of the nature of forgiveness.

---

24. Jean-Luc Marion, "A Phenomenological Sketch of the Concept of Gift," in *Postmodern Philosophy and Christian Thought*, Merold Westphal, ed. (Bloomington: Indiana University Press, 1999), 122–43. I will be combining Marion's ideas with Levinasian understanding and developing them in my own words. Marion may not concur with my conclusions, but the inspiration for my reflections on the gift comes primarily from Marion.

7

The Truth of the Gift: Grace

Gift and Economy

Let me begin unfolding the truth of the gift with an interaction among I's where there is no gift. Bob buys groceries. The cashier takes Bob's money and gives Bob his food. Bob buys food because he needs to eat, and the owners of the grocery store sell food in order to generate the income they need to live (or some such). In the exchange of money for food there is no gift, only *economy*, a tit-for-tat exchange of goods. Such economies of exchange, most far more complex, are perfectly familiar and unproblematic features of our world. Just as clearly, precisely because economies involve a tit-for-tat exchange, economies do not support the giving of any gift.

This illustrates a general principle: insofar as there is an economy of exchange, there is no gift. Say, for instance, that out of the blue Bob gives his friend Sallie an expensive and beautiful glass vase. The next day Sallie reviews a stack of applications for a good job at her company and she discovers Bob's son, Steve, is among the applicants. Sallie understandably wonders if the vase was a gift or a clandestine attempt to initiate an economy and establish expectations of a tit-for-tat exchange. Even if Bob was unaware his son had applied, until Sallie learns Bob did not know, she will quite reasonably wonder if Bob has really given her a gift, for insofar as there is an economy of exchange, there is no gift.

For clarity, I will speak of "presents" instead of "gift" and "presented" instead of "given" to refer to that which is commonly called a "gift given" without truly being "gift" or "given" because it is in fact part of a tit-for-tat economy. To be sure, in some instances a present presented and taken is perfectly appropriate and creates no ambiguity. For instance, I may present a present to strangers at a university hosting me for a visit. It is common knowledge that such institutional niceties are, wholly appropriately, parts of an economy of exchange. Or say I am going to a Christmas party at the house of friends. My "hostess gift" may be in part a true gift and in part an expected part of an economy of exchange. In such cases everyone is aware of the ambiguities, so there is no impropriety. In any case, people usually have a clear sense of the degree to which the gift has not been given, and they realize that the gift has not been given insofar as there is economy.

Consider now a scenario where the gift may have been given. Bob gives a bike to his young daughter, Becky, for her birthday. Becky loves the bike and says an excited "thanks" to her Dad. Has the gift been given? Or, despite the fact that one is dealing here with a birthday gift, is this only another economy? Let me consider this question in relation to Bob (the giver/presenter), the bike (the present), and Becky (the recipient/taker). Did Bob give the gift or present a present? Is the bike the gift or a present? Did Becky receive the gift or take a present?

The Presenter in Contrast to the Giver

First, let's say Bob was annoyed at having to spend time and money getting the bike but got it anyway because it was expected of him as a father. In this case, economy wholly displaces gift, for the only reason Bob presents the present is in order to avoid judgment. Perhaps he also presents it in order to get appreciation from Becky and/or social recognition. Perhaps Bob gets neither his daughter's appreciation nor social recognition, for his daughter is ungrateful—perhaps she is an ingrate or perhaps she senses her father's real motives—and no one else cares. Bob may still get his due, for Bob can still get *from himself* the satisfaction of knowing that, despite his daughter's ingratitude and society's indifference, he has done his duty as a father. In all these instances we are dealing with wholly economic dynamics.

Significantly, there is economy and no gift even if Bob's motivations are idealistic. Let us say, for instance, that Bob, in full poetic authenticity, wants to self-create himself as a good father, as a generous donor, or the like. Even in such idealistic cases of authentic self-creation there is no gift, for since one's ultimate motivations relate to one's own poetic project, the return comes in the creation of one's desired identity.

All these returns—the daughter's thanks, the daughter's appreciation, societal recognition, self-affirmation, desired self-creation—are reasons that explain why Bob got his daughter the present. They all create one tit-for-tat economy or another. None involve true gift, for all are part of economic dynamics and so name goals Bob pursues ultimately *for himself*. In short, in answer to the question of why Bob gave a present, all sphere of nature explanations (e.g., all psychological, sociological, and anthropological explanations) and all poetic explanations (i.e., explanations in terms of an I's project of authentic self-creation) depend upon the dynamics of economies of exchange.

In sum, neither sphere of nature explanations nor explanations in terms of I's self-creating allow for gift. For sphere of nature explanations always involve causal relations and conserve value in an economy of exchange, and poetic self-creation flows wholly from an I freely self-creating in accord with I's own poetic ambitions. There is, then, no place in sphere of nature explanation or in poetic self-creating for the truth of the gift. Since naturalistic and secular streams of modern Western rationality acknowledge only sphere of nature and/or poetic realities and explanations, they have no way of conceiving or affirming the reality of the gift. As discussed above, this is why predominant streams of modern Western philosophy and science deny the reality of *agape*.

Whence the Gift?

If the gift does not have its source in either natural causes or the self-creating of poetic I's, from what or in whom does the gift originate? Levinas was awakened to the I-transcending spiritual reality of *agape* by the horrors of the Holocaust. I attempted to invoke the same awakening using Elie Wiesel's haunting narrative of the boy murdered on the gallows. I approached that story in conversation with Heidegger's undercutting of naturalistic rationality and, following Levinas, I argued that our response to the horror undercut the hegemony not only of the naturalistic I but also of the secular I. For we do not begin neutrally and decide to be horrified by the hanging of that boy; we from the first find ourselves taken hostage by the Face of that boy. From the first we find ourselves seized by "No!" to violation of his Face. In our having been seized in and by love for the Face of the boy, the truth of the reality of the sphere of *agape* is forcefully unveiled.

Discussion of the gift, by contrast, typically places us in pleasant present/giving contexts. The reality of the gift, however, undercuts the hegemony of the natural and the secular I's just as surely as the violation of a Face. Indeed, while our reactions vary dramatically according to context, *in both instances of horrific violation and instances of joyful giving of presents one is seized in and by the very same spiritual reality: agape*. In the concrete historical context of violation of a Face, the faithful I seized in and by love sees evil, is horrified, and is immediately moved to resist. In the concrete historical context of the flourishing of a Face, the faithful I seized in and by love sees good, is joyful, and is immediately moved to affirm and enhance the good. In both cases I am awakened to the reality of *agape* and I share love that I first receive. The *agape* in and by which I have been seized *is itself the source of the gift*. In this sense, as Marion says, the gift gives itself.[1] In the light of this realization I can describe how the gift is shared by discrete I's using sphere of nature realities.

The Giver

Apart from all economies, what is it for Bob truly to give Becky the gift? We should think of how we have been seized when we have truly given a present. Perhaps we have seen the stranger in need, or our friend, or our child, and we have found ourselves seized in and by love for them. In awful circumstances, we have been seized by an urgent concern and acted to help. In happy circumstances, the desire to express our love wells up around us, and before we know it, we're reaching out to give a hug, or sending a text, or buying the perfect present. Just so, insofar as Bob truly gave the gift, he was seized in and by love for Becky. He did not harden his heart, and he gave Becky a present signifying the truth of the gift. To give a bike, not a baseball glove, a green bike, not a blue one: those were Bob's decisions. What was not a product of Bob's decision was his love for Becky.

Bob did not begin in a neutral stance vis-à-vis Becky and decide to love; Bob found himself seized in and by love for Becky and called to respond. The originating love in and by which Bob found himself seized was neither the product of Bob's poetic self-creating nor the negation of his poetic capacities. For, since the love in and by which Bob was seized for Becky is Bob's unique election by love for Becky, and since Bob *could* harden his heart, Bob's love for Becky is the authentic realization of the spiritual reality of *agape* within the natural and poetic worlds. Thereby Bob truly gave/shared the gift.

The real gift, the love for Becky given to Bob, the love signified by the bike, flows from the having been seized. Bob loves Becky in and through the love in and by which he has been seized and to which he has not hardened his heart. Bob receives his love for Becky. Every true giver gives a gift they have first received and not resisted. Thereby, the extranatural, extrapoetic reality of *agape* is authentically incarnated in a concrete historical relationship between a giver and a recipient via some natural sign (i.e., some present). Thus we rightly recognize the reality of *agape* whenever we find ourselves

---

1. Marion's exact quote is, "The gift *itself* gives in giving the giver" (Jean-Luc Marion, "A Phenomenological Sketch of the Concept of Gift," in *Postmodern Philosophy and Christian Thought*, Merold Westphal, ed. [Bloomington: Indiana University Press, 1999], 134).

seized in and by love for the Faces of others, even if we are only called to give a smile. That is the source and the truth of the gift.

The Present and the Gift

Let us now consider the gift and the present. The bike or the vase or even a nonmaterial present (e.g., I volunteer at the soup kitchen) is always part of an economy of exchange. This is clear in relation to the common sense that a present must be appropriate. If Bob spends his annual income and gives his neighbor Sallie not a vase but a brand new sports car, then not only will he be unsuccessful in giving her a gift, but he will be unsuccessful in instantiating an economy. The gift of a sports car to Sallie would be too big, laughable, and likely unwelcome. Or say out of the blue Bob gives Sallie a dinner fork. Now the gift is too small, a bit bizarre, and insufficient to initiate an economy.

The reason there is a sense that a present must be "just right" is because the present is expected to be an appropriate part of an economy of exchange. Too big, and the present demands too much in return and becomes a burden. Too small, and the present fails to live up to minimal requirements and the recipient feels jilted, perhaps offended. Every present has some value in the world and is received—too big, too small, bizarre, just right—in accord with that value and thereby participates in some economy of exchange.

At the same time, even if one thinks in terms of the sphere of *agape*, the concrete signification of the gift must always be some sphere of nature reality (i.e., phenomenal or epiphenomenal), or else no signification of the gift will ever appear at all. Since I's are physically and existentially discrete (e.g., we are not telepathic), there is no gift-relation between I's without some signifying present (e.g., the bike, the food or clothing, a hug, a smile). That is, *the gift must be present in a present if the gift is to become visible to a recipient.* On the one hand, if there is no signification (i.e., no present), there can be no gift that appears to any other I. If there is no present, then no sharing of any gift can be realized between two I's. On the other hand, every present is part of an economy, and if the present is considered to be in and of itself the gift, then those who see the present neither see, give, nor receive the gift.

For instance, Bob *gives* the gift but Becky only *takes* the bike. In such cases, insofar as he is not hardened from the scars of like previous disappointment, Bob will feel the tragic absence of the gift, the heart-rending absence of a loving, Face to Face relationship with his daughter. Or Becky desperately wants the gift from her father, but Bob only *presents* a bike. In such cases, insofar as she is not hardened from the scars of like previous disappointment, Becky will feel the tragic absence of the gift, the heart-rending absence of loving, Face to Face relationship with her father.

Once the relationship between the gift and the giver is unfolded, the relationship between the gift and the present (e.g., the bike) becomes clear. The bike is not in and of itself the gift. The bike is the manifestation of the gift within the spheres of nature and of self-creating I's. The bike is carefully chosen, bought, and given because of the gift. Some present is necessary if there is to be any expression of the gift. At the same time, the present itself is never the gift. The gift is the love for Becky given to, received by, and signified by Bob. The present, when truly given, is a concrete, visible sign of the gift.

In sum, while the gift cannot appear in the world if there is no present, the present is never the gift. The gift, an extranatural, extrapoetic reality, remains invisible in the sphere of nature in its presence in the present, hidden precisely where it is revealed to poetic I's who are response-able and awakened to the sphere of *agape*.

The Taker in Contrast to the Recipient

It is as recipients of presents that the reality of the economy of exchange is often most powerfully experienced. Even if it is just the need to say "thank you" in order to reestablish equilibrium, you feel the force of the economy. As studies of reciprocal altruism make clear, even some nonhuman mammals feel the force of tit-for-tat economy. When you take a present you typically feel you owe a proportionate return. This is a manifestation of the invisible but potent expectation of reciprocity built into economies of exchange. With the recipient just as with the giver, if one thinks solely in terms of the sphere of nature and/or in accord with authentically self-creating/poetic I's, all taking of presents will be understood wholly in accord with economies of exchange.

If Becky is not merely to take the present, but to receive the gift, she must receive the love signified by the present. This love is not, first or last, Bob's love, but the love in and by which Bob has been seized for Becky. Becky truly receives the gift insofar as she does not harden her heart to having been seized in and by the same love. When those who are awakened remember times they have truly been given and received gifts, what they primarily remember is not the present they received, no matter how delightful or valuable. What they primarily remember is what filled them with joy, the gift manifest through the present. They certainly may have been happy about the present, but they were joyful over the love received with the giver, over the shared entry into the transcending joy of the Face to Face.

Becky could harden her heart and *take* the present (instead of receiving the gift). Insofar as Becky does not harden her heart to having been seized in and by love, however, she authentically receives the gift when she receives Bob's present. Insofar as Bob and Becky both authentically receive and give the gift, that is, insofar as both have been seized in and by love for the other, Bob and Becky are Proximate, united in the transcending glory of the Face to Face.

Bob's surrender to having been seized and giving would be realized whether or not Becky truly received the gift. Bob's giving would be true even if Becky only took the present. When Becky truly receives the gift, however, Bob's love is made complete, for, again, in mutual love one for the other, the relationship is made whole. This is not the closure of some tit-for-tat economy of exchange, for neither Bob nor Becky is the source of or "have" the love. Each was given the love they share for the other. Neither hardened their heart, and so the hidden truth of the gift was realized between their discrete Faces through sphere of nature significations (the bike, Becky's gleeful "thank you"). This love is Paul the apostle's love "made complete" through shared surrender to the very same love one for the other. This is the love made complete that sustains the unity of the *koinonia*, where discrete Faces, united in and by the extranatural, extrapoetic reality of *agape*, enjoy the transcending communion of the Face to Face.

This, then, is the truth of the gift: not that we initiate, decide, or create love, but that if we do not harden our hearts we find ourselves seized in and by love. In short, the gift given, the gift signified by the bike, and the gift received are all the same transcending gift, the gift of having been seized in and by love that is *not from oneself* and that is *for all Faces*, the gift of *agape*.

In sum, economies of exchange may accompany but are never themselves a part of the gift. Insofar as one only affirms naturalistic or secular rationality, the essential dynamics of any purported "gift, giving, receiving" will always boil down to some economy of exchange or another. Insofar as one thinks within the conceptual boundaries of the sphere of nature and/or poetic self-creation, then, there is no possibility of understanding the truth of the gift or the reality of true giving and receiving. For this reason, those who affirm naturalistic or secular forms of rationality cannot affirm the reality of the gift. To be sure, however, they may well have experienced the truth of the gift, they may recognize our affirmation of the reality of *agape* to be both reasonable and necessary to the most adequate description of ultimate reality, may come to affirm the sphere of *agape* and the reality of the gift, may overtly surrender to having been seized in and by love. In short, they may hear this testimony, surrender to its truth, and know salvation.

We who affirm an encompassing sphere of *agape* and the truth of the gift should not deny economies of exchange. Even when a true gift is truly given, one or several economies (e.g., reciprocal "altruism," poetic self-satisfaction) may also be in play. For instance, even fathers who are genuinely seized in and by love for their children may also be motivated by a desire to self-create themselves as good fathers. Surely kinship "altruism" is in play in Bob's special regard for his daughter. <u>There is nothing wrong with such idealistic, poetic aspirations or conditioned responses. While economy of exchange dynamics may accompany the gift, however, they are not part of the reality of the gift.</u>

I expect all these dynamics, once named, to be familiar. Most people readily distinguish between a present truly received—the sense of solidarity, communion, thankfulness, transcending joy—and a present (the bike itself, the ring itself, the money itself) not received but only taken. Most people also readily distinguish between presents truly given and attempts to buy their love or to put them in debt.

Equally clear corollaries could be unfolded. For instance, highly desirable presents can threaten the truth of the gift for both giver and recipient. When the gift is signified by a warm smile or by something thoughtful and meaningful but materially worthless, there is little danger an economy will obscure the truth of the gift. On the other hand, if the gift is signified by something expensive, such as a new car or a large diamond ring, then the danger that the gift will be betrayed by an economy becomes palpable. <u>In general, the more valuable the present the greater the threat that an economy will betray the gift, for valuable presents have great potential to focus attention upon the present itself and away from the gift.</u> The point is not to forgo the giving of expensive presents, but to recognize and mitigate the threat that an economy will obscure the truth of the gift for both givers and recipients.

More corollaries could be unfolded, but I have said enough to distinguish economies of exchange from the truth of the gift and to explain how the spiritual reality of *agape* may be made manifest among poetic I's in and through the sphere of nature. Economies are in and of themselves an important part of daily life. At the same time, insofar as you are engaged in an economy, you are not participating in the transcending glory of the gift.

The personal danger lies in the possibility of a life wholly taken up in economies. That is, in a life filled only with people with whom one is in wholly economic relationships, in a life devoid of loving relationships. A lesser but still significant tragedy is the fate of modern Western thinkers who have indeed surrendered to having been seized in and by love for Faces but who, betrayed by naturalistic or secular understanding, cannot clearly name and affirm the transcending reality of the *agape* in and by which they have been seized.[2]

2. See, in this regard, one of the twentieth century's most influential and poignant analyses of gift giving, Marcel Mauss's *The Gift: the Form and Reason for Exchange in Archaic Societies* (W. D. Halls, trans. [New York: W. W. Norton & Company, Inc., 1990]—first published in French in 1950). The tensions I am describing are clear and poignant in Mauss (see especially the final chapter). For an uncompromising secular perspective, see Mary Douglas's agape-denying "Foreword" to Norton's 1990 edition

The societal danger lies in the sociopolitical development of cultures in which the reality of the sphere of *agape* is systematically denied (e.g., due to the predominance of naturalistic and/or secular rationality). Insofar as the reality of *agape* is denied, powerful sphere of nature drives to privilege personal survival, to gain as much power as possible over and against others, and to gain self-centered pleasures are all left unchecked by affirmation of moral reality, personal response-ability, ethical responsibilities, and the truth and transcending glory of having been seized in and by love for all Faces.

We who are awakened and realize the reasonableness of affirming the reality of the sphere of *agape* realize that ultimately all giving, all grace, flows from the sphere of *agape*. No sphere of nature/poetic I, then, is the source of the gift. Every giver incarnates and shares/gives love they have first received. In this sense, while within the sphere of nature and among poetic I's we distinguish givers from recipients, with regard to the truth of the gift and the sphere of *agape*, givers and recipients stand in the same relationship to the gift, to the reality of *agape*. Insofar as we do not harden our hearts we all, givers and recipients, incarnate *agape* and live Proximate one to all others, united in the transcending communion of the Face to Face, awakened to our spiritual unity in the *koinonia*, alive to the primordial encompassing reality of *agape* in which we live and move and have our spiritual being.

The Parable of the Prodigal Son

The truth of the gift, or grace, and the contrast between relationships grounded in economies (i.e. delimited to the spheres of nature and poetic I's) and relationships grounded in the gift (i.e., awakened to the sphere of *agape*) is a major theme of Jesus' parable of the Prodigal Son (Luke 15:11–32). In relation to discussion of the gift, the key figure in the parable is the father. From an economic perspective, the father's actions are unreasonable, even unjust. Those who are awakened, however, see a man who has wholly surrendered to having been seized in and by love. As will become clear, the father is a paradigm of the faithful, gift-giving I, while both sons are paradigmatically economic takers. I will now attempt to flesh out the significance of the gift in conversation with Jesus' poignant parable.

In the parable of the Prodigal Son, a father, a prosperous Jewish farmer, has two sons. In accord with contemporary law, when a father with two sons dies

---

of Mauss's work. Marion's work on the gift is inspired by Jacques Derrida's reflection upon Mauss in *Given Time: I. Counterfeit Money*, Peggy Kamuf, trans. (Chicago: University of Chicago Press, 1992).

the elder son receives two-thirds of his estate, the younger son one-third.[3] The transfer may be instituted before the father's death, a useful alternative if the father is in failing health. The transfer of property is absolute. Once a parent transfers their property, they are dependent upon their children. In this parable the father is in good health when his younger son asks him to divide his estate. When the father accedes to the request, the younger son gathers his inheritance and departs. The prodigal's actions say that his father is dead to him.

The prodigal squanders his wealth and soon finds himself destitute in a distant land. At this point the prodigal "came to himself." This is what came to him: he is starving while his father's hired hands have food to spare. The prodigal devises a plan of action. He decides to go to his father and say he has sinned against heaven and against his father. He will affirm he is no longer worthy to be called son, and he will ask his father to treat him like a hired hand. Then, like the other hired hands, he too will have food to spare.

The prodigal's actions make clear that he understands his relationship to his father in wholly economic terms. From the younger son's economic perspective, once his father handed over the inheritance, the father/son relationship was over. The prodigal, thinking in economic terms, knows he no longer has the right to be "son," so he decides to propose a new economic relationship: he will be "hired hand." The prodigal's hope is that he will be given the status of "hired hand" and enter into a hired hand/employer relationship. His goal is to save himself from starvation. What is loudly *not* named as being any part of the prodigal's coming to himself is any remorse, change of heart, intention to apologize and request forgiveness, or any hope or even any desire to enter into a loving father/son relationship. According to the text, the prodigal thinks wholly in terms of economy and self-interest.

Plan in place, the prodigal heads home. His father sees him from a distance and having been filled with compassion (*esplagchnisthe*, ἐσπλαγχνίσθη), the father runs to his son, a culturally inappropriate act signaling great feeling, and hugs and kisses him. The father looks foolish when viewed in terms of economies of exchange. This is how the father would have looked to the prodigal, who had only ever seen his father's face, never his Face. Considering the father's material success and his consistent and pithy interactions with his sons in the parable, however, it is reasonable to conclude the father is no fool. Like most people who discern when their gifts have been not received but taken, the father surely realizes his son has only ever seen his face, that is, has only ever seen an economic father/son relationship. The father had been

3. I here merely note the sociocultural sexism that may be at play in the absence of any mention of a wife or daughter in this parable. Significantly, the logic of agape the parable advocates would delegitimize any sexism.

and continues to be seized in and by love for the Face of his son. His wisdom is manifest when his words and acts are viewed in the light of his having been seized in and by love for the Faces of his sons.

The father realizes that his own face (in contrast to his own Face) is prominent because he is a successful landowner and so he himself represents a large inheritance for both sons. We are not told, but it is wholly reasonable to conclude, that the father realizes that this was one of those cases in which the value of the present was obstructing awakening to the gift. If that is the case, then the father's giving over of the inheritance is the father's attempt to get through to his younger son by removing the obstacle, rendering his own face worthless in the hope of better exposing his Face. The running, embrace, and kissing are all authentic responses of a father wholly seized in and by love for the Face of a son perhaps gone forever, perhaps captive, perhaps dead, but now physically safe and proximate. Given that the father takes all these actions before the prodigal says a word, these gifts are also maximally vulnerable, poignantly blatant, screamingly desperate attempts by the father to manifest his Face.

Is it enough? Will his younger son finally be awakened by the gift, finally have ears for the *Saying* and the Proximity of his father's Face, finally enter the transcending glory of the Face to Face?

We are not privy to the prodigal's thoughts. To this point he has thought in exclusively economic terms, so he is most likely happy but stunned. Is he awakened? He repeats his prepared statement verbatim, dropping only the "hired hand" part. Did he hold the "hired hand" card back in case his father was foolhardy enough to make a better offer? Does he view the robe and signet ring as unexpected plunder? Does he plan on playing his father for a fool? Or is the younger son finally awakened by his father's desperate acts of love? By the time he spoke his pre-planned statement, "I have sinned against heaven and against you," had that said been transformed into a *Saying*? Did he awaken to having been seized in and by the same love?

In sum, does the prodigal son *take a present* and remain cut off from loving relationship from his father and all others? Or does he *receive the gift*, for the first time enter into loving, Proximate relationship with his father, and enjoy the transcending communion of the Face to Face? We dearly hope for awakening, but the question remains forever open, for we hear no more about the prodigal son.

The parable's focus turns to the elder son. The elder brother honored the economic relationship with his father, remaining with the estate and evidently continuing to respect the authority of his father. The elder brother's reactions to his father and his younger brother's return, however, make clear that he, *just like the prodigal,* has never seen the Face of his father (or of his brother). The elder brother's understanding is wholly economic. Just as the prodigal, thinking in terms of economy, cannot now see himself as son, so the elder brother, thinking in terms of economy, cannot now see the prodigal as brother. Thus when he addresses his father he stresses his own fidelity to the rules of an economic relationship and pointedly refers to the prodigal as "this son *of yours*."

The elder brother, thinking in terms of economy, can only see how flagrantly his father has violated the economies of exchange, beyond all rights giving unjustified status to and even celebrating the prodigal and thereby making a mockery of the elder brother's relationship with his father which, *just like the prodigal*, the elder brother understands wholly in terms of economy. When the elder brother complains of working "like a servant" and uses terms like "obedience" and "orders," he betrays that he has always understood himself to be in a "hired hand" relationship to his father, the major difference from the other hired hands lying in his right to inheritance. The elder son honored the economy while the younger son dishonored it, but both brothers understood the father/son relation wholly in terms of economy. The elder brother, just like the prodigal, never discerned the Saying of his father's Face, never received the gift, never enjoyed loving, Proximate relationship with his father, never knew the transcending joy of the Face to Face.

The father responds to his elder son with pained but hopeful declarations of Proximity, a plea for eyes to see, and an explanation that is wise in the light of awakening. First, the declarations of Proximity: Do you not know that all that I have is yours? That I am always with you? Then an explanation that is wise in the light of awakening: In concrete contexts of joy, those who are awakened are joyful. Can you not understand that *"your brother,"* perhaps gone forever, perhaps captive, perhaps dead, has returned? We who are awakened are joyful, we do not decide to celebrate, we make no economic calculation, we are joyful, we cannot but rejoice.

Does the elder son finally hear the Saying of his Father? Does he finally gain eyes to see? Does he finally receive the gift and enter into the glory of the transcending communion of the *koinonia*, Face to Face with his father (and, ideally, with his brother)? Or, continuing to think in wholly economic terms, scandalized by his father's violation of tit-for-tat economy, will the elder brother perhaps be pushed over the edge and "go prodigal" himself? The question remains open, for in the wake of the father's final, desperate, love-drenched pleas, we hear no more about the elder brother. At the end of the parable we are left anxious but hopeful for the awakening of both brothers, for both have been lost to wholesale economy. Did wholesale economy prevail? Or was there awakening to the truth of the gift? Jesus deliberately constructs the parable so as to leave the question forever open, for his real question and concern is not only about or for the parable's brothers.

8

Justice, Grace, Forgiveness

Should we not take seriously the elder brother's complaint about the injustice of the father? Is there not a way in which the father's actions, however ideal when considered from the perspective of *agape*, are unjust? What of real-world evildoers? What of protecting the innocent and vulnerable? What of justice, which is, after all, quite rightly about economy (e.g., to each their due)? Christians may express this concern in worry not only over the fact that the father acts out his radical acceptance of the prodigal before the prodigal even speaks, let alone confesses, but over the fact that there is no sacrifice, no substitutionary atonement anywhere in the parable. Forgiveness is not the focus of the parable—indeed, it to some degree slips in unnoticed in the course of the parable's testimony to the truth of the gift. This will prove to be no accident. Let me address these questions in the course of unfolding the dynamics of forgiveness in relation to having been seized in and by love for all Faces.

Forgiveness

Without explicit note I named the reality of forgiveness above when I described the way in which Levinas was seized in and by love for the Faces of Nazi soldiers. Insofar as I have been seized in and by love for Faces apart from any consideration for faces, insofar as I do not harden my heart, I find myself seized even by the Faces of faces who are enemies of the good. Christians discuss this astounding reality, the reality of having been seized in and by love for all Faces, even the Faces of enemies of the good, in terms of grace and forgiveness. The terms "grace" or "gracious love" are used to emphasize the

133

extraethical character of *agape*. Grace specifies love that is not deserved, love beyond justice, beyond any tit-for-tat economy, love that includes even enemies. "Forgiveness" specifies the gracious character of the love always already (i.e., "fore") "given" to enemies of the good in the having been seized. Insofar as *agape* is, as we have seen, by definition beyond every economy, "grace" names an intrinsic dimension of *agape*.

In other words, that which is given in fore-given-ness is precisely the gift of having been seized in and by love for every Face. This gift of gracious love is given fore because the having been seized first has us, and since the love of the having been seized is gracious love, love even for enemies of the good, then insofar as we have surrendered to having been seized in and by this love we have already forgiven all Faces. Forgiveness, then, no more originates in me than love originates in me. *Agape* is already gracious love (in this sense, "gracious love" is a redundancy stressing an important point). In not hardening my heart to having been seized in and by love I authentically receive gracious love: love and forgiveness for all Faces.

Forgiveness Not Forgetting

It is critical not to confuse "forgiveness" with "forgetting." *Forgiveness* vis-à-vis *Faces* does not imply *forgetting* vis-à-vis *faces*. To forgive is to be seized in and by love for the Faces of others despite the complicity and culpability of their faces. To forgive is to awaken and not harden one's heart to the truth and reality of the sphere of *agape*. To forgive, then, is reasonable and realistic. To forget would be unrealistic, for it would ignore the reality of the spheres of nature and of poetic I's. Fidelity to Faces in the world requires realistic attention to the complicity and culpability of faces. Affirmation of the free will of poetic I's, who may harden their hearts, and of the sphere of nature, with its often brutal, amoral struggles for survival, should preclude pie-in-the-sky naivety. To ignore the realities of the spheres of nature and of poetic I's would be to forget justice and would hinder loving response to real suffering and evil and loving defense of those who are afflicted or persecuted.

While we love all Faces, then, we do not forget faces. And for the sake of the moral, for the sake of love, for the sake of other vulnerable, persecuted, or suffering Faces, we resist evil. Never, insofar as we have not hardened our hearts, do we take action out of hatred or vengefulness. We do, however, take action—coercive, even violent action—in order to protect other Faces, for forgiveness of Faces does not imply forgetfulness about faces.[1] Thus Levinas,

---

1. This is Levinas's "third," which refers to the third or the three millionth Face beyond any one Face, and so requires consideration of questions of justice among Faces.

the French army officer, was seized by the Faces of Nazi soldiers he nonetheless literally fought against.

Let me take care to say that the recognition that we ourselves are beloved means that if someone tries to violate your Face, you should be just as responsible to your own beloved Face as you would be to any other Face. That means that you are responsible to take decisive, perhaps even violent action in defense of your own face.[2] There is nothing good, loving, or faithful about allowing oneself to be taken advantage of or abused. The love that moves us to affirm and defend other Faces should equally move us to affirm and defend our own beloved Faces (accordingly, again, you may sacrifice your life for a friend of the good, but, all else equal, you should not compromise your well-being or lose your life in aid of an enemy of the good).[3]

Forgiven

In surrender to having been seized in and by gracious love I receive forgiveness for every Face, *including my own*. My surrender to having been seized in and by the other's Face is never done for myself. In my surrender to having been seized in and by love for others' Faces, however, I am nonetheless also surrendering, indirectly but decisively, to having been seized myself in and by

2. For Levinas we are in a morally asymmetrical relationship with the Face of the other, such that the Face of the other always takes absolute and unqualified priority over our own Face. Because every other Face seizes me absolutely and directly, Levinas in his theory can countenance no violence toward even unjust faces in defense of the face of one's own Face. That is, there is no place for any measure of coercive or violent self-defense in Levinas. Thus Levinas theorizes a love that is not only self-forgetful but also self-negating. One can see how problematic this understanding would be in, for instance, cases of domestic abuse. Because Levinas understands us to be taken hostage directly by the Faces of others, he locates the decisive asymmetry between oneself and the Faces of others. In contrast to Levinas, however, I explicitly understand us to be seized not directly by the Faces of others but *in and by love* for all Faces. As explained, it is in this moment of having been seized in and by love that our own response-ability, and hence our own Faces, which are never directly visible to us, become manifest. In having been seized in and by love, then, each of us is, indirectly but decisively, seized not only in and by love for other Faces, but seized also in and by love for our own Face. This means, for instance, that victims of abuse *should* take decisive and appropriate action in fidelity to the love they have received for their own Faces.

3. My neo-Levinasian affirmation of self-defense flows from a spiritual stance that differs from modern affirmations of self-defense and self-sacrifice based upon appeal to self-assertion or assertion of the intrinsic value of the atomistic I. For my call to defense and affirmation of self flows from the "yes" of having been seized in and by love for all Faces, and this includes, indirectly but decisively, having been seized in and by love for my own Face.

gracious love. In the most intense moments of having been seized in and by love, whether moments of joy or of horror, our attention is wholly absorbed by the Faces of others. While such moments are self-forgetful, however, they are not self-negating. To the contrary, such moments are typically remembered as the most significant and, in happy instances, the most cherished moments of our lives. In the dynamic of having been seized in and by love we are manifest to ourselves not only as poetic I's but as response-able, moral, loving, beloved, spiritual I's elected by gracious love.[4] We receive gracious love for ourselves when we do not harden our hearts to having been seized in and by love for the Faces of others.

In other words, having forgiven others and having been forgiven myself are both dimensions of the gift of having been seized in and by gracious love. What is revealed in our having been seized in and by love for all other Faces despite their complicity and culpability, no matter how awful, is the gracious character of the love by which we too have been seized. That is, what is revealed in gracious love for others—despite their complicity and culpability, no matter how awful—is gracious decisive love for my own Face despite my own complicity and culpability, no matter how awful. By contrast, those who harden their hearts cut themselves off from the Faces of others and cut themselves off from unselfish love for their own Faces. They cut themselves off from their own response-ability, from their own moral, spiritual being, and they cut themselves off from having been seized in and by love, from forgiveness and having been forgiven, and from the joy of transcending, Face to Face communion, from *koinonia*.

This is what Jesus means when he says that insofar as we do not forgive others from our hearts we will not be forgiven. Jesus is not referring to a tit-for-tat economy. Jesus is speaking of the consequence of hardening one's heart to having been seized in and by love. I am cut off from forgiveness insofar as I do not forgive, not because there is a tit-for-tat relationship between having forgiven others and having been myself forgiven, but because both follow from precisely the same surrender to having been seized in and by gracious love. In my surrender to the gift of having been seized in and by love, in my receiving of the gift, I find myself not only having forgiven others but also living my own having been forgiven-ness.

---

4. Levinas says the reality of having been seized in and by love for the Face of another "is also election and love reaching [the one] who is invested by it in [his or her] uniqueness qua responsible one" (Emmanuel Levinas, *Of God Who Comes to Mind*, Bettina Bergo, trans. [Stanford: Stanford University Press, 1986], ix).

The Parable of the Unforgiving Steward

The relationship among surrender, gift, and forgiveness are unfolded in Jesus' parable of the Unforgiving Steward (Matt. 18:21–35). Jesus tells the parable in response to a query from Peter. Peter asks Jesus how many times he should forgive, "As many as seven times?" Jesus answers: not seven, but seventy times seven. This is hyperbole, not a directive to forgive people four hundred and ninety times. Jesus is telling Peter that when it comes to forgiveness, he needs to stop thinking in terms of economy and start thinking in terms of the gift. In traditional theological language, Jesus is telling Peter that he needs to move from the realm of law (justice) to the realm of grace (*agape*). Jesus then tells the parable of the Unforgiving Steward.

A steward owes a king an astronomical amount of money (on the order of an ordinary elementary school teacher owing twenty million dollars). The king, as was customary, orders the man and his family to be sold along with all his possessions in order to collect as much payment as possible. The steward falls before the king and begs for mercy. The king is seized by compassion for the man, forgives the debt, and releases him. Shortly after being released, the steward comes upon a man who owes him money and who begs the steward for mercy. The steward, unmerciful, has the man thrown into prison. When the king learns of this he summons the steward, tells him he has learned that he did not show mercy as he received mercy, and hands him over to be "tortured" until he pays his entire debt.

In economic terms, the parable directly contradicts Jesus' admonition to forgive seventy times seven times. The king does not even forgive twice. The absurdity of the economic interpretation is meant to force us to think in terms of the gift and forgiveness. Significantly, "seized by compassion" is a translation of the Greek aorist passive verb *splagchnistheis* ("σπλαγχνισθεὶς," literally "seized by compassionate movement of one's inward parts"). This is essentially the same word used to describe the compassion by which the father was seized for the prodigal (*esplagchnisthē*, "ἐσπλαγχνίσθη"). In other words, the king had surrendered to having been seized in and by love for the Face of the man, and so the economy, the massive debt, was as nothing.

The king forgives the servant his impossible debt just as the father forgives the prodigal his impossible debt. The parable of the Unforgiving Steward, however, is the tale of a prodigal who did not receive the gift, who plays his father for a fool, whose heart is later revealed in mistreatment of his father's hired hands. It is clear that the steward did not receive the king's gift, because to receive the gift requires surrender to the same love, a move from economy to *agape*, from law to grace. When the steward does not forgive as he was forgiven, it becomes clear that he remained within the economy (by their fruit you will know them), that he had *taken* the king's present and *not received* the gift.

The king's anger, then, is not only *at* the steward over his throwing of his own debtor into prison, but also *for* the steward. That is, the king is seized in and by love for the steward's Face. The king, however, now realizes that the steward does not understand and never did receive the gift. The steward has eyes only for the economy. He took the present. He played the king as a sucker. In the steward's own eyes, he remains impossibly indebted to the king, for the steward still lives wholly in the realm of law and justice, not in the light of *agape*.

The king, moreover, cannot make the steward receive the gift. This is the meaning of the "handed over to be tortured." In our context the allusion to torture is rightly disturbing. In Jesus' day it would have been unsurprising. The point here has nothing to do with affirming torture by the authorities, for the torture this parable is talking about is self-imposed. Those who have surrendered to *agape* will neither see in the torture an economy satisfied nor smile at justice served upon a mean-spirited ingrate. They will lament a man caught in the torture of living with a hardened heart, living complicit in this vale of tears without forgiveness, isolated from loving relationships, isolated from the Face to Face, cut off from the transcending communion of *koinonia*.

We can hope that the steward may somehow yet, perhaps on the far side of destitution, realize the true nature of the king's gift, which *endures* (the decisive factor is the hardness of heart of the steward, not any change of heart on the king's part; there is no reason to conclude that the king stopped surrendering to having been seized in and by love for the steward's Face). We can hope that the steward may yet receive the gift and know the transcending communion of the Face to Face. As it is, Jesus uses the steward to caution those who harden their hearts to the Faces of others, who are not forgiven because they do not forgive, who wound not only others but also themselves. The parable of the Unforgiving Steward is the sad tale of those lost to wholesale economy.

Notably, to be myself forgiven does not depend upon the surrender of others, for forgiveness flows not from others but from having been seized in and by gracious love. Others do not forgive us, but insofar as they have surrendered to *agape*, they have authentically received forgiveness for us and, indirectly but decisively, for themselves. While to be myself forgiven does not depend upon the awakening of others, there are significant stakes in others' awakening, for with mutual awakening our joy in and with others can be made complete. The lost are found. We can celebrate and participate in the transcending joy of the *koinonia* (Proximity and Face to Face communion).[5]

5. At the same time, my position does not denigrate but celebrates the physical, the aesthetic, and the enjoyment of physical realities and pleasures.

In sum, forgiveness describes the reality of having been seized in and by love for Faces in contexts involving complicity and wrongdoing. In forgiving and having been forgiven what has been given both to others and to us is the same gracious love. In *agape*, we find ourselves having forgiven others and having been forgiven ourselves beyond any economy, including the economy of justice.[6] Insofar as we have been awakened and have surrendered to the glory of having been seized in and by love for the Faces of others, we are already forgiven and beloved members of a spiritual communion.

In contrast to philosophies that attempt to ground themselves in the atomistic I, in this philosophical spirituality one is affirmed and filled with joy and delight because one does not live over and against all those who are other, but precisely through surrender to having been seized in and by love for them. I am not initially awakened to love for my own Face but to the Faces of others; the having been seized in and by love for my own face is decisive but revealed indirectly. Value, meaningfulness, joy, communion, *koinonia*, my own Face as precious, response-able, moral, spiritual, beloved, forgiven, an essential and infinitely valuable aspect of the Face to Face: all are delivered *through* surrender to having been seized in and by love for the Faces of all the innumerable other creatures (people, other animals, all the plants—the more the richer!) that fill every nook and cranny of our enchanted world.[7]

The glory of this awakening describes, philosophically, spiritual salvation. This is salvation to the spiritual meaningfulness of life, to the reality of the gift, to Proximity, to the transcending glory of the Face to Face, to participation in the *koinonia*. Notably, it is also salvation from sin, salvation from complicity and culpability, salvation from the otherwise wrenching "No!" we must confess in answer to the question, "Is it righteous to be?"

Living by Grace

In accord with the argument to this point, it is clear that in this fallen world my existence is not righteous. We each emerge into existence already complicit (original sin), and there is nothing we or anyone else can do to justify

---

6. Theologians discuss this relationship between justice and *agape* in terms of law and grace.

7. A note on the relationship between the moral and the aesthetic: aesthetic good is the delight of a Face in something other than a Face (e.g., in a painting, music, a sunset, or perhaps the face of a human Face [delight in a great personality or physical attractiveness]). Since a Face is primordially response-able to having been seized in and by love for other Faces, moral good has priority over aesthetic good. This is why violation of the moral simply voids any competing aesthetic appeal—as if an awakened Face could delight in a context that involves the violation of the Face of another. (So, for instance, no evil is ever appreciated as beautiful.)

ourselves. Wiesel was right to say that there is no *answer* to Auschwitz—nothing can make it right, nothing can compensate for it and all the other evils suffusing this vale of tears, nothing can justify anyone's existence, and nothing lets us affirm the whole of existence as good. Levinas was right that blank eyes still stare accusingly upward from open pits. No one can or should try to answer the modern "problem of evil" by articulating a tit-for-tat economy in which some counter-balancing good (e.g., life in heaven after death) or evil (e.g., the murder of an innocent upon a cross) fulfills an *economic* demand for justice.

Wiesel was also correct, however, to affirm that even in the face of Auschwitz there is response in responsibility. Levinas, furthermore, was right to discern behind responsibility response-ability. And behind response-ability, Levinas was right to discern the extranatural, extrapoetic reality of the sphere of *agape*, that is, to discern having been seized in and by love for all Faces. Levinas, moreover, having surrendered to having been seized in and by love for the Face of every face, realized that he had been seized in and by love even for the Faces of Nazis. That is, Levinas realized that within the gift of *agape* lies the glory of forgiveness for all, love even for those who are and remain enemies of the good. In the Christian vernacular, Levinas discerned *grace*, love for those who are not deserving, love beyond any and every tit-for-tat economy, love for we (all of us) who are not righteous, love for we (all of us) who have no "right to be." We who surrender to having been seized in and by love receive, for others and for ourselves, forgiveness.

In a word, speaking in a Christian key wholly consonant with Levinas's Jewish spirituality, it is not righteous for any of us to be, but we can live by grace. We can live in surrender to having been seized in and by love for all Faces. We can live beloved and forgiven. At the same time, we remain complicit and culpable, and at times willfully violate the well being of Faces. In other words, law and justice are endemic to the spheres of nature and of poetic I's, gracious love is endemic to the sphere of *agape*, and we live in a reality best understood in terms of all three spheres. So there is an enduring and irreducible incommensurability between my complicity and culpability insofar as I understand myself, on the one hand, in relation to the spheres of nature and of poetic I's and, on the other hand, in relation to the sphere of *agape* (gracious love).

This enduring incommensurability provides a philosophical reading of sixteenth century reformer Martin Luther's talk of living simultaneously forgiven and sinful (*simul iustus et peccator*). This describes the inescapable predicament of we who live "in the world" (i.e., in the sphere of nature and poetic I's) even as we live by faith (i.e., live surrender to having been seized in and by gracious love). This describes the continuing triumph of grace amidst the enduring reality of evil, the continuing pertinence of justice despite the extranatural, extrapoetic reality of *agape*.

In sum, in our having been seized in and by love for every Face, our own forgiveness is always already given. It is given beyond any explanatory ethical logic within history, without any initiative on our part, and apart from any of those (often bloody) would-be expiatory mechanisms that traffic in tit-for-tat economies. Insofar as one lives in the light of having been seized in and by love for every Face, one lives having been seized in and by love even for enemies of the moral. One lives the freedom and affirmation of having forgiven and having been forgiven. And in relation to those who also see our Faces, one lives the transcending joy of Face to Face communion, a member of the *koinonia*. We do not reason our way to, conclude, or infer this reality. It is the gift of *agape*. Even as we remain complicit and culpable within a fallen world, we can live awakened to the gift, awakened to *agape* already having seized us, and we can reasonably and rightly confess our faith, that is, our election by and surrender to the gift of gracious love. We can and should give thanks for it, testify to it, and strive to act ever more fully in its light.

Gallows as Cornerstone and the Reasonableness of Faith

As Wiesel and Levinas illustrate, awakening to having been seized in and by love for Faces flows as powerfully from pain and sorrow as from joy and happiness. At the heart of every impassioned "no!" to concrete evil or suffering lies surrender to having been seized in and by love. "No!" comes in response to the violation of our foundational and unshakable sense of what, seized in and by love, we would desire for a Face. Evil is derivative, for evil is "*agape*-violated." The passion of the "no" is the passion of *agape*.

The reality of *agape*, then, far from being compromised or contradicted by the suffering and evil suffusing reality, is powerfully manifest in every "No!" For every "no" is at heart a passionate, loving response to Faces violated. *Agape* is spiritually alpha and omega, for the reality of *agape* is profoundly manifest and endures not only in moments of joy, but amidst horror over the violation of Faces. Far from being overcome by evil, it is only in light of *agape* that evil, *agape* violated, is manifest as such. To be sure, on occasion an evil or injury can be so extreme that it is psychologically or physically (e.g., brain injury) debilitating, cutting off our response-ability. This makes clear our vulnerabilities as physical beings in a fallen world. It does not speak against the reality of *agape*.

Because of all this it is not surprising that it is often precisely when we witness the most horrendous violation of Faces that we find ourselves most powerfully seized in and by love. When overcome by horror we do not question the reality of the evil, so in such moments we have no question about the reality of *agape*. That is why a gallows or cross can horrify us and simultaneously be the cornerstone of surrender to having been seized in and by love, that is, the cornerstone of faith.

God Is Love

The unveiling of the transcending spiritual reality of *agape* and the ultimate nonreality of evil is the unveiling of *agape* as the one, only, and ultimate spiritual reality, wholly good, alpha and omega. At this point in the argument, then, we can reasonably affirm not only the independent and primordial reality but also the significance of *agape* for I's—including the reality and character of grace, faith, election, having forgiven, having been forgiven, Proximity, meaningfulness, good, the transcending communion of the Face to Face, and participation in the *koinonia*. Insofar as "God is love" is interpreted strictly (i.e., "God *is* love" / "love *is* God"), this unveiling of the independent reality of *agape* and its significance has been an unveiling of the reality and significance of God.[8]

This love in and by which we are seized is intensely personal, but it is not yet God as a person, that is, as the discrete and independent center of consciousness and agency imagined and treasured by many people of faith and typical of Christian theology. Since faith in this God, however, is wholly continuous with traditional faith in the personhood of God, and since I have undercut modern Western naturalistic and secular reasons for foreclosing upon the possible reality of such a God, I may have opened steps along a path to affirmation of the personhood of God. Of course, it would be critical to delineate the precise meaning of "personal" when applied to God. In any case, affirmation of a personal God lies beyond the bounds of this philosophical inquiry. Nonetheless, God as unfolded reasonably within this philosophical spirituality in terms of *agape* is substantial and significant. For instance, God in the sense unfolded here is wholly sufficient for understanding the meaning and significance of "God" in the selected verses from 1 John 4, which, as I said in my preface, proclaim the essence of the faith I am here striving to unfold:

8. This is not an argument, in the modern sense, for the existence of God. (Whatever else God is, the classic religious traditions agree that, contrary to modern presumption, God is not the possible conclusion of any human argument.) But in the precise sense in which we have delineated the profound influence and significance of God in our lives (i.e., of the primordial and ultimate reality of love for all Faces in and by which we always already find ourselves seized), there is no good or reasonable basis for hardening our hearts to God.

> Beloved, let us love one another, because love is from God; everyone
> who loves is born of God and knows God. Whoever does not love
> does not know God, for God is love. . . . In this is love, not that we
> loved God but that [God] loved us . . . God is love, and those who
> abide in love abide in God, and God abides in them.[9]

I have little doubt that the author of 1 John thought of God as a person.
The meaning of "God" within the bounds of this philosophical spirituality,
however, is sufficient to affirm not only the meaning and significance of God
in these passages, but the significance of God in relation to faith, good, evil,
fall, original sin, election to works of love, forgiveness of others and oneself,
salvation from sin and to the transcending glory of the Face to Face, and the
glory of the *koinonia*.

In this philosophical spirituality "God" is an *icon* opening our gaze to the
extranatural, extrapoetic reality of the sphere of *agape*. "God" designates the
primordial, transcending reality that proceeds neither from me nor from the
Face of any other, but that seizes me in gracious love for all Faces and, in
instances where the face of another Face is likewise awakened to my Face, that
lifts us up into the transcending joy of Face to Face communion (the *koinonia*
where our joy is made complete).[10]

In sum, while this philosophical spirituality cannot assert the reality of the
personhood of God, the God reasonably unveiled is substantive, vitally significant, and engages us in a supremely intimate and personal way. In surrender to this God one finds passion for what is loving and good, abhorrence for
what is evil, and also forgiveness and the glory of living Face to Face, the joy
of *koinonia*. At this point, then, we are not only justified in affirming, but we
have added significant vistas of meaningfulness to the conclusion I claimed I
would defend in the preface: namely, that based solely upon what is reasonable and good according to common public standards, every person of faith
can be utterly confident that it is wholly reasonable and good to affirm, give
thanks for, live, and testify to faith in God.

In a different way, we have arrived at a conclusion similar to that reached
by Descartes. Where Descartes concludes that "knowledge of our own minds

9. 1 John 4: 7–8, 10a, 16b.

10. Speaking technically, I am here gesturing to what I consider to be Jean-Luc
Marion's essential supplement to Levinas, namely, his explication of the givenness—
from without the fourfold causation—of the gift. Here again, see especially Jean-Luc
Marion, "Sketch of a Phenomenological Concept of Gift." I should specify that combining the concepts of Levinas and Marion in this fashion is a strong move that creates
an understanding different from either of their projects. Still, I think my understanding is consistent with the spirit of their projects. In any case, I have been profoundly
influenced by and am indebted to their work.

and of God . . . are the most certain and evident of all possible objects of human knowledge for the human intellect," we are now warranted in claiming that we can be as sure of our existence as freely self-creating, poetic I's and of the reality of *agape* as we are sure of the reality of the physical universe. We would never say that God "can be demonstrated by reasoning that has no other source but our own mind," and we would not exactly say, "God may be more easily and certainly known than the things of this world." We can quite reasonably say, however, that God, the reality of *agape* in and by which we have been seized for all Faces, is as immediately and surely known as the things of the sphere of nature.

Let me quickly stress that true spiritual passion is never focused upon defending this conclusion *per se*. For true passion is the passion of having been seized in and by love for all Faces, that is, the passion is not focused upon affirmation of any belief but upon concern for all Faces, and in our particular context our concern over the ways in which modern Western naturalistic and also secular reason obstruct awakening to faith. What has and should motivate attempts to articulate and defend the reasonableness of faith is the passion of the having been seized. In accord with passion for all Faces, the goal here has been to clear away conceptual obstructions and to help to awaken lost, confused, or uncertain Faces, to testify to the reality of the gift of having been seized in and by gracious love, to the possibility of living beloved and forgiven, to the glory of living Face to Face, and to the joy of living in *koinonia*.

Finally, note that the appeal to general revelation defended here is wholly consistent with the claims of Paul as cited by Descartes (i.e., Romans 1:19–20). For based upon this argument it is wholly reasonable to maintain, exceptional circumstances aside, that with regard to all poetic I's, "*what can be known of God* [that which falls within the bounds of what is generally considered to be good and reasonable] *is plain to them* [reacting appropriately to the horror of the concentration camps is not conceptually complicated or difficult], *because [God] has shown it to them* [i.e., the gift gives itself; God gives Godself; *agape* gives *agape*; grace begets grace]. *Ever since the creation of the world his eternal power* [the spiritual power manifest in the having been seized] *and divine nature* [*agape*; gracious love], *invisible through they are* [the spiritual, sphere of *agape* reality of the gift is not visible in the sphere of nature], *have been understood and seen through the things [God] has made* [the gift is essentially hidden yet manifest in the presence of a present, that is, if there is no present, then there is no gift, but the present is not the gift; or, I see a physical horror and I see it as horror because I am spiritually seized in and by love for all Faces]. As Paul goes on to say, *what the law requires* [the *Saying* of God, the command of the Face, the wholly direct and intimate having been seized in and by love for all Faces] *is written on human hearts* [faith is not unreasonable, but it is not a product of reason, the source of faith is the *agape* that, exceptional circumstances aside (e.g., brain injury) seizes us all—though we may resist and efface it].

Understood in this fashion, and based solely upon what is reasonable and good according to common public standards, this philosophical spirituality legitimates Paul's affirmation that, with regard to poetic I's, "what can be known of God is plain to them, because God has shown it to them. Ever since the beginning of the world [God's] eternal power and divine nature, invisible though they are, have been understood and seen through the things [God] has made" (Romans 1:19-20).

Resurrection, Universal Reality and Creaturely Diversity, and Jesus on the Essence of Saving Faith

Life after Death: Open Pits and the Gift

What was his name? When did he last see his parents? What did he do at his last pre-war birthday party? Did he have brothers and sisters? Would he have married, had children? The mortal evil was useless for that boy in the gallows. For those awakened by love, the vertigo returns. Fidelity to *agape* keeps the pits open. Faith and love do not relieve but intensify the wrenching violation. Hope for perfect peace, peace even for that boy, peace even for those staring sightless up from open pits, that hope is not absolutely negated, but it is most certainly not realized or realizable in this world. In accord with what we can understand and say now, their suffering was useless, unjustifiable. Our vision of the whole remains fractured. None of this opposes faith. To the contrary, all of this follows precisely *from* faith, from surrender to having been seized in and by love for all Faces.[1]

As we remember the murder of that boy and the multitude of others whose lives have been brutal and brief, a loving question arises about and for them.

---

1. "Fearing God," Levinas says, "primarily means fearing for the other." Elsewhere he says, "I cannot describe the relation of God without speaking of my concern for the other. When I speak to a Christian, I always quote Matthew 25 [the parable of the Sheep and the Goats]; the relation to God is presented there as a relation to another person. It is not a metaphor: in the other, there is a real presence of God. In my relation to the other, I hear the Word of God. It is not a metaphor; it is not only extremely important, it is literally true. I'm not saying that the other is God, but that in his or her Face I hear the Word of God" (Levinas, "Philosophy, Justice, and Love," in *On Thinking-of-the-Other: entre-nous*, Michael Smith and Barbara Harshav, trans. [New York: Columbia University Press, 1998], 117, 109–10).

Namely, the question of the possibility of some good life after death arises forcefully and appropriately in the form of a burning hope for them all. This question arises in the wake of having been seized in and by love in a fashion utterly distinct from the way in which it arises for those, like Heidegger and Rorty, who ground meaningfulness in the novelty or creativity of the atomistic I. If the self-creating I is the source of all meaningfulness in I's world, then the death of I is a total disaster. For those whose concern is above all for themselves, the question of life after death arises forcefully in terms of concern over one's own death as the paramount threat to one's ultimate concern: one's own life.

Heidegger and Rorty, in accord with modern naturalistic and secular rationality, reject any possibility of life after death. While the philosophical spirituality unfolded here does not foreclose upon that possibility, the literal resurrection of individual beings to heaven would seem to require a God who is a person, a possibility about which it appears we could have confidence only in the wake of some sort of special revelation. Notably, there is no essential dynamic of progress built into my understanding of the relationship among the three spheres.[2] That is, I have uncovered no dynamic that would lead one to conclude that the sphere of *agape* will eventually transform the basic character of the sphere of nature or transform the hearts of all poetic I's. Indeed, watching asteroids hitting Jupiter some years ago (asteroids that would have destroyed virtually all life on Earth), it became easy to imagine how at any moment human history and all memory of it could be forever destroyed (e.g., via asteroids, nuclear accident, nuclear war).

None of this derails salvation through faith, the gift of grace, unfolded in this philosophical spirituality. The dynamics of awakening and surrender to having been seized in and by gracious love for all Faces (including, indirectly but decisively, our own), the transcending glory of the Face to Face, release into the reality of having forgiven and having been forgiven, glorious lives of *Saying* in *koinonia*, the reality of *agape*: all of it stands even if, consistent with all appearances, our deaths and the death of that boy mark totally, without exception and forevermore, the ends of our faces and Faces. In accord with this philosophical spirituality, none of our affirmations, none of our joy, none of our delight, none of our actions, and none of our decisions depend upon any belief, expectation, hope, or even any thought of life after death.

The very idea of life after death, moreover, can pose a threat to spiritual awakening, for it is a dangerously valuable present for mortals easily consumed by concern for self. The very idea of resurrection to life after death

---

2. This distinguishes my position from that typical of process philosophy and theology, to which I am otherwise very close.

can direct my attention to *my* possible survival after death, can accentuate my self-interested desires, thereby helping to cut me off from awakening, from the gift, from the Faces of others, from true salvation. As a spiritual discipline, it is wise to dismiss utterly any thought of one's own possible resurrection. Nonetheless, insofar as the pits still gape open, insofar as the vertigo returns, insofar as the question of life after death arises out of love and concern for an innumerable host of afflicted, persecuted, and executed others, and insofar as nothing in this philosophical spirituality forecloses upon the possibility of life after death, it would be mean-spirited not at least to *hope* in some sort of resurrection to a good life after death for that boy and a host of all kinds of Faces (children, kittens, cockroaches, and saplings).

Under the pull of that desperate hope, we might dare to ask even the personally dangerous question of whether there is any *reason* to hope for some sort of resurrection to good life. We may grasp the slimmest of reeds. *The primordial and ultimate spiritual reality of agape*, taken together with the realization that we are seized in and by love for *particular* Faces, gives us a slim basis for hoping in good life for individuals after death.[3] This may be why so many of the world's faith traditions, whether they speak of heaven or the Pure Land, have developed a conviction that somehow the spiritual reality of *agape* is finally triumphant even for that boy, that finally the vertigo is defeated, that the "yes" of *agape* is fully realized for every Face. This may be wishful thinking (of a most generous sort). I think, however, that we can quietly affirm hope, sheer hope, not something we conclude, believe, demand, expect, cling to, need, use as a basis for choosing among actions, utilize in a theodicy or tit-for-tat economy, or use to affirm our vision of the whole, but sheer hope, reasonable hope, hope first and foremost *for the sake of others*, in some sort of resurrection to good life after death.

Is Christian Belief an Essential Aspect of Christian Faith?

I have described faith as living surrender to having been seized in and by gracious love for all Faces. Insofar as I do not harden my heart, love has and *Says* me, and I live having been seized in and by love; that is, I live faith, which is the gift of grace. Faith is not a product of my choice or intention,

---

3. The insistence upon the primordial and ultimate worth of *each* Face may mark the root distinction between monotheistic and monistic religions. My denial of an independent reality of evil marks a point of continuity among all of the world's major religious traditions, monistic and monotheistic alike, in contrast to dualistic understandings (e.g., Manicheeism), which assert a primordial good/evil binary, or naturalistic understanding, which denies both good and evil in the classic realist/idealist/ religious sense.

not my assent to or affirmation of some set of claims, not in any sense my work, but wholly given. Beliefs, in contrast to faith, are our ideas, our systems of ideas, our affirmations, *said* that we create *about* faith. In this sense, the essence of Christian faith does not require affirmation of Christian beliefs, or even knowledge of the name "Jesus," for faith is not Christian belief but what Christian belief is *about*. Faith is living surrender to having been seized in and by gracious love. Motivation for loving action, the saving forgiveness and the glory of living Face to Face, and the transcending joy of communion in the *koinonia*: all are received with the gift of faith.

This distinction between the essence of Christian faith, on the one hand, and Christian belief, on the other, can sound radical, but it is precisely this understanding of faith that Jesus unfolds in his parable of the Sheep and the Goats (Matthew 25:31–46). This parable is especially susceptible to misreading, for it deals with an incredibly valuable present: the sheep are ushered into eternal glory—while the goats are dismissed into eternal torment. The present (i.e., eternal glory) is so potent in its potential to seize our self-interested attention that it can distract powerfully from the parable's stunningly precise delineation of the character of faith and of the gift. Indeed, the present of heaven is so dangerously desirable (and the possibility of hell so terrifying) that its corrosive effect pervades not only readings of this parable, but Christian understanding generally. For this reason, as I suggested above, Christian belief in a literal heaven after death is spiritually dangerous—even if, as we can rightly *hope*, there is a literal heaven after death.

The parable of the Sheep and the Goats is frequently read as a fearsome warning and a guide to gaining eternal life. If you want to be a sheep and go to heaven, then you should be a Christian and obey Jesus' commands to feed the poor, visit the sick, and so forth. If you reject Jesus and his teachings, then you are going to hell. The point of the parable, so the story goes, is that you should believe in Jesus and his teachings (usually some specific list of beliefs is specified) so you can go to heaven.

Such wholly self-centered, economic "spirituality" *does* consider Christian beliefs to be necessary for faith that is in essence Christian, that is, such "spirituality" is indeed exclusively Christian. The parable, however, says no such thing. In the parable only one set of questions separates sheep from goats: Did you feed the hungry, clothe the naked, welcome the stranger, visit the sick and imprisoned (e.g., those in debtors' prison)? According to the parable, it does not matter if you are Jew, Gentile, Samaritan, Christian, Muslim, Buddhist, Sikh, Roman, Greek, Confucian, Apache, or Alpha Centurion. The question is, did you feed, clothe, welcome, visit? In a word, have you lived surrender to having been seized in and by love for the Faces of others? Have you lived faith?

In this parable Jesus makes startlingly clear the intimate relationship among awakening, surrender, response-ability, and responsibility. We cannot directly see in the sphere of nature whether or not anyone—the king, the steward, the father, the prodigal, the elder brother—has truly accepted the gift. We can only discern this spiritual reality indirectly. True faith bears fruit in the actions of poetic I's in the sphere of nature. I's who have surrendered to having been seized in and by the Faces of others immediately and without any other reason feed, clothe, welcome, and visit.

People can, of course, act in such ways without faith. People can act in accord with a decision to assent to a certain ethic or system of beliefs, or perhaps because they want to self-create themselves in the image of a saint. Or, as with the tempting misreading of this parable, people can act in accord with an economic calculation in expectation of fulfilling some tit-for-tat economy that earns eternal life in heaven. This would be the economic calculation of goats, those who are *surprised* that they failed to feed, clothe, and visit when they know full well that they gave those *presents*, not understanding that what they failed to receive and share was *the gift*.

In a word, if I give food to you in order to gain eternal life, I have not even seen, let alone been seized in and by love for, your Face. I have used your face as an opportunity for my own face. My motivation is wholly self-centered. On this rationale, even God—here construed as an economically (tit-for-tat) motivated being with supernatural power to grant me life in heaven (though this is not the motivation or power of *agape*)—on this rationale even God is reduced to a means I use in order to gain reward for myself.

That is why Jesus stresses the surprise not merely of the goats but also, and just as significantly, *the surprise of the sheep*. The surprise of the sheep is essential, for it signals that sheep do not act out of economic calculation (e.g., do not act in order to gain eternal life), do not act in accord with assent to a set of ethical or religious beliefs, do not act in order to create themselves in a desired image. Sheep act out of faith, the gift of grace, which means the sheep did not harden their hearts to having been seized in and by love for the Faces that in their concrete, historical lives elected them. Without any calculation, without any thought of God or religious duty, in direct response to having been seized in and by love for others' Faces, they acted lovingly. Because of the purity of their faith they were not aware of having done anything to serve God. They responded directly to having been seized in and by love for others' particular Faces.

Precisely in response to the Faces of others, the sheep responded to God—"just as you did it to one of the least of these . . . you did it to me" (Matt. 25:40). They responded to God, however, only insofar as they were not conscious of doing anything for God, hence their *essential* surprise (which is indexed to the essential hiddenness of the gift/God/*agape*). The parable names the subtle doubling that we unfolded in our description of surrender to having been seized in and by love for the Faces of others. We began with what is most obvious, immediate, and forceful: our having been taken hostage by the Faces of others. When we explored the precise dynamics of this having been taken hostage, however, we discerned the reality of *agape*, of gracious love, and so we realized that in not hardening our hearts to the Faces of others we were surrendering to having been seized *in and by love* for their Faces. Surrender to their Faces was surrender to love and, insofar as this love *is* a reality and *is* God, we realized that surrender to having been seized in and by love for their Faces is precisely surrender to God.

Acting in response to having been seized in and by love for their Faces, then, giving the gift, which includes giving appropriate presents, is acting in surrender to God—but only so long as we do not think in terms of surrender to God.[4] That is why the surprise, the hiddenness of God, is essential. Precisely as we surrender to having been seized in and by love for "the least of these" (an emphasis directed against economic valuing), we surrender to God; and precisely as we act for "the least of these," we act in fidelity to God. We give presents in giving the gift we have first received. Thereby we, in our living, become the Saying of *agape*, the Saying of God in the world, and, with those likewise awakened, live Face to Face, delivered unto the transcending glory and fellowship of the *koinonia*.

On this reading, the line dividing those who see the I as the absolute center of all value and meaningfulness, in contrast to those awakened and seized in and by love for all Faces, marks an essential boundary between those who do and do not enjoy faith in God. This line does not correlate with the lines commonly drawn between people of faith and atheists. There are people who do not affirm any beliefs about God (they may even claim to be atheists) who nonetheless surrender to having been seized in and by love for all the Faces by which they have been elected. These people therefore act in response to their election by love. If faith is living surrender to having been seized in and by love for all Faces, then these people are living faith in God (surprised sheep).[5] Meanwhile, there are those who say they believe in God yet *do not* live surrender to having been seized in and by love for all the particular Faces by which they have been elected. These people do not live faith in God

---

4. So, Jesus says, when giving alms do not let your right hand know what your left is doing (Matt. 6:3).

5. This describes Richard Rorty, whose passion for the Faces of the marginalized and questing after a solidarity with others that was stronger than death was, sadly, subverted *in his theory* (not in his clear passion for justice) by his secular philosophy (there is no path from contingency and irony to solidarity).

(surprised goats). This line between those who are and those who are not faithful to God correlates with the line Jesus draws between the sheep and the goats—and let us remember, true sheep *mourn* lost goats.

In Jesus' famous parable of the Sheep and the Goats, then, Christian belief is not part of the essence of the faith at the heart of Christianity. Ideally, of course, one both lives surrender to having been seized in and by love and also has accurate beliefs about God. Nonetheless, while beliefs are vitally important, beliefs are not faith. Beliefs are about faith, and distinctively Christian belief is not necessary for living surrender to having been seized in and by love. Distinctively Christian belief, then, is not necessary for living what Jesus portrayed as true faith in God, not necessary to what Jesus portrayed as the essence of faith.

I am making a strong, universalistic claim insofar as, working within a Western philosophical context, I am nonetheless claiming to have unfolded the essence of reasonable faith and to have identified it with the essence of reasonable Christian faith (and, insofar as Levinas represents Judaism, with the essence of reasonable Jewish faith). I have argued that sphere of *agape* spiritual truths are no more relative than sphere of nature scientific truths. I have argued that "sphere of *agape*" truly names a dimension of ultimate reality and that "faith" names poetic I's living surrender to *agape*. My argument is distinctly Western and Christian, but I am claiming it has universal relevance.[6] If I am correct, while there may be considerable cultural and aesthetic diversity, insofar as any religious tradition is true (and I would expect the world's classic religious traditions all to be largely true), then the essence of that tradition's faith (e.g., Buddhist, Jain, Hindu, Islamic) will be continuous with the essence of Christian faith (and vice-versa) insofar as, in each case, faith is understood within the bounds of what is considered to be reasonable and good by common public standards.

At the same time, it is not only possible, but considering the transcending character of the reality, unsurprising that, just as science, justifiably, long utilized two incommensurable vocabularies (i.e., wave and particle vocabularies) in order to most fully describe and engage the reality of light, so people of faith will utilize diverse systems of beliefs in order to most fully name and incarnate the significance of the transcending reality of *agape*. Indeed, just as we are fortunate to have, for instance, diverse poems, paintings, and plays all truly but incompletely describing vital dimensions of existence—the beauty of a mountain stream, grief over the loss of one's child, love for a spouse, the horror of battle—so we may be fortunate that there are diverse systems of

6. Instead of "Christian," one might say, "Judeo-Christian," but out of respect for Judaism, and despite the profound influence of Levinas, I will simply say, "Christian."

religious belief striving faithfully to unveil, name, and incarnate surrender to having been seized in and by love.

The world's great faith traditions can be seen as historically deep, highly refined, multi-authored poems, all of which are responses to the same reality of *agape* and all of which are striving and largely succeeding, if imperfectly and incompletely, to testify to and responsibly to incarnate that same transcending reality. Nonetheless, while there is ample space and reason to celebrate diversity, insofar as the world's classic faith traditions have been truthfully developed in response to the spiritual dimension of ultimate reality, namely, the sphere of *agape*, the essence of the faith their beliefs all strive to articulate should be commensurate. There is no place here for affirmation of moral or spiritual relativism. To the contrary, insofar as various religions disagree over the essential character of the sphere of *agape* (i.e., the essence of faith), they cannot be equally true.

In sum, my exploration is delimited to the sphere of general revelation. Within the sphere of general revelation, one will always use vocabularies and speak in terms of beliefs that have been conditioned by one historical trajectory or another. In that sense, my argument is distinctly Western and Christian (or, said cautiously, Judeo-Christian). In accord with the philosophical spirituality defended here, however, I reasonably understand my ideas, though distinctly Western and Christian, to be responses to and descriptions of a dimension of ultimate reality, the sphere of *agape*. Insofar as my Christian beliefs are true, then, they are true to a universal reality. By the same reasoning (*mutatis mutandis*), Buddhist, Jain, or other beliefs may well be equally true. Since we are dealing with the same ultimate reality, insofar as the beliefs of diverse faiths are equally true, they will be commensurate. Again, there is no place here for affirmation of moral or spiritual relativism with regard to the essence of faith.

While this philosophical spirituality is distinctly Western and Christian and articulates and affirms the essence of Christian faith to be reasonable and true, it does not claim that only Christianity is true or that only Christians are truly faithful. As illustrated in relation to the parable of the Sheep and the Goats (and this is equally true with regard to the parables of the Prodigal Son, the Unforgiving Steward, and the Good Samaritan [see below]), this understanding of the relationship among transcending spiritual reality, the essence of faith, and belief(s) is consistent with the teachings of Jesus.

To be sure, some theological affirmations that are essential to classic Christian confession apparently do lie beyond the reach of any philosophical spirituality, for example, belief in the personhood of God (as noted above), life after death, discreet divine intervention within the sphere of nature, the uniquely unique (i.e., ontologically *sui generis*) identity of Jesus as the Son of

God: all would seem to require some sort of special revelation. None of these affirmations are necessarily unreasonable, but they appear to lie beyond the parameters of general revelation. Such beliefs may be an essential part of the Christian belief system, but they are not part of the essence of Christian faith.

I now conclude with an attempt to add clarity and nuance to my defense of the essence of reasonable faith—and also to add support to my claims that the essence of reasonable faith is wholly commensurate with the essence of Christian faith—with a reading of the globally celebrated parable Jesus offers in hopeful, loving response to a lawyer: a poor, lost goat who comes to test Jesus but who ends up revealing his concern to "justify himself" and inherit eternal life, namely, the parable of the Good Samaritan (Luke 10:25–37).

The Parable of the Good Samaritan

The parable of the Good Samaritan is Jesus' interpretation of "love your neighbor as yourself." Jesus' parable is part of his ministry to a lawyer who wants to "justify himself" and gain "eternal life." A "lawyer" in this context is an expert in Jewish law, that is, in Torah. Jesus begins by eliciting from the lawyer and then affirming the standard two-fold summary of the Torah. First, love God with all your heart, soul, strength, and mind. Second, love your neighbor as yourself. "Do this," Jesus affirms, "and you will live." There was no contemporary debate over this two-fold summary of the Law, but there was debate over who counted as neighbor. Two interpretations of the Law were prominent: "neighbor" could designate either "all Jews" or "all Pharisees." While the two-fold summary of the Law was uncontroversial, there was disagreement about which of these two interpretations of "neighbor" was correct. So the lawyer, wanting to "justify himself," asks, "who is my neighbor?"

For centuries, commentators, noting that in Jesus' day Samaritans were considered to be enemies by Jews and noting that in the parable the Samaritan was the neighbor, have read the parable as a call to radically expand the parameters of "neighbor."[7] Who is neighbor? Answer: everyone, even those who profess other faiths, even members of rival peoples. This interpretation is certainly not incorrect. Moreover, Jesus' portrayal of an ethnic enemy as

---

7. On Samaritans as enemies and for an excellent brief survey of some problematic and common tendencies in interpreting the parable, see Amy Jill-Levine, "The Many Faces of the Good Samaritan—Most Wrong," *Christian Ethics Today*, 20, no. 1 (Winter 2012), 20–21. (The essay also appeared in the Jan/Feb. 2012 issue of the *Biblical Archeological Review*.) Note that Jill-Levine understands "neighbor" in the parable in the ordinary sense, thereby joining a virtually universal consensus that stretches at least back to St. Augustine, who in his interpretation gives the ordinary meaning of "neighbor" and interprets the parable accordingly (*On Christian Doctrine*, I.XXX.31).

the one who fulfilled the Law is significant, especially given the historic and enduring power of "us" versus "them" sectarian impulses, for the parable makes clear that anyone, regardless of national or religious identity—whether Buddhist, Muslim, Christian, or Apache or whether American, Israeli, Palestinian, Iranian, Russian, or Chinese—may prove to be neighbor.

To think Jesus is only extending the category of "neighbor," however, is to miss the depth of his spiritual genius. Jesus realizes that what is keeping the lawyer from true living ("do this and you will live") is the lawyer's all-consuming self-interest. For the lawyer any "neighbors," whoever they might be, will only be means useful for achieving his own self-interested desire for eternal life. Indeed, there is reason to worry that the lawyer follows the first command about loving God for the same reason. That is, there is reason to worry that even God is reduced to a means used to achieve the lawyer's own desired end: eternal life. Jesus realizes that the lawyer, and for that matter all who accept the standard framing of the debate over "who counts as neighbor?" and who try to determine whom they have to love, are confused about the reality and character of "love." Accordingly, it is the reality and character of "love" that is clarified and movingly conveyed by the parable.[8]

Jesus displaces the standard debate by radically changing the meaning of "neighbor." Again, Jesus tells the parable in answer to the question, "Who is my neighbor?" Jesus' audience is listening for his answer to that question. The expectation, naturally, is that the key to Jesus' answer will lie in the identity of the person in the parable who is in the role of neighbor. Namely, the answer will lie in the identity of the man in the ditch. For first-time hearers, by the time Jesus has finished describing the risky, time-consuming aid rendered by the Samaritan, the dramatic tension has heightened. The priest passed by. The Levite passed by. The Samaritan stopped, rendered aid, and delivered the man to safety. Who was in the right and, more importantly, why?

Most people, and no doubt most of Jesus' listeners, were sufficiently awakened to have resonated with the Samaritan's response to the Face of the man in the ditch. The climactic answer to the question of "neighbor," however, turns upon the as-of-yet-unanswered question of the identity of the man in the ditch. What is the identity of the man in the ditch? Who counts as neighbor?

The parable, however, is over. We never learn the identity of the man in the ditch. Instead, Jesus asks the lawyer, "who proved neighbor?" This

8. Note: affirmation of love in the *agape* sense does not entail rejection or condemnation of "love" in the aesthetic/*eros* sense. Modernity has no problem with love in the aesthetic/*eros* sense. I am addressing, by contrast, modernity's conceptual eliding of *agape*/altruism in the classic, universal sense. (Notably, this is a sense beyond the bounds of kinship, reciprocal, or group "altruisms.")

is an abrupt and profoundly disorienting turn. It is also brilliant, for Jesus is attempting to stimulate a profound reorientation in the lawyer's understanding of the two-fold love command by radically changing the meaning of "neighbor" and thereby provoking awakening to *agape*, to having been seized in and by love.

Jesus' question regarding "neighbor" directs focus away from any other (e.g., the man in the ditch) and toward the one who was seized in and by love for another (e.g., the Samaritan). For Jesus, the meaning of "neighbor" has nothing to do with the identity of the man in the ditch. *In the parable not only is "neighbor" not every other, "neighbor" is not any other.* In contrast to standard definition, in the parable "neighbor" names the spiritual orientation of the Samaritan, the spiritual orientation of the one who was seized by compassion for the man in the ditch, the spiritual orientation of those who are awakened and who have not hardened their hearts to having been seized in and by love for the Faces by which they have been elected.

"Neighbor" in the spiritual sense does not name the sociocultural identity of any other, does not name the *face* of any other. "Neighbor" names the I awakened to the Faces of others, the I who lives surrender to having been seized in and by love for all Faces. This I acts in the world in response to election by the Faces of others. This I, in Levinas' beautiful words, is moved by love, "to fear injustice more than death, to prefer to suffer than to commit injustice, and to prefer that which justifies being over that which assures it."[9]

"Neighbor" names those who, seized in and by love, feed the hungry, welcome the stranger, clothe the naked, care for the sick, visit the imprisoned. That is, "neighbor" names sheep. "Neighbor" names not only the Good Samaritan, but also the prodigal's father and the king who forgave the steward, all of whom were seized in and by gracious love for the Faces of others. In all three cases—Samaritan, prodigal's father, forgiving king—the phrase translated "was moved with pity," "was filled with compassion," or "out of pity," the reality I am designating, "having been seized in and by love," translates the same Greek verb (ἐσπλαγχνίσθη/*esplagchnisthē* or σπλαγχνισθείς/*splagchnistheis*).[10] "Neighbor" describes I's who have not hardened their hearts to having been seized in and by love for the Faces of all others.

Note the passive character of the love in and by which neighbors find themselves seized. The Samaritan is not the source of the love. Nor is the Samaritan obeying any command in the sense of *choosing* to be obedient to a

---

9. Levinas, "Ethics as First Philosophy," in *The Levinas Reader*, Sean Hand, ed. (Cambridge, MA: Basil Blackwell, 1989), 85.

10. See Luke 10:33 (Samaritan), Luke 15:20 (prodigal's father), and Matt. 18:27 (forgiving king).

concept, principle, text, or divine being. The Samaritan is directly seized in and by love for the Face of the wounded man. Jesus makes this point by moving counter to expectations and telling a parable to a Jewish audience in which a Samaritan proves neighbor. He also gives us only that information about the man's face (namely, that he is injured) that is necessary to understand the concrete responsibilities entailed by election by his Face.

There is a stark contrast between this understanding of love and love insofar as it can be understood by naturalistic or secular rationality. Insofar as naturalistic or secular rationality can affirm love at all, it must begin with "self-love" in the sense of self-concern and self-interest. Because of the influence of secular rationality, for many modern Western thinkers, including even many Christians, it seems "love your neighbor as yourself" must be interpreted in accord with the logic of self-love in the self-interested sense. That is, it seems that in order to understand the command to "love your neighbor as yourself," you must begin with "self-love" in the sense of self-concern and self-interest, and then you must decide to obey a command from an external authority to extend that same kind of love to others.

This way of understanding the command divides "love your neighbor as yourself" into two parts and reverses their order. That is, the command is read as saying, "just as much as you love yourself, you must love your neighbor." Since there is no *agape* in this modern understanding, the question, "why obey this command?" immediately arises, and since one's ultimate appeal can only be to self-interest, this question must be answered in some selfish, spiritually devastating sense (e.g., the lawyer's self-interested reason, "in order to gain eternal life").

By contrast, if you grasp that "love your neighbor as yourself" names and calls for surrender to the gift, you realize the love that is the concern and compassion of the having been seized in and by love for others is precisely and simultaneously the love in and by which you also find yourself seized. The love of the "as thyself" names the love in and by which we are seized for ourselves, and this is precisely the same love in and by which we are seized for others. This love for yourself in and by which you are seized is passionate about your own flourishing, but this is not passion that flows from selfish concern for your own flourishing. The love you enjoy for yourself is not selfish self-love, for it is not love that originates in you. The love you enjoy for yourself is the gift, the gracious love in and by which you have been seized for all Faces, including your own. This love of self is not selfish because it does not originate in you at all, let alone in self-love in the selfish sense, for this love of self is the gift of love.

The fact that it is often in the wake of having been seized in and by love for others that one is awakened to having been seized in and by nonselfish love for oneself is cliché in ministry, mission, and social service circles. When I work for others I find myself, even if I too am caught in devastating circumstances, filled with a sense of meaningfulness and certainty of purpose. And insofar as good results, I am filled with joy. That is, insofar as one begins to live "love your neighbor," one finds *oneself* having been seized in and by love. One finds that one has oneself, indirectly but decisively, received the gift of being loved. In doing likewise, one receives and lives the gift of the "as thyself," for one is seized in and by the same love.

Accordingly, folks come back from mission trips inspired, excited, loving, loved, gifted, full of a sense of purpose and meaningfulness. They can hardly wait to do it again, and they say things like, "I went there to give. I thought they were the needy ones, but it turns out that I was more needy than I ever imagined. I received not only far more than I gave, but far more than I thought I could ever receive." Acting as neighbors, doing likewise, they taste what it is to be neighbor, what it is in this world right now to be living eternally, and they are filled with joy, happiness, and love. That is, they receive love for themselves, receive themselves as beloved (i.e., receive the "as thyself").

On this reading, Jesus (like Levinas after him) is saying that Torah does not delineate the love commands expecting that we will "love" out of obedience to the dictates of Torah. The scriptures testify to a command that seizes us with absolute intimacy, the Saying of Faces. The scriptures strive to awaken us to that Saying, to awaken us to having been seized in and by love for all Faces. In Jesus' parable, "love your neighbor as yourself" names a command that seizes us in utter immediacy and orients our desire, it names the Saying of Faces, desire *from* love and *for* all, *agape*, the gift, having been seized in and by love for all Faces (all others and your own).

Agape commands us with absolute intimacy and directness. It is not, however, an external command to obey an objective imperative, let alone an inducement to act in selfish pursuit of potential reward. Moreover, as the two who passed by illustrate, the command of love is not irresistible. It does not negate poetic autonomy. I's can harden their hearts. Ominously, I's who have over time repeatedly hardened their hearts may barely hear the Saying of Faces.[11] There is, again, an asymmetry in poetic I's having been seized in and

11. Although, as I am arguing, spiritual realities are not wholly linguistic products of human history, their articulation in language can enhance sensitivities to their reality and thereby give them real influence within history. On the other hand, the disappearance of language articulating spiritual realities can facilitate a deadening of spirit and hardening of heart at a sociocultural level. This could be a consequence of the predominance of naturalistic and secular rationality in modern Western societies, for these rationalities deny spiritual realities and marginalize wholesale the spiritual insights of the world's classic religious traditions.

by love for all Faces. Our autonomy is not primary, but neither is it negated: we cannot choose to love, but we can choose whether or not to harden our hearts. The autonomy and authenticity of poetic I's is affirmed, then, even as the independent reality of *agape* that first seizes I's is recognized.

Insofar as we can harden our hearts, the love we receive and give is authentically our love, but this love is not something we initiate, cause, create, choose, or give from ourselves. The love we live in word and act is always a love in and by which we first find ourselves seized. We find ourselves having been seized in and by love for those who are afflicted and suffering (in which case we find ourselves immediately/intimately troubled and moved to help) and also by those who are happy and rejoicing (in which case we are immediately/intimately joyful and smiling). Insofar as we are seized by Faces without regard to faces, we also find ourselves seized in and by love not only for other humans, even enemies of the good, but also for cats, dogs, horses, seals, sparrows, rats, ants, and (hopefully) all manner of other creature—even, in our most spiritually sensitive moments, by trees and flowers of the field.

Loving God with all our heart, soul, mind, and strength, then, is not something we initiate. Loving God begins in the love that first seizes us and to which we surrender. Indeed, loving God with all our heart, soul, mind, and strength names the radical passivity of allowing oneself to be seized fully in and by love for all others and acting in fidelity to that love.[12] On this reading, this is why Jesus says that the second great command, "love your neighbor as yourself," is like the first, "love God with all your heart, strength, soul, and mind."[13] For faith is living surrender to having been seized in and by gracious love for all Faces. Since faith is surrender to love for all or, in other words (insofar as God *is* love), surrender to God for all, loving God with all one's heart, strength, soul, and mind is precisely surrender to having been seized in and by gracious love for my neighbor and for myself (and so what you do for the "least of these" you do for God).

This reading of Jesus' interpretation of "love your neighbor as yourself" is supported by two striking aspects of Jesus' exchange with the lawyer. First, in the New Testament, "eternal life" typically signifies an already realized state

12. Or, in terms familiar from common Christian testimony, "I did not choose God, I found myself chosen," or I "received" or "accepted" Christ, all of which on this understanding signifies not (in standard modern style) affirmation of a set of truth claims, beliefs, or doctrines (i.e., "faith" is not "deciding to believe in"), but opening oneself as fully as possible to having been seized in and by the same love that seized the Samaritan.

13. Jesus does not say the second command is like the first in Luke, but in Matthew (22:39), where it is Jesus who names the two great commands in response to a lawyer's question.

of affairs. That is, while in the New Testament "eternal life" does sometimes refer to a future life after death, life after death is not the essential characteristic of "eternal life," for "eternal life" usually names a present reality. One lives eternal life in the here and now. Jesus tells the lawyer, however, that if he keeps the two great commands he "will" (future tense) receive eternal life. If "eternal life" for Jesus does not essentially specify life after death, why does Jesus use the future tense in "do this and you will live"?

An answer becomes apparent in light of the second striking aspect of Jesus' interchange with the lawyer. The parable defines the love in the two love commands in terms of spiritual orientation, the orientation of sheep, surrender to having been seized in and by compassion, a way of *be*-ing. Jesus, however, does not say "go and *be* likewise" but "go and *do* likewise." This is because Jesus brilliantly relates autonomous decision, action, and *agape*, which is neither self-interested nor the direct product of a decision. As the incompatible verb tenses make clear, you cannot decide to having been seized in and by love. You cannot, for instance, decide to love the homeless. You can, however, decide to work in a soup kitchen. As you get to know and open your heart to homeless folk in the context of acting in loving ways toward them, you should begin to find yourself awakened to their Faces. You should find yourself having been seized in and by love for them. In this sense, service for others can work as a concrete spiritual discipline that stimulates awakening and purifies faith.[14]

Jesus is wholly cognizant of the lawyer's real spiritual condition, and Jesus realizes the essential spiritual transformation can only be achieved indirectly. Jesus' concrete exhortation to the lawyer in terms of what he should *do*, then, is pedagogically brilliant. Jesus urges the lawyer to "do likewise" hoping that even if the lawyer engages in service for selfish reasons, he nonetheless will, in the course of his concrete rendering of aid, be awakened, surrender to having been seized in and by love for the Faces he is helping, and find himself, indirectly but decisively, beloved. Jesus is hoping that the lawyer will thereby receive the peace of having forgiven and of having been forgiven, enter into the transcending glory of seeing Face to Face, live in Proximity, live in a community formed and sustained in and by *agape*, and participate in the transcending joy of the *koinonia*. This is the eternal living Jesus has in mind when he says "do this and you will live," and it describes the glory of living wholly reasonable faith.

---

14. All spiritual disciplines should likewise work indirectly; the spiritual point of a spiritual discipline (it may also have a practical point, for instance, feeding the hungry) is not the discipline itself, nor the resolve to pursue it, but the indirect facilitating of initial or enhanced surrender to having been seized in and by love.

Jesus, God Incarnate and Crucified

I have been striving to unfold the essence of reasonable Christianity, which is to say, the essence of Christian faith insofar as it falls within the bounds of what is commonly considered to be good and reasonable. I think there is considerably more potential for philosophical spirituality to contribute to distinctly Christian thought (and I would expect the same potential to be present vis-à-vis other faiths), so I will finish with a very brief illustration of the promise of this approach for distinctly Christian thought. Namely, I will note some delimited but still significant ways in which the fruits of a philosophical spirituality can help Christians think about Jesus as God incarnate. And I will describe a critical aspect of what it is to be a follower of Jesus (a Christian) and to see the cross as a central icon of distinctly Christian faith.

It is common for Christians to speak of the final week of Jesus' life as Passion Week. What precisely is the passion of Passion Week? Neither crucifixion nor suffering are themselves passions. Nor is the passion of Passion Week a passion for the cross or death. (There is no reason to think Jesus was sadistic or suicidal.) Thinking within the bounds of this philosophical spirituality, the passion of Passion Week is the passion of Jesus, *agape* incarnate, *agape* so perfectly incarnated in Jesus that Jesus remains true to this passion for every Face to the death, even death on a cross.

The civil and ecclesial authorities did not execute Jesus so that humanity's sins might be forgiven, in order to appease God, or as some sort of bloody payment in a tit-for-tat economy. Jesus was executed because he lived surrender to having been seized in and by love for all the Faces that surrounded him, and so he spoke clearly and forthrightly about that which was loving and good and against what was unloving and evil. Jesus thereby threatened powerful figures and systems of exploitation and oppression, and precisely as one would expect in a fallen, selfish, and violent world, those figures and systems responded to the threat by crucifying him.

Jesus did not falter. The passion of Passion Week was a passion so true and resolute that it endured and in the end, facing the ultimate test, proved stronger even than the desire to live. The triumph manifest in the cross is the triumph of surrender to the passion of having been seized in and by love, that is, it is the triumph of faith over desire for personal well being and survival. In the words of Levinas, in Jesus' fidelity to having been seized in and by love for every Face that surrounded him, even unto death on a cross, we see a man who in the passion of *agape* was led "to fear injustice more than death, to prefer to suffer than to commit injustice, and to prefer that which justifies being over that which assures it."[15]

---

15. Levinas, "Ethics," 85; see also "Nonintentional Consciousness," 132.

Jesus was manifest as the incarnation of *agape* not only in his death but also in his life. According to the testimony of the gospels, Jesus so thoroughly lived surrender to having been seized in and by love for all Faces; so thoroughly lived gift, not economy; so completely was the living incarnation, the presence of the gift; that those who had "eyes to see"—that is, those who did not harden their hearts—immediately awakened and received the gift in his presence. In encounter with Jesus people saw themselves seen and beloved. In precisely the way we so dearly hoped for on behalf of the prodigal, the elder brother, and even the unjust steward, many (though certainly not all) recognized the divine gift hidden and shared in Jesus' presence. In this way, they received faith, the faith of Jesus, faith which is the gift of grace. That is, they received the gift of having been seized in and by love for all Faces, including their own Faces, and so they received forgiveness for their sins and (right then) eternal life, the glory of Face to Face communion, entry into the joy of the *koinonia*.

In this sense, to be a Christian, a follower of Jesus, is not essentially to assent to certain assertions about Jesus, that is, it is not essentially to hold certain beliefs. To be a Christian *is* essentially having accepted the passion of Jesus Christ as one's own. That is, to be a Christian is essentially living surrender to having been seized in and by love. Within the boundaries of reason, when we Christians take communion, remember the broken body and shed blood, affirm the cross of Jesus as an icon of our faith, and confess ourselves to be followers of Jesus, we not only affirm the force of *agape* engendering the screamed "no!" before the torture and murder of an innocent man. We also celebrate a surrender to having been seized in and by love for all Faces so utterly and completely that it remained faithful unto death, even death on a cross. And we confess our desire for so pure and strong a faith, our desire for so utter and complete a surrender to having been seized in and by love for all the Faces that daily elect us.

In sum, in a fashion akin to Paul the apostle, for Christian faith insofar as I have unfolded it here within the bounds of what is reasonable and good according to common public standards, these three are spiritually ultimate: faith, hope, and love. The greatest of these is *love*, the transcending, enveloping *agape* in and by which we find ourselves seized. Then comes *faith*, our living surrender to having been seized in and by love for every Face, including our own. In faith we receive the gifts of love, that is, the gifts of God: forgiveness and having been forgiven-ness, passion for every Face (the potentially costly passion of Passion Week), our own Faces as beloved, the glory of living Face to Face, and the transcending joy of communion in the *koinonia*. Finally, standing before the enduring fissure of all the useless suffering, haunted by visions of sightless eyes staring up from open pits, remembering all those murdered Faces, we reasonably and passionately *hope*. We hope that, in some way beyond our present imagining, transcending, enveloping *agape* is the final, triumphant word for each and every Face.

It is now clear why we can answer the question "Is faith reasonable?" with a sure and spiritually resonant yes. For we now understand why, given the current state of human understanding and based solely on what is reasonable and good according to common public standards, every person of faith can be utterly confident that it is wholly reasonable and good to affirm, give thanks for, live, and testify to faith in God. In other words, wholly in accord with common public standards of what is good and reasonable, the awakened rationality of this philosophical spirituality allows us in full confidence to proclaim the reasonableness and surpassing significance of faith (not only of Christian faith) and to testify to how faith in God empowers us, fills us with joy, and inspires loving action.

Bibliography

Aristotle. "Physics." In *The Basic Works of Aristotle*, edited and translated by Richard McKeon. New York: Random House, 1941.

Augustine. *On Christian Doctrine*. Translated by D.W. Robertson Jr. New York: Macmillan Publishing Company, 1958.

Beauchamp, Tom and James Childress. *Principles of Biomedical Ethics*, 6th ed. Oxford: Oxford University Press, 2009.

Brooke, John Hedley. *Science and Religion: Some Historical Perspectives*. Cambridge: Cambridge University Press, 1991.

Burtt, E. A. *Metaphysical Foundations of Modern Science*. New York: Doubleday & Company, Inc, 1954.

Butterfield, Herbert. *The Origins of Modern Science*, revised edition. New York: The Free Press, 1997.

Calvin, John. *Institutes of the Christian Religions*. Edited by John McNeill. Translated by Ford Lewis Battles. Philadelphia: The Westminster Press, 1960.

Caputo, John. *Deconstruction in a Nutshell: A Conversation with Jacques Derrida*. New York: Fordham University Press, 1997.

Critchley, Simon. *The Faith of the Faithless: Experiments in Political Theology*. New York: Verso, 2012.

Davidson, Donald. *Essays on Actions and Events*. Oxford: Clarendon Press, 1980.

_____. "On the Very Idea of a Conceptual Scheme." In Donald Davidson, *Inquiries into Truth and Interpretation*, 183–98. Oxford: Clarendon Press, 1990.

Dawkins, Richard. *The Blind Watchmaker: Why the Evidence of Evolution Reveals a Universe without Design*. New York: W. W. Norton & Company, 1986.

Dennett, Daniel. *Breaking the Spell: Religion as a Natural Phenomenon*. New York: Viking Penguin, 2006.

_____. *Consciousness Explained*. New York: Back Bay Books, 1991.

_____. *Darwin's Dangerous Idea*. New York: Touchstone, 1995.

_____. *Freedom Evolves*. New York: Penguin Books, 2003.

Derrida, Jacques. *Deconstruction and the Possibility of Justice*. Edited by Drucilla Cornell, Michel Rosenfeld, and David Gray Carlson. New York: Routledge, 1992.

_____.*Given Time: I. Counterfeit Money*. Translated by Peggy Kamuf. Chicago: The University of Chicago Press, 1992.

Descartes, René. *The Philosophical Writing of Descartes*, Vol. 1. Translated by John Cottingham, Robert Stoothoff, and Dugaid Murdoch. Cambridge: Cambridge University Press, 1985.

_____. *The Philosophical Writings of Descartes*, Vol. 2. Translated by John Cottingham, Robert Stootthoff, and Dugaid Murdoch. Cambridge: Cambridge University Press, 1984.

Dostoevsky, Fyodor: A Novel in Four Parts with Epilogue. Translated and annotated by Richard Pevear and Larissa Volokhonsky. New York: Vintage Classics, 1991.

Douglas, Mary. "Foreword." In Marcel Mauss, *The Gift: The Form and Reason for Exchange in Archaic Societies*. Translated by W.D. Halls. New York: W. W. Norton & Company, Inc., 1990.

Dupre, Louis. *Passage to Modernity: An Essay in the Hermeneutics of Nature and Culture*. New Haven: Yale University Press, 1993.

Freud, Sigmund. *Future of an Illusion*. New York: W.W. Norton & Company, Inc., 1989.

Grant, Edward. *Planets, Stars, and Orbs: The Medieval Cosmos, 1200–1687*. Cambridge: Cambridge University Press, 1994.

Hawking, Stephen. *A Brief History of Time*. New York: Bantam, 1998.

Heidegger, Martin. *Being and Time*. Translated by John Macquarrie and Edward Robinson. San Francisco: HarperSanFrancisco, 1962.

_____. *Being and Time*. Translated by Joan Stambough. Revised by Dennis Schmidt. Albany: State University of New York Press, 2010.

Hume, David. *Dialogues concerning Natural Religion*. Edited by Martin Bell. New York: Penguin Books, 1990.

_____. *A Treatise of Human Nature*. Edited by L. A. Selby-Bigge, 2nd ed. Revised by P. H. Nidditch. Oxford: Clarendon Press, 1975.

Husserl, Edmund. *Logical Investigations, Volume 1*. Translated by J.N. Findlay. New York: Routledge, 2001.

Janicaud, Dominique. *Le tournant theologique de la phenomenologie francaise*. Paris: Editions de l'Eclat, 1991.

_____. *Phenomenology and the "Theological Turn": The French Debate*. Translated by Dernard Prusak. New York: Fordham University Press, 2001.

Johnson, Phillip. *Defeating Darwinism by Opening Minds*. Downers Grove, IL: Intervarsity Press, 1997.

Kane, Robert. *The Significance of Free Will*. New York: Oxford University Press, 1998.

Laplace, Pierre-Simon. *A Philosophical Essay on Probabilities*. Translated by F.W. Truscott and F.L. Emory. New York: Dover, 1951.

de Lazari-Radek, Katarzyna and Peter Singer. *The Point of View of the Universe: Sidgwick and Contemporary Ethics*. Oxford: Oxford University Press, 2014.

Levinas, Emmanuel. "Being-Toward-Death and 'Thou Shalt Not Kill.'" In Emmanuel Levinas, *Is It Righteous to Be? Interviews with Emmanuel Levinas*, 130-139. Translated by Andrew Schmitz. Edited by Jill Robbins. Stanford: Stanford University Press, 2001.

_____. "Ethics as First Philosophy." In *The Levinas Reader*, 75–87. Edited by Sean Hand. Cambridge, MA: Basil Blackwell, 1989.

_____. "Interview with Myriam Anissimov." In Emmanuel Levinas, *Is It Righteous to Be? Interviews with Emmanuel Levinas*, 84-92. Translated by Jill Robbins and

Thomas Loebel. Edited by Jill Robbins. Stanford: Stanford University Press, 2001.

_____. "The Name of a Dog, or Natural Rights." In Emmanuel Levinas, *Difficult Freedom: Essays on Judaism*, 151–53. Translated by Sean Hand. Baltimore: John Hopkins University Press, 1997.

_____. "Non-Intentional Consciousness." In Emmanuel Levinas, *On Thinking of the Other: entre-nous*, 123–32. Translated by Michael Smith and Barbara Harshav. New York: Columbia University Press, 1998.

_____. *Of God Who Comes to Mind*. Translated by Bettina Bergo. Stanford: Stanford University Press, 1986.

_____.*Otherwise Than Being or Beyond Essence*. Translated by Alphonso Lingis. Pittsburgh: Duquesne University Press, 1981.

_____. "Philosophy, Justice, and Love." In Emmanuel Levinas, *On Thinking-of-the-Other: entre-nous*, 103–21. Translated by Michael Smith and Barbara Harshav. New York: Columbia University Press, 1998.

_____. *Proper Names*. Translated by Michael B. Smith. London: Athlone Press, 1996.

_____. "Signature." In Emmnuel Levinas, *Difficult Freedom: Essays on Judaism*, 291–95. Translated by Sean Hand. Baltimore: The John Hopkins University Press, 1997.

_____. "Useless Suffering." In Emmanuel Levinas, *On Thinking of the Other: entre nous*, 91–101. Translated by Michael B. Smith and Barbara Hershey. New York: Columbia University Press, 1998.

Levine, Amy-Jill. "The Many Faces of the Good Samaritan—Most Wrong." *Christian Ethics Today* 20:1 (Winter 2012): 20–21.

Lindberg, David C. *Beginnings of Western Science*. 2nd edition. Chicago: University of Chicago Press, 2008.

Lindberg, David and Ronald Numbers, eds. *God and Nature: Historical Essays on the Encounter Between Christianity and Science*. Berkeley: University of California Press, 1986.

Locke, John. *A Letter concerning Toleration*. Amherst, NY: Prometheus Books, 1990.

Malka, Salomon. *Emmanuel Levinas: His Life and Legacy*. Translated by Michael Kigel and Sonja M. Embree. Pittsburgh: Duquesne University Press, 2006.

Marion, Jean-Luc. *God without Being*. Translated by Thomas Carlson. Chicago: University of Chicago Press, 1991.

_____. "A Phenomenological Sketch of the Concept of Gift." In *Postmodern Philosophy and Christian Thought*, 122–43. Edited by Merold Westphal. Bloomington: Indiana University Press, 1999.

Mauriac, Francios. "Forward to *Night*." In Elie Wiesel, *The Night Trilogy*, translated by Marion Wiesel, 15–19. New York: Hill and Want, 2008.

Mauss, Marcel. *The Gift: The Form and Reason for Exchange in Archaic Societies*. Translated by W.D. Halls. New York: W. W. Norton & Company, Inc., 1990.

McDowell, Josh. *Evidence That Demands a Verdict*. San Bernardino, CA: Here's Life Publishers, Inc., 1972.

Moore, G. E. *Principia Ethica*. Cambridge: Cambridge University Press, 1903.

Nagel, Thomas. *Mind and Cosmos: Why the Materialist Neo-Darwinian Conception of Nature Is Almost Certainly False*. Oxford: Oxford University Press, 2012.

Rorty, Richard. *Contingency, Irony, and Solidarity*. Cambridge: Cambridge University Press, 1989.

_____. "Introduction: Antirepresentationalism, Ethnocentrism, and Liberalism." In Richard Rorty, *Objectivity, Relativism, and Truth*, 1–17. Cambridge: Cambridge University Press, 1991.

_____. *Philosophy and the Mirror of Nature*. Princeton: Princeton University Press, 1981.

_____. "Truth and Freedom: A Reply to Thomas McCarthy," *Critical Inquiry 16* (Spring 1990): 633–43.

Ryle, Gilbert. *The Concept of Mind*. Chicago: The University of Chicago Press, 2002.

Skinner, Quentin. "Who Are 'We'? Ambiguities of the Modern Self." *Inquiry: An Interdisciplinary Journal of Philosophy* 34 (June, 1991): 133–53.

Smilansky, Saul. *Free Will and Illusion*. Oxford: Oxford University Press, 2000.

Taylor, Charles. "How Is Mechanism Conceivable?" In Charles Taylor, *Human Agency and Language: Philosophical Papers 1*, 164–86. Cambridge: Cambridge University Press, 1985.

_____. *Sources of the Self: The Making of the Modern Identity*. Cambridge, MA: Harvard University Press, 1989.

Weiner, Eric. "Americans: Undecided About God?" *New York Times*, December 11, 2011, SR5.

Wiesel, Elie. *The Night Trilogy*. Translated by Marion Wiesel. New York: Hill and Want, 2008.

_____. "Preface to the New Translation." In Elie Wiesel, *The Night Trilogy*, translated by Marion Wiesel, 5–13. New York: Hill and Want, 2008.

Wilson, David Sloan. *Unto Others: The Evolution and Psychology of Unselfish Behavior*. Cambridge, MA: Harvard University Press, 1999.

Index of Names